The Struggle over State Power in Zimbabwe

The establishment of legal institutions was a key part of the process of state construction in Africa, and these institutions have played a crucial role in the projection of state authority across space. This is especially the case in colonial and postcolonial Zimbabwe. George Hamandishe Karekwaivanane offers a unique long-term study of law and politics in Zimbabwe, which examines how the law was used in the constitution and contestation of state power across the late-colonial and postcolonial periods. Through this he offers insight on recent debates about judicial independence, adherence to human rights and the observation of the rule of law in contemporary Zimbabwean politics. The book sheds light on the prominent place that law has assumed in Zimbabwe's recent political struggles for those researching the history of the state and power in Southern Africa. It also carries forward important debates on the role of law in state-making, and will also appeal to those interested in African legal history.

George Hamandishe Karekwaivanane is a Lecturer in African Studies at the University of Edinburgh. He was perviously a Research Fellow in the Centre of African Studies at the University of Cambridge. He holds a DPhil from the University of Oxford.

African Studies Series

The African Studies series, founded in 1968, is a prestigious series of monographs, general surveys, and textbooks on Africa covering history, political science, anthropology, economics, and ecological and environmental issues. The series seeks to publish work by senior scholars as well as the best new research.

Other titles in the series are listed at the back of the book.

The Struggle over State Power in Zimbabwe

Law and Politics since 1950

GEORGE HAMANDISHE KAREKWAIVANANE

University of Edinburgh

CAMBRIDGE
UNIVERSITY PRESS

CAMBRIDGE
UNIVERSITY PRESS

University Printing House, Cambridge CB2 8BS, United Kingdom

One Liberty Plaza, 20th Floor, New York, NY 10006, USA

477 Williamstown Road, Port Melbourne, VIC 3207, Australia

4843/24, 2nd Floor, Ansari Road, Daryaganj, Delhi – 110002, India

79 Anson Road, #06-04/06, Singapore 079906

Cambridge University Press is part of the University of Cambridge.

It furthers the University's mission by disseminating knowledge in the pursuit of education, learning, and research at the highest international levels of excellence.

www.cambridge.org
Information on this title: www.cambridge.org/9781107190207
DOI: 10.1017/9781316996898

First published 2017

Printed in the United Kingdom by Clays, St Ives plc

A catalogue record for this publication is available from the British Library.

Library of Congress Cataloging-in-Publication Data
Names: Karekwaivanane, George Hamandishe, 1980–, author.
Title: The struggle over state power in Zimbabwe: law and politics since 1950 / George Hamandishe Karekwaivanane.
Description: New York: Cambridge University Press, 2017. |
Series: African studies; 139 |
Includes bibliographical references and index.
Identifiers: LCCN 2017035384 | ISBN 9781107190207 (hardback)
Subjects: LCSH: Political questions and judicial power – Zimbabwe – History. |
Justice, Administration of – Zimbabwe – History. | Zimbabwe – Politics and government. | Political culture – Zimbabwe. | BISAC: HISTORY / Africa / General.
Classification: LCC KTZ170. K37 2017 | DDC 347.6891–dc23
LC record available at https://lccn.loc.gov/2017035384

ISBN 978-1-107-19020-7 Hardback

For my brother Nicholas who died far too soon, and is sorely missed

Contents

Figures

Tables

Acknowledgements

This book began as a doctoral project at Balliol College, University of Oxford. My studies there were made possible by a scholarship from the Clarendon Fund and Mr Hakeem Bello Osagie. I am grateful to my sponsors for their generosity, and to Balliol College for providing me with an academic home during the course of my studies. I would also like to thank the administrators of the Beit Fund and the Smuts Memorial Fund who provided research grants that financed my fieldwork trips to Zimbabwe and within the United Kingdom. The work of converting my doctoral thesis into this monograph was carried out at the Centre of African Studies of the University of Cambridge. The Centre provided an intellectually stimulating and collegial environment in which to do the further research and writing that was necessary to produce this book. I am grateful to all my colleagues in Cambridge who helped to create this environment and contributed in many different ways to the writing of this book. These include Harri Englund, David Maxwell, Victoria Jones, Jessica Johnson, Ruth Watson, John Iliffe, John Lonsdale, Christopher Clapham, Chris Warnes, Zoe Groves, Adam Higazi, Justin Pearce, Andrea Grant, Sharath Srinivasan, Adam Branch, Devon Curtis, Rachel King, Duncan Omanga and Christine Noe.

In writing this book, I benefitted immensely from the numerous informants who welcomed me into their homes and shared their life stories with me. Their lives and actions made this study such a rewarding experience to research and write about, and I hope that I have done justice to their memories. I am also grateful to the archivists whose help was crucial in enabling me to access the diverse and rich set of documents on which I have drawn for this study. Livingstone Muchefa, Tafadzwa Chigodora and Blessed Magama offered invaluable assistance in locating material in the Zimbabwean archives. Similarly, Lucy McCann was a huge help in my efforts to access the documents in Rhodes House library. I am also grateful to Advocate

Kennedy Sibanda and Gogo Constance Mabusela who allowed me to access their private archives for the 1970s and 1980s.

My heartfelt thanks go to Jocelyn Alexander who supervised my doctoral studies; I could not have wished for a better mentor, and hope that I will someday come to embody the same combination of intellectual rigour and affability. It is unlikely that I would have made it as far as my doctoral studies were it not for my Masters supervisor at the University of Zimbabwe, Dr Joseph Mtisi. Under very trying economic and political circumstances in Zimbabwe, he continued to inspire and encourage my fellow students and I to work hard and aim higher. My examiners David Anderson and David Maxwell provided invaluable advice on how to transform my theses into a book, and have continued to be important pillars of support in my ongoing academic journey, and I am very grateful to them.

In the process of writing this book, I benefitted from stimulating discussions with, and the valuable comments I received from, colleagues at the University of Oxford, the University of Zimbabwe and the University of Cambridge where I was able to present different parts of it. Their questions and comments helped me to refine my ideas and to think in new ways about my project. I also benefitted from the intellectual generosity of several friends who read and gave valuable comments on sections of this book. These include Sarah-Jane Cooper-Knock, Mhoze Chikowero, Susanne Verheul, Joseph Mujere and Glen Ncube. I alone, however, bear the responsibility for any of its shortcomings.

Travelling on this academic journey was made possible by the unwavering support of my family. My parents spared nothing to ensure that my siblings and I had a solid education, and they have continued to encourage my never-ending educational pursuits. My research trip to Chamburukira with my father remains one of my most-treasured memories of the fieldwork for this book. My siblings, Zivanai, Nicholas (who unfortunately passed away before this book was published), Redemptor and Trish, have always been a source of encouragement to be the best I can be. Last, but certainly not least, I am grateful to Kudzai and Tapiwanashe who have been a welcome distraction from my academic labours, and have been a constant source of support and affection which helped to see this project through to the end.

An earlier version of Chapter 5 appeared as an article in *Africa* (Karekwaivanane 2016), and an article in *Politique Africaine* (Karekwaivanane 2015) drew on data presented in Chapters 6 and 7.

Abbreviations

ANC	African National Congress
BSAC	British South Africa Company
BSAP	British South Africa Police
CAS	Capricorn Africa Society
CCJP	Catholic Commission for Justice and Peace
CYL	City Youth League
DC	District Commissioner
ICU	Industrial and Commercial Workers Union
IDAF	International Defence and Aid Fund
ILIC	Interdenominational Legal Information Centre
IRA	Inter-Racial Association
LRF	Legal Resources Fund
MIA	Ministry of Internal Affairs
MP	Member of Parliament
NAD	Native Affairs Department
NC	Native Commissioner
NDP	National Democratic Party
NLHA	Native Land Husbandry Act
PC	Provincial Commissioner
PNC	Provincial Native Commissioner
PO	Presiding Officer
RF	Rhodesian Front
RICU	Reformed Industrial and Commercial Workers Union
SRANC	Southern Rhodesian African National Congress
TLA	Tribal Land Authority
UANC	United African National Council
UDI	Unilateral Declaration of Independence
YWCA	Young Women's Christian Association
ZANLA	Zimbabwe African National Liberation Army

ZANU	Zimbabwe African National Union
ZANU (PF)	Zimbabwe African National Union – Patriotic Front
ZAPU	Zimbabwe African People's Union
ZIPRA	Zimbabwe People's Revolutionary Army

Introduction

In 1968, four guerrilla fighters, Thomas Mutete Makoni, Jonathan Maradza, Amidio Chingura and Joseph Muyambo, were tried in the Salisbury High Court for possession of arms of war.[1] The four had entered Rhodesia from Zambia with rifles, pistols, landmines, hand grenades and TNT, and hid them at a homestead in Mrewa district. However, the arms were discovered by the police, and the men were subsequently arrested and prosecuted. When the matter came to trial, Makoni and his colleagues refused to secure the services of a lawyer to represent them or to call any witnesses to speak in their defence. Instead, they chose to stage a moral defence. When they took the stand, they did not deny that they had brought the weapons into the country. What they did reject, however, was the state's efforts to frame their actions within a discourse of crime and terrorism. They articulated their political grievances as Africans living under colonial rule, and asserted the legitimacy of their decision to take up arms against the repressive Rhodesian settler state. Their position was summed up in the following terms by Muyambo when he entered his plea: 'I disagree with the suggestion that I committed a crime by entering this country with arms because I came into this country to release our country from bondage.'

For his part, Justice Lewis, who presided over the case, was at pains to limit their testimony to matters deemed relevant by the court. He repeatedly rebuked them for their 'long political harangue', pointing out that 'the legislature does not regard that as a lawful excuse; lawful authority or reasonable excuse means lawful permission to have possession of these weapons'. However, throughout the trial, the guerrillas rejected these efforts to constrain their testimony. Despite Lewis's

---

[1] National Archives of Zimbabwe (hereafter NAZ), S3385, Salisbury High Court Criminal Cases 11496–11502, *Regina v. Thomas Mutete Makoni et al.* The four were part of the Zimbabwe African National Liberation Army (ZANLA), the armed wing of the nationalist party Zimbabwe African National Union (ZANU).

best efforts, Makoni and his colleagues were able to make use of the dock as a platform from which to articulate critiques of the Rhodesian government and, in effect, place it on trial. The four men eloquently enumerated the oppressive policies of the Rhodesian government, and refused to recognise the legitimacy of the legal proceedings they were being subjected to, which, they argued, sought to preserve racial domination. It was on these grounds that Chingura declared: 'I strongly dispute the rights of this court to sentence me to death.' In his final words to the court, Makoni echoed Chingura's sentiments in asserting: 'I know that your lordship is about to pronounce the death sentence upon me now. I still maintain that I have not been lawfully tried.'

A number of things are notable about the exchanges during this legal encounter between the four guerrilla fighters and the Rhodesian judge. The first is their deployment of the idea of law for diametrically opposed purposes. Although Justice Lewis invoked the law in order to enforce the settler state's efforts to suppress African political demands, Makoni invoked it in order to assert them. The statements by the judge and the defendants also indicated a fundamental disagreement about what made law 'lawful', and underlying them were contrasting understandings about law and justice. On the one hand, Justice Lewis adopted a rigidly formalist stance, and sought to apply the strict letter of the law without regard to the political and moral arguments articulated by the four guerrilla fighters. On the other, Makoni and his colleagues' position was informed by a substantive understanding of justice, one that was concerned with the fairness of the outcomes of trials, and the morality of the laws that the courts enforced.

The exchanges between Makoni and his colleagues, and Justice Lewis were by no means unique. From the 1950s, law increasingly provided both the language and the locale for debates between Africans and settler authorities over the political questions that were vexing the Rhodesian body politic.[2] As settler rule was challenged by the rise of African nationalism, successive colonial governments increasingly resorted to employing the law to quell political dissent. At the same time, African men and women from different walks of life mobilised the law instrumentally and discursively in their struggles with the state and with each other. In numerous instances, they made use of legal spaces in order to articulate

---

[2] S. Engle Merry, 'Resistance and the Cultural Power of Law', *Law and Society Review*, 29 (1995), 14.

their alternative visions of the social and political order in the country, and legal ideas came to play a significant role in shaping African political imaginaries. At the heart of this book is an analysis of these multiple ways that law was used to constitute and contest state power in Zimbabwe between 1950 and 2008. In doing so, this book provides a social and political history of law in Zimbabwe, and takes forward key debates about how scholars have sought to understand the relationship between law, state power and agency in African history.

Law and the Constitution of State Power

Studies of the role of law in asserting state power in African history have adopted two main approaches. The first emphasises the coercive uses of the law, and this was a central feature of the Marxist and Dependency theory–inspired work of the 1970s and 1980s that examined the emergence of capitalist production in colonial Africa. In the agrarian history literature, for example, law figures as one of the key instruments by which the colonial state undercut African agrarian livelihoods. Through legal measures, colonial governments effected land dispossession, imposed a range of taxes and compelled Africans to enter into wage labour.[3] The work on labour history has similarly pointed to the coercive role of the law in building a labour system that provided cheap African labour for the mines, plantations and industries.[4] Legislation such as pass laws, vagrancy laws, and the Master and Servants Act enabled employers to establish stringent disciplinary regimes in the workplace and compel Africans to work despite the sub-economic wages and the poor living and working conditions.

---

[3] G. Arrighi, 'Labour Supplies in Historical Perspective: A Study of the Proletarianization of the African Peasantry in Rhodesia', *Journal of Development*, 6 (1970). See also R. Palmer and N. Parsons (eds), *The Roots of Rural Poverty in Central and Southern Africa* (Berkeley, 1977); and C. Bundy, *The Rise and Fall of the South African Peasantry* (London, 1979).

[4] Jeffery Crisp, *The Story of an African Working Class: Ghanaian Miner's Struggles, 1870–1980* (London, 1984); C. van Onselen, *Chibaro: African Mine Labour in Southern Rhodesia, 1900–1933* (London, 1976); R. Turrell, 'Kimberly: Labour and Compounds, 1871–1888', in S. Marks and R. Rathbone (eds), *Industrialisation and Social Change in South Africa: African Class Formation, Culture, and Consciousness, 1870–1930* (Essex, 1982); and A. Clayton and D. C. Savage, *Government and Labour in Kenya 1895–1963* (London, 1974).

What emerges clearly from the agrarian and labour history literatures is the way that law enabled, rather than constrained, the power of colonial states over the African populations they ruled.

The coercive operation of the law has also been captured fairly graphically in the literature on colonial violence, which demonstrates the intimate connection between law and violence. Studies of corporal punishment, in particular, reveal the ways that violence and ideas about racial difference were embedded in colonial legal systems.[5] As Anupama Rao and Steven Pierce aptly observe, 'the body of the colonized was a critical site both for maintaining colonial alterity and enacting colonial governance'.[6] Equally, the histories of the turbulent period of decolonisation have demonstrated that law underwrote some of the extreme cases of violence at the end of colonial rule. This was often achieved through the invocation of states of emergency which sanctioned brutal operations to quell African political opposition.[7] These studies have also shown how the courts were frequently enlisted to punish African opposition to colonial rule, all too often through the use of the capital sentence. This comes out clearly in David Anderson's work on the last years of colonial rule in Kenya. 'British Justice in 1950s Kenya', he notes, 'was a blunt, brutal and unsophisticated instrument of oppression.'[8]

From the 1990s, however, a new approach had begun to emerge in the literature, one that paid more attention to the subtler ways that law was employed by colonial authorities. These studies dwelt

---

[5] A. Rao and S. Pierce, 'Discipline and the Other Body: Correction, Corporeality, and Colonial Rule', *Interventions*, 3 (2001). See also S. Pete and A. Devenish, 'Flogging Fear and Food: Punishment and Race in Colonial Natal', *Journal of Southern African Studies(JSAS)*, 31 (2005); D. Anderson, 'Punishment, Race, and "The Raw Native": Settler Society and Kenya's Flogging Scandals, 1895–1930', *JSAS*, 37 (2011); D. Killingray, 'The "Rod of Empire": The Debate over Corporal Punishment in the British African Forces, 1888–1946', *Journal of African History (JAH)*, 35 (1994); and S. Pierce, 'Punishment and the Political Body: Flogging and Colonialism in Northern Nigeria', *Interventions*, 3 (2001).
[6] Rao and Pierce, 'Discipline and the Other Body', 61.
[7] D. Anderson, *Histories of the Hanged: The Dirty War in Kenya and the End of Empire* (London, 2005); C. Elkins, *Britain's Gulag: The Brutal End of Empire in Kenya* (London, 2005); O. J. M. Kalinga, 'The 1959 Nyasaland State of Emergency in Old Karonga District', *JSAS*, 36 (2010); and M. Munochiveyi, *Prisoners of Rhodesia: Inmates and Detainees in the Struggle for Zimbabwean Liberation, 1960–1980* (New York, 2014).
[8] Anderson, *Histories of the Hanged*, 7.

on the symbolic, legitimating and 'productive' functions of the law, and drew inspiration from the works of scholars such as Antonio Gramsci, Michel Foucault and Pierre Bourdieu. Although Gramsci and Foucault did not devote much attention to the subject of the law, their insights into the nature and exercise of power significantly influenced the way scholars have tried to understand law and its relationship to state power in colonial contexts. In the case of scholars who draw on Gramsci, it is his concept of hegemony that has proved most useful. For Gramsci, domination was not achieved solely by coercion.[9] Rather, ruling classes strove to elicit the consent of the ruled to their subordination, and this was achieved through the control of civil society, which was used to disseminate a world view that naturalised the dominance of the ruling class. Drawing on these insights, scholars have tried to explore the ways that colonial states used law to aid their hegemonic projects. However, historians of Africa, for the most part, agreed that colonial states were not hegemonic, not least because the colonial experience was characterised by a significant amount of violence.[10] In addition, as Diana Jeater points out, 'colonial rulers [we]re clearly of a different culture, and their norms and values [we]re easily recognized as not part of the "natural" social order of the society at large'.[11]

As a consequence, there has been a move away from Gramsci's original idea of an overarching hegemony, towards the idea of a 'fragmented hegemony'.[12] This reformulation of the concept of hegemony has been effectively applied to law by Sally Engle Merry who contends that:

Instead of an overarching hegemony, there are hegemonies: parts of law that are more fundamental and unquestioned, parts which are becoming challenged, parts which authorize the dominant culture, and parts which offer liberation to the subordinate. Law cannot be viewed as either hegemonic or

---

[9] D. Litowitz, 'Gramsci, Hegemony and the Law', *Brigham Young University Law Review*, 515 (2000).

[10] D. Engels and S. Marks, 'Introduction: Hegemony in a Colonial Context', in D. Engels and S. Marks (eds), *Contesting Colonial Hegemony: State and Society in Africa and India* (London, 1994). See also R. Guha, *Dominance without Hegemony: History and Power in Colonial India* (Cambridge, MA, 1997).

[11] D. Jeater, *Law, Language and Science: The Invention of the "Native Mind" in Southern Rhodesia, 1890–1930* (Portsmouth, 2007), 4.

[12] Litowitz, 'Gramsci, Hegemony and the Law', 536.

not as a whole, but instead as incorporating contradictory discourses about equality, justice and persons.[13]

Richard Rathbone's work on the Gold Coast provides an example of the partial hegemony of English law amongst the coastal trading elite. He concludes that, due to its utility in commercial transactions: 'English law, its language, assumptions and great texts had been absorbed into the culture of much of the Southern Gold Coast, but that implied no necessary acceptance of the totality of the system which had introduced it.'[14] He further points out that: 'While colonial law acquired a degree of acceptance and even had a strong influence on the sensibilities of the modern elite, that acceptance was partial and conditional.'[15] The value of this concept of fragmented hegemony, especially for the study of African legal history, lies in the way it draws us to redirect our efforts towards the search for instances where law has been used to authorise social and political hierarchies, or to generate consent, while remaining attentive to the unstable and incomplete influence of law. It is this thinking that informs part of the analysis of the law within this book.

Notwithstanding the valuable insights that these two different approaches to understanding the role of law in African history proffer, the picture they each provide is incomplete in important respects. By downplaying the repressive nature of law in favour of its symbolic and constitutive power, we risk missing intimate relationship between law and violence in colonial Africa. By the same token, studies that focus on physical coercion alone miss (or dismiss) other important aspects about the law that can be just as consequential. These include the ways it is deployed discursively, or the ways that courts are used as sites for performances whose reach and impact can be extended and amplified by the media. Significantly, the operation of law in colonial Africa was often simultaneously repressive and productive, coercive and constitutive. This book, therefore, attends to the ways that law was used

---

[13] S. E. Merry, 'Courts as Performances: Domestic Violence Hearings in a Hawai'i Family Court', in M. Lazarus-Black and S. F. Hirsch (eds), *Contested States: Law, Hegemony, and Resistance* (New York, 1994), 54. See also D. Anderson, 'Policing the Settler State: Colonial Hegemony in Kenya, 1900–1952', in Engels and Marks, *Contesting Colonial Hegemony*, 263.

[14] R. Rathbone, 'Law, Lawyers and Politics in Ghana', in Engels and Marks, *Contesting Colonial Hegemony*, 246–47.

[15] Ibid., 247.

to command and to demand, as well as constitute and legitimise the social and political order in Zimbabwe between 1950 and 2008.

The balance in the use of law for coercion or legitimation, and the level of success that the state achieved, varied over time. As such, the approach I take is not simply to merge two ways of thinking about the law, but rather to examine this shifting balance between coercion and legitimation over time. In addition to rendering a more nuanced picture of the role of law in colonial and post-colonial Zimbabwe, this approach presents a further analytical advantage. It offers a useful window onto the continuous process of making and remaking the state. Thinking about how, when and why the balance in the use of the law shifted over time casts a light onto the shifting and often fragmented nature of colonial states. Law was not simply a tool in the hands of the state, it was also central to the constitution of the state itself. The establishment of legal institutions in the early colonial period was part of the process of state construction, and these institutions were central to the projection of state authority across space. In addition, the effort to establish colonial courts as the final arbiters of justice in African colonies was part of the effort to establish the state as the apex of society. Furthermore, as Thomas Hansen and Finn Stepputat point out, the construction of states entailed 'the institutionalization of law and legal discourse as the authoritative language of the state and the medium through which the state acquire[d] discursive presence and authority to authorize'.[16]

Although law was important in the constitution of states, it was often the source of division within them. Historians have long noted that colonial states were 'bearer[s] of complex and conflicting values, with internal tensions and disputes about the most appropriate way to rule'.[17] This book demonstrates that law was one source of this internal tension. Different branches of the state in colonial and post-colonial Zimbabwe were constantly at loggerheads over the content and administration of the law. For much of the colonial period, the tension was concentrated between officials of the Native Affairs Department who sought to cultivate personalised forms of authority

---

[16] T. B. Hansen and F. Stepputat, 'Introduction: States of Imagination', in T. B. Hansen and F. Stepputat (eds), *States of Imagination: Ethnographic Explorations of the Postcolonial State* (London, 2001), 7.

[17] Cited in J. Alexander, *The Unsettled Land: State-making and the Politics of Land in Zimbabwe, 1893–2003* (Oxford, 2006), 11.

over Africans, and those of the Justice Department who insisted on rule-bound conduct. However, after independence, the key tensions were between senior members of the executive and the judiciary. These tensions, I argue, were rooted in their divergent views about the relationship between law and the legitimate exercise of state power.

Colonial States and Indigenous Legal Systems

In reflecting on the role of law in the making of state power, it is important to consider the place of indigenous legal systems, as colonial and post-colonial officials often sought to draw them into the service of the state. Martin Chanock's study of 'customary law' in Northern Rhodesia and Nyasaland was important in driving the debate on this subject.[18] Chanock challenged the prevailing view amongst anthropologists in the 1970s that 'customary law' was a carry-over from the pre-colonial African past. He argued, instead, that it was a fabrication of the colonial period that arose out of a coincidence of interests between colonial officials and male African elders. On the one hand, colonial officials were concerned about the breakdown of law and order that followed the undermining of 'traditional' leaders, as well as the need to mobilise African labour. On the other, male elders were anxious to regain their control over women and youth. This had been eroded by colonial laws that enabled young women to resist patriarchal control, as well as the new avenues for wealth accumulation created by the colonial economy which gave young men greater independence from their elders. The result of the alliance between colonial officials and male elders, Chanock argues, was the freezing of what had hitherto been a flexible body of practices within African society into rigid codes which came to be recognised as 'customary law'. Chanock's arguments about the invention of 'customary law' were very influential in shaping subsequent studies, and were later applied to Southern Rhodesia by Elizabeth Schmidt in her pioneering work on the history of Shona women in Mashonaland Province.[19] Like Chanock, she argues that

---

[18] M. Chanock, *Law, Custom and Social Order: The Colonial Experience in Malawi and Zambia* (Cambridge, UK: 1985). See also F. G. Snyder, 'Colonialism and Legal Form: The Creation of "Customary Law" in Senegal', *Journal of Legal Pluralism*, 49 (1981).

[19] E. Schmidt, *Peasants, Traders and Wives: Shona Women in the History of Zimbabwe, 1870–1939* (London, 1992), 104–13.

there was a window of emancipation for African women as a result of the application of the 'repugnancy clause' by colonial officials. However, this window closed due to the 'creation' of 'customary law' and the reassertion of patriarchal control.

An important shortcoming of the work by Chanock and Schmidt is that they allocate too much power to colonial administrations, and see far more success in their projects than may have been achieved in reality. Sally Falk Moore's research among the Chagga in Tanzania shows that codification did not necessarily rigidify 'customary law'. Although it retained the outward appearance of being unchanging, it was in fact responsive to changing social and economic conditions. 'In the colonial period', she argues, 'the Native Authorities could make new rules. "Customary law" could be added to, bits of it replaced. It could be reinterpreted. Parts of it could remain unused. But as labelled, it was an entity which was conceived as static.'[20] Sarah Berry has similarly questioned the view that the attempts to invent 'customary law' were successful.[21] In her study of access to land in the Gold Coast, she observes that the rise in the value of land due to increased agricultural commercialisation, made access to land the focus of struggles within African society. In this context: 'Colonial "inventions" of African tradition served not so much to define the shape of the colonial social order as to provoke a series of debates over the meaning and application of tradition which in turn shaped struggles over authority and access to resources.'[22]

Brett Shadle's research on the codification of 'customary law' in colonial Kenya is particularly instructive. He shows that administrative officials in Kenya were in fact opposed to codification, for fear that a 'crystallized, unalterable customary law would allow them little room to adjust the law in order to control local African courts and, by extension, African societies.'[23] His detailed analysis of the proceedings in African courts in Gusii reveals that even after codification, court elders

---

[20] S. Falk, Moore, *Social Facts and Fabrication: Customary Law on Kilimanjaro* (Cambridge, 1986), 317.
[21] S. Berry, 'Hegemony on A Shoestring: Indirect Rule and Access to Agricultural Land', *Africa*, 62 (1992).
[22] Ibid., 328.
[23] B. L. Shadle, '"Changing Traditions to Meet Current Altering Conditions": Customary Law, African Courts and the Rejection of Codification in Kenya, 1930', *JAH*, 40 (1999), 413.

'followed a much more nuanced customary law in the courts than the one spelled out in colonial texts.'[24] He thus concludes that: 'Customary law and African courts, which colonial officials believed to be basic to the reproduction of state legitimacy and authority, lay largely outside the purview of the state.'[25] Given that the Southern Rhodesian state had greater capacity than its Kenyan counterpart, I would not go so far as to conclude, as Shadle does, that customary law and African courts were 'largely outside the purview of the state'. However, his broader observations are relevant to Southern Rhodesia, where Law Department officials were opposed to the idea of chiefs being accorded judicial powers. As a consequence, contrary to Schmidt's claims, there was no codification of 'customary law'. In addition, when the Rhodesian Front government did try to actively make use of chiefs' courts during the late 1960s and 1970s, it was but one of many actors vying to shape what actually happened in those courts. Chiefs, their followers, and nationalist parties all had their own agendas. As a consequence, the state often lost the struggle to influence chiefs' courts.

A second shortcoming in the approach taken by Chanock is the underlying 'legal centralist' perspective that views the colonial legal system as a single entity, incorporating statute law and invented 'customary law', both of which are tied to the state. This perspective not only tends to overstate the success of 'invention', it also underplays the distinct nature of the legal systems involved, as well as the complex, and at times antagonistic, relationships which developed between them over time. This is especially the case in Southern Rhodesia where neither 'Indirect Rule' nor codification was implemented. As Diana Jeater's work on the early colonial period in Southern Rhodesia has shown, there existed distinct African legal systems with their own legal procedures, concepts, and jurisprudential foundations, all of which proved to be resilient in the face of colonial incursion.[26]

It is therefore necessary to rethink the idea of the invention of 'customary law', as well as the legal centralist assumptions that undergird the work by Chanock and others.[27] As such, I adopt the alternative

---

[24] Ibid, 414.
[25] Ibid, 430.
[26] Jeater, *Law, Language and Science . . .*
[27] See also K. Mann and R. Roberts, 'Introduction', in Mann and Roberts (eds), *Law in Colonial Africa* (London, 1991), 8–9.

approach of legal pluralism because of the way it decentres the state as a source of law, while remaining attentive to the ways that 'state law penetrates and restructures other normative orders through symbols and through direct coercion and, at the same time, the way non-state normative orders resist and circumvent penetration or even capture and use the symbolic capital of the state.'[28] This perspective provides a better lens through which to view the shifting and mutually constitutive relations between the different legal systems in colonial and post-colonial Zimbabwe than 'legal centralism', or ideas of top-down invention.

Law and African Agency

Thinking about the role of law in the constitution of state power in colonial Africa raises a number of questions about African responses. Could law be used by Africans in pursuit of their own interests? What room, if any, existed for resistance within the legal arena? Three points are worth making in answering these questions. First, the use of law as a mode of rule rendered it available for use by the ruled in pursuing their interests, at times in opposition to the rulers. This inherent 'weakness' of law as a mode of rule is made clear by Edward Thompson who argues that law could occasionally provide access to justice for subordinate social groups:

If law is evidently partial and unjust then it will mask nothing, legitimize nothing, contribute nothing to any class's hegemony. The essential precondition for the effectiveness of the law, in its function as ideology, is that it shall display an independence from gross manipulation and shall seem to be just. It cannot seem so without upholding its own logic and criteria of equity; indeed, on occasion, by actually being just.[29]

Another weakness, already alluded to, is the fact that law was often a source of division within the colonial state. As John Comaroff points out, the existence of tensions within the colonial state provided opportunities for Africans to make use of the law in contesting the actions

---

[28] S. E. Merry, 'Legal Pluralism', *Law and Society Review*, 22 (1988), 871.
[29] E. P. Thompson, *Whigs and Hunters: The Origins of the Black Act* (New York, 1975), 263.

of state officials.[30] However, such tensions did not necessarily make colonial rule any less exploitative.

Second, as Africans' legal consciousness became more sophisticated, they were able to use the law to contest state power in multiple ways. Courts, as Susan Hirsch points out:

… are "complex sites of resistance" in part because they have the potential to play pragmatic, ideological, and symbolic roles in contestations over power … this complexity is generated as well by the fact that people use courts to contest multiple relations of power, reworking understandings of gender, race, class, and other hierarchies sometimes simultaneously. Thus, oppositional practices in courts, emerging in response to a range of dominations, assume many forms and generate diverse outcomes.[31]

Hirsch's study of cases brought before Islamic courts in Kenya shows how Muslim women were able to use these courts in order to contest two different sets of power relations. In the first instance, the cases they brought challenged patriarchal control. At the same time, by making use of Islamic courts, as opposed to state courts, they were also resisting state efforts to incorporate Muslim communities into its secular legal system. Merry has also demonstrated that subordinated individuals could harness the symbolic power of the law in their efforts to challenge oppressive structures and relationships.[32] In addition, they could mobilise the language of law in clashes with the state and appropriate state-instituted legal spaces for their own performances.

Third, there is a need to be cautious in determining whether, and at what point, we should classify particular instances of African legal agency as resistance. This is because the use of the courts sometimes yielded contradictory results. Derek Peterson's study of marital disputes that were heard in church courts during the early colonial period in Tanganyika shows how litigants represented themselves in ways that harnessed the authority of these courts in their favour. However,

---

[30] J. Comaroff, 'Colonialism, Culture and Law: A Foreword', *Law and Social Inquiry*, 26 (2001), 311. See also F. Cooper and A. Stoler, 'Introduction Tensions of Empire: Colonial Control and Visions of Rule', *American Ethnologist*, 15 (1989).

[31] S. Hirsch, 'Khadi's Courts as Complex Sites of Resistance: The State, Islam and Gender in Post-colonial Kenya', in M. Lazarus-Black and S. F. Hirsch (eds), *Contested States: Law, Hegemony, and Resistance* (New York, 1994), 120.

[32] Merry, 'Resistance and the Cultural Power', 15.

he points out that '[t]his mode of agency did not work against power. Kaguru and Gogoi litigants contracted with colonialism.'[33] By appealing to these courts, they effectively invited closer church involvement in their lives. Stephen Ellman has also argued that 'anti-apartheid lawyering' in South Africa had the unintended result of legitimising the legal system among some groups of Africans.[34] This, he adds, was not necessarily harmful in the long run as it contributed to the legitimacy of the South African legal system after apartheid. These studies both raise important questions about the efficacy of resisting the state by means of its own laws and legal institutions.

In this book, I build on these observations in my analysis of the ways that individuals wielded the doubled-edged sword of law in Zimbabwean history, and how successful they were in doing so. However, I also take the study of African legal agency further in important respects. The existing literature has done well to explore the increasingly complex ways that law has been used as a resource by African litigants. Writing about legal agency in this way assumes a degree of legal consciousness; however, this a subject which is hardly entered into in the literature.[35] It is therefore necessary to pay closer attention to the development of legal consciousness and the factors that facilitated it. I argue that the development of African legal consciousness, and the strategies that Africans employed in the legal arena in colonial and post-colonial Zimbabwe were connected to the evolution of the state's own uses of the law – the two impelled each other. The Rhodesian settler state's decision to rely on law as a mode of rule, made it necessary for Africans to develop the sufficient legal consciousness to engage with it and be able to 'speak law to power'. As Africans became fluent in the language of the law and capable of frustrating the state's designs by the early 1960s, this triggered the passage of more repressive laws and the tightening of the procedures and regulations that guided the administration of the law.

---

[33] D. R. Peterson, 'Morality Plays: Marriage, Church, and Colonial Agency in Central Tanganyika, ca. 1876–1928', *American Historical Review*, 111 (2006), 1009

[34] S. Ellman, 'Law and Legitimacy in South Africa', *Law and Social Inquiry*, 20 (1995).

[35] I have adopted Sally Engle Merry's definition of legal consciousness as 'the ways ordinary people understand the legal system and their rights to use it'. S. Engle Merry, 'Anthropology, Law and Transnational Processes', *Annual Review of Anthropology*, 21 (1991), 361.

This shift in the state's tactics was accompanied by corresponding shifts in African's legal strategies by the mid-1960s.

This study also underscores the importance of moving the scholarly focus beyond the uses of law as a resource, and uncovering the imaginaries, the ideas of personhood, as well as the alternative visions of the social and political order that animated African legal agency. An important imaginary that informed the outrage behind much of the legal action instituted against the state was that of rights-bearing citizenship.[36] This imaginary was important in driving Africans' legal challenges in the 1960s and 1970s, when the Rhodesian Front government sought to discursively construct Africans as ethnicized, custombound subjects.[37] It was equally important after independence, when the ZANU Patriotic Front (PF) government sought to define members of opposition parties such as ZAPU and the Movement for Democratic Change as being outside of the nation, and posing a threat to it. In a direct challenge to these efforts, many civil society and opposition activists asserted their status as rights-bearing citizens and sought the protection of the law and courts, which they believed they were entitled to. I should add, however, that my focus on formal legal institutions, and what may be characterised as the 'rationalist' ideas of rights, has been influenced by my sources and the limitations of space. It is not my intention to underplay the importance of alternative sources of African political imaginaries and ideas of personhood such as religion. Indeed, this book is best read alongside, and not in opposition to, studies that explore these alternative social spheres.

The analysis of the mobilisation of ideas about law and rights-based citizenship undertaken in this book also allows for a contribution to the efforts by scholars to proffer ways that human rights might be reinvigorated as a basis for making claims in post-colonial Africa. A growing disenchantment has rightly come to surround the subject of human rights in contemporary Africa. Richard Falk, for example, has

---

[36] J. Alexander, 'The Political Imaginaries and Social Lives of Political Prisoners in Post 2000 Zimbabwe', *JSAS*, 36 (2010).

[37] See M. Mamdani, *Citizen and Subject: Contemporary Africa and the Legacy of Late Colonialism*, (Princeton, 1996); Cooper and Stoler, *Tensions of Empire*, and J. Comaroff, 'Governmentality, Materiality, Legality, Modernity: On the Colonial State in Africa', in J. Deutsch, H. Schmidt and P. Probst (eds), *African Modernities: Entangled Meanings in Current Debate* (Oxford, 2002), 107–34; and L. White, *Unpopular Sovereignty: Rhodesian Independence and African Decolonization*, (Chicago, 2015), 38–43.

pointed out how the discourse of human rights has often been devalued through its appropriation by powerful states in order to 'validate non-defensive uses of force'.[38] Harri Englund has also shown how a narrow understanding of human rights that limits them to political rights has undermined their utility as a basis for making social and economic claims by the poor.[39] What is more, this limited conception of human rights fails to challenge the global neoliberal economic orthodoxy that is partly responsible for inequality and poverty in Africa. In addition, Michael Neocosmos has argued that contemporary human rights discourse tends to encourage political passivity and the delegation of the struggle for rights to non-governmental organisations.[40]

The increasing appropriation of scholarly critiques of human rights by authoritarian governments in order to justify their repressive actions underscores the need for scholars to contribute to the search for solutions. This is particularly so in post-2000 Zimbabwe where the ZANU (PF) government has been adept at articulating these critiques, while meting out violence to its political opponents. In response to criticisms of its repressive actions, the government argued that it was being 'demonised' for championing the economic rights of Zimbabweans through its efforts to achieve a more equitable distribution of land. In addition, it made the counter-accusation that the countries and organisations that criticised it were employing human rights discourse in order to pursue a 'regime change agenda'.

There is thus a critical need, as Englund points out, 'to offer the intellectual resources for thinking beyond the particular human rights discourse' that has become dominant among activists, donors and non-governmental organisations in many African countries.[41] Englund's work on local notions of obligations makes an important contribution to this search for alternatives ideas and discourses. For Neocosmos, part of the solution lies in adopting a 'politics which prescribes rights and entitlements and demands them from the state'. In illustrating this, he points to the 1955 Freedom Charter adopted by South Africa's

---

[38] R. Falk, 'The Power of Rights and the Rights of Power: What Future for Human Rights?', *Ethics and Global Politics*, 1–2 (2008).

[39] Englund, *Prisoners of Freedom*.

[40] M. Neocosmos, 'Can a Human Rights Culture Enable Emancipation? Clearing Some Theoretical Ground for the Renewal of a Critical Sociology', *South African Review of Sociology*, 37 (2006).

[41] Englund, *Prisoners of Freedom*, 200.

African National Congress. The Freedom Charter, he argues 'was not a human rights document which passively enjoined people to petition the state for the rights due to them by virtue of simply being alive; it was and still is a document which calls on people to engage in politics to fight for their rights ...'[42] Neocosmos' central argument is about the need for an active political struggle for rights. However, there is a second point which is implicit in his argument, and to which this study speaks. Briefly stated, the *struggle* for rights in Africa has a much longer history than is often acknowledged. As I show in this book, the struggle for rights in Zimbabwe goes at least as far back as the mid-twentieth century, and the demands for rights-bearing citizenship were articulated individually and collectively and were very much a part of the nationalist struggle. One way of reinvigorating the contemporary struggles for rights is to sever the tie with the post-Cold War neo-liberal orthodoxy, and re-contextualise them within this longer history of political struggles and the older discourses of rights.

Methods and Sources

This book focuses on legal struggles between Africans and the state, and amongst Africans themselves in Zimbabwe between 1950 and 2008. This period witnessed important socio-economic and political changes that, in turn, fuelled conflicts between Africans and the state and amongst Africans themselves. And very often these conflicts found their way into the courts. These changes included the ambitious top-down efforts to restructure African agriculture in the 1950s which triggered a crisis in state legitimacy; the moves to use chiefs re-legitimise the state and draw their courts more firmly into the service of the state during the 1960s and 1970s; the rise of African nationalism and the bitter anti-colonial war that culminated in Zimbabwean independence in 1980; the progressive efforts by the new ZANU (PF) government to transform the inherited legal system that went alongside its brutal efforts to silence dissent; as well as the rise of a strong opposition political movement in the late 1990s, and the concerted efforts by ZANU (PF) to hold on to power at all costs. By covering the colonial and the post-colonial period, the book examines the continuities and changes

---

[42] Neocosmos, 'Can a Human Rights Culture', 376.

in the way that successive governments employed the law to constitute state power, and how citizens deployed it to contest that same power.

The key source material for this book has been court records, and I have focused on two major sets of cases. The first are cases that occurred in the rural areas and which often concerned access to land and the regulations governing its use, as well as the negotiation of gender relations. The second are the overtly political cases that related to the battles between the government of the day and its political opponents. I have selected these cases partly because they were amongst the most prominent cases of the period; as such they provide a valuable window onto the important struggles of the day and the role law played in these struggles. In addition, these cases allow me to examine the development of legal consciousness and its expression as legal agency, in both rural and urban areas. With respect to interpreting these cases, I have tried to understand these legal struggles in the context of broader social and political struggles. I have thus focused on the events leading to the court case, the case's passage through the legal system, and its significance in relation to broader struggles. At another level, I have used legal disputes as a way of exploring African legal agency and the underlying ideas that animated it. I have, therefore, paid close attention to the statements made by African litigants as well as their courtroom 'performances'.

In writing about legal struggles in this way, one is confronted with a familiar problem facing historians of colonial Africa: that of striking a balance between portraying African agency and colonial violence. On the one hand, highlighting African agency risks underplaying the extent of colonial violence; on the other, an emphasis on state violence can occlude African agency. I have, therefore, tried to chart a path between these two extremes. Nevertheless, it is important to underscore the fact that the legal encounters I discuss were generally between unequally matched parties. The Rhodesian state had substantial coercive power, and as settler rule was increasingly challenged, it resorted to more and more violence. Equally, the post-colonial state was never hesitant to bring the full force of its coercive might down upon its perceived enemies, regardless of what the law said. As such, citizens' legal victories were often short-lived as the state found alternative, often extra-legal, means to achieve its goals. However, it is important to note that whether people won or lost in their courtroom struggles with the state, this was only one dimension of the legal struggles. As the law was being used instrumentally, discursively and 'performatively', defeat at one level could often be translated into victory at another. Importantly, the law was never the only means by which the struggles in question were being pursued. In the 1960s and 1970s, for example, the anti-colonial war was underway.

Studying the colonial period through the prism of legal struggles also runs the risk of giving the impression that colonial power could always be negotiated with or that it was always, or primarily, rule-bound. The legal arena, like other 'sites of struggle' such as the plantation, the mine compound, the village, or the township, has its own unique possibilities and limitations for historical actors and, indeed, for historians. To this end, I have tried to show how litigants' fortunes varied depending on the court they were appealing to, the period and the 'crime' in question. Pursuing legal action often required resources which many citizens did not always have. As such, there is often a risk that focusing on struggles in the legal arena narrows the focus onto elites who had the means to institute legal action. In order to avoid an elite bias, I have widened the net by focusing on cases instituted by individuals and by the state. Due to the legalism of the Southern Rhodesian state, there were frequent legal skirmishes between Africans from all walks of life and state officials, and these increased with the implementation of the Native Land Husbandry Act of 1951 and the rise of African nationalism. In addition, during the 1960s and 1970s, organisations such as the International Defence and Aid Fund (IDAF), Christian Aid, the Catholic Commission for Justice and Peace, and Amnesty International provided financial assistance to enable thousands of Africans involved in politically related cases to access legal representation. Similar assistance was provided from the late 1990s by organisations such as the Zimbabwe Human Rights NGO Forum and the Zimbabwe Lawyers for Human Rights.

Court records, it should be pointed out, have a number of limitations. They often record the 'narrow thread of organised dispute' at the expense of the 'broader lattice of contention'.[43] In addition, while they are amongst the few instances in which African voices are captured in the colonial archive, 'these voices speak in ways which

---

[43] D. W. Cohen, '"A Case for the Basoga": Lloyd Fallers and the Construction of an African Legal System', in K. Mann and R. Roberts, *Law in Colonial Africa* (London, 1991), 239–53.

have been profoundly shaped by the procedures of the court and by the circumstances surrounding the transformation of testimony into text.'[44] Not only have they been filtered by translation and transcription, but litigants often frame their cases to meet the 'discursive traditions' of the court. These limitations were evident in many of the cases I came across in the archives. However, African litigants were not always bound by these courtroom conventions, and those instances where they challenged them were especially significant. As the opening vignette shows, by the late 1960s, nationalists and guerrillas were rejecting the conventions of the Rhodesian courts. This rejection signified the loss of legitimacy of the law and the courts.

I have tried to mitigate the limitations of court records by consulting a diverse set of sources which include newspapers, government correspondence, as well as autobiographies and memoirs. I have also relied extensively on Parliamentary Debates which provided access to the policy considerations that informed the laws, as well as the key debates about the legislation. An added advantage of Parliamentary Debates was their consistent availability across the period covered in this book. By following debates on the different laws that were passed to govern the conduct of politics, I have been able to track and compare the ways that successive administrations viewed the relationship between law and the legitimate exercise of state power. In addition, by combining Parliamentary Debates with court records and other sources, it was possible to trace legislation from the time of its formulation, the debates over it, its implementation, and the resultant legal encounters between Africans and the state.

I have also relied significantly on oral history. I conducted interviews with fifty-five informants who included litigants, lawyers, judges and politicians. These interviews were important in filling the gaps in the archival record, and guiding my interpretation of the archival sources. However, the collection and interpretation of the interviews themselves were not always a straightforward matter. Many of the interviews were undertaken between 2010 and 2011, in the aftermath of the violent and contested election of June 2008, which deepened the political polarisation in the country. Despite the relative political and economic stability during the period I conducted my interviews, the

---

[44] R. Roberts, 'Text and Testimony in the Tribunal de Premiere Instance, Dakar, during the early Twentieth Century', *JAH*, 31 (1990), 450.

political landscape was still characterised by political contention and suspicion. This political context often coloured the ways that the past was remembered by my informants, and it also influenced what I was able to ask and what informants were willing to disclose. My informants in rural districts such as Zaka, for example, were more comfortable talking about the legal struggles during the colonial period than those after independence.

The political context also influenced the accounts of the lawyers I interviewed. The human rights violations, lack of respect for the rule of law and erosion of judicial independence by the Zimbabwean government since 2000 gave rise to a narrative amongst human rights activists and lawyers, which traced these problems to the early years of the ZANU (PF) rule. In some cases, informants maintained that the administration of the law during the Rhodesian years was better than the 1980s. However, a closer examination of the events in the 1980s shows that the developments in the legal arena during these early years of the ZANU (PF) government cannot be reduced to a story of repressive law. In addition, the extreme violence of the 1980s was followed by relative stability in the 1990s. There is also little to suggest that the administration of the law during Rhodesian years was 'better' than that in the first decade of independence. I have, therefore, treated these accounts as narratives that were shaped by my informants' social and political backgrounds.

Chapter Outline

The main body of this study consists of eight chapters. Chapter 1 provides the historical backdrop against which the legal developments from 1950 onwards must be understood. It briefly recounts the history of the Southern Rhodesian legal system between 1890 and 1950, focusing on its establishment and operation. Among other things, it highlights the tensions that emerged between the Native Affairs and the Law Departments over the content and the administration of the law. In addition, the chapter sets out the evolution of colonial policy on indigenous legal systems during the first six decades of colonial rule. Lastly, it examines Africans' increasing engagement with the colonial legal systems and underscores the importance of attending to the underlying ideas that animated their legal agency. Chapter 2 focuses on the Rhodesian Front government's attempts to draw on 'customary law' to reconstitute the state's legitimacy in the 1960s and 1970s in the wake of the crisis brought about by the implementation of the Native Land Husbandry Act of 1951. I argue that this belated turn towards chiefs was accompanied by an attempt to discursively construct Africans as ethnic subjects that were bound by customary obligation, as opposed to rights-bearing citizens who were protected by the law from the arbitrary exercise of state power. However, I show that these efforts failed due, in large part, to the defiance of villagers across Rhodesia who tenaciously contested the unwelcome impositions of the state.

In Chapters 3 and 4, I shift the focus from the sphere of custom onto that of politics, and examine the legal responses of successive settler governments to the rise of African nationalism. Chapter 3 focuses on the period between 1950 and 1964, and analyses the colonial government's attempt to come to terms with the rising political agitation by Africans, as well as some of the early legal encounters between the settler government and African nationalists. In it I show that the laws which were passed in order to criminalize African political activity emerged out of lengthy debates within settler society about the principles that were supposed to guide the relationship between law and the legitimate exercise of state power. The chapter also illustrates the increasingly sophisticated forms of legal agency exhibited by nationalists who managed to use the courts to contest the efforts by state officials to silence them. However, the success of nationalists in the courts led to growing calls by colonial officials for more repressive laws by the early-1960s. Chapter 4 picks up the story from the mid-1960s, and explores the role that law played in the political sphere during the fifteen years leading up to Zimbabwean independence in 1980. I argue that the assumption of power by the Rhodesian Front led to a decisive shift in the government's use of law away from legitimation towards coercion. The period witnessed the build-up of a substantial legal armoury which was used to ruthlessly suppress African political dissent. It also saw the cementing of the 'state of exception' as a feature of Rhodesian statecraft. This shift in the state's use of the law, I argue, was accompanied by a corresponding shift in the attitudes of nationalists and guerrillas towards the Rhodesian legal system.

In Chapter 5, I carry the theme of African legal agency forward by examining the involvement of African lawyers in the struggles in the legal arena between 1950 and 1980. I argue that these lawyers not only exercised legal agency themselves, but also enabled other Africans to exercise it. The chapter highlights the important role they played as 'translators' of the law. On the one hand, they translated the concepts and stipulations of state law for their clients; on the other, they translated their clients' grievances into the language of the law. In doing so, these lawyers not only helped their clients to assert their legal rights, they also contributed to the development of their legal consciousness and helped to trigger shifts in their ideas of personhood.

Chapters 6 and 7 examine the two contrasting dimensions of transformation and continuity that characterised developments in the legal sphere during the first decade of independence. In Chapter 6, I explore the ways the new ZANU (PF) government tried to transform the inherited legal system in which law, violence and racial domination had become intricately intertwined. In the same way that Chapter 1 sets out colonial officials' efforts to use the law to construct a particular social, economic and political order, this chapter shows how the post-colonial government used the law in its attempt to remake this old order and enact its modernising vision. It explores three key areas of legal reform during this period: the 'Africanisation' of the legal system, the reorganisation of 'customary law' courts, and reforms to the legal status and rights of women. The reforms of this period, I argue, opened up new avenues for the exercise of legal agency, and this was especially the case with the laws that elevated the legal status of women. In Chapter 7, I turn to the continuities in the legal arena focusing on the political sphere. I demonstrate that the ZANU (PF) government embraced the practices of the settler governments that preceded it and used the law to brutally quell political opposition. These continuities were the result of a combination of the institutional legacies of the settler state, the party's own authoritarian tendencies, the longstanding animosity between ZANU (PF) and ZAPU, as well as the political calculations of the 1980s. Although citizens tried to use the law to challenge state repression, during the 1980s law proved to have limited effectiveness as a shield. Not only was the government unwilling to entertain legal arguments that stood in the way of its objectives, the circumstances of the period were such that the dock had limited value as a platform from which to challenge the state or to draw attention to its misdeeds.

Lastly, Chapter 8 examines the ways that political struggles have been fought out in the legal arena in Zimbabwe since the late 1990s.

In it, I challenge the view that the explanation for these struggles lies in the global context of the post-Cold War moment. Instead, I argue that while the global ideological currents of the post-Cold War period did inflect the legal struggles in Zimbabwe, to fully understand them we must look much further back in history. I demonstrate that the 'authoritarian rule of law' implemented by the ZANU (PF) after 2000 can be traced to much older state practices which became embedded during the turbulent last decades of settler rule, and were later refined by the ZANU (PF). Similarly, the use of law by citizens for pragmatic and ideological reasons was part of a much older set of political repertoires.

1 | *Laying Down the Law: A Historical Background, 1890–1950*

Introduction

The immediate impetus for the colonisation of Zimbabwe was the search for the famed 'Second Rand'. Having failed to secure profitable gold mines in Witwatersrand, Cecil John Rhodes and his partners in the British South Africa Company (BSAC) began to look northwards to the lands between the Limpopo and the Zambezi which were thought to possess rich gold deposits that rivalled those found in the South African Transvaal.[1] The search for this 'Second Rand' was spearheaded by the BSAC which had been granted a Royal Charter in October 1889 to colonise the territory on the behalf of the British monarchy. Among other things, the Royal Charter charged the BSAC with the responsibility of establishing governmental structures in the new territory, and one of the first tasks that it undertook was to establish a legal system.

This chapter provides an overview of the establishment and operation of that legal system between 1890 and 1950, and makes four main points. First, it demonstrates that the establishment of the legal system was an integral part of the colonial project which proceeded incrementally and provoked tensions within the state and the settler community. Second, it contends that the interaction in the legal sphere between the imposed and the indigenous legal systems is best understood using the framework of legal pluralism. Third, it argues that law played an important role in the creation and maintenance of the social, economic and political order envisioned by colonial authorities. Finally, it intervenes in the debates over African interaction with the colonial system, by making the case for an analysis of African legal agency that goes beyond opportunism, and takes account of the

---

[1] I. Phimister, *An Economic and Social History of Zimbabwe, 1890–1948: Capital Accumulation and Class Struggle* (London, 1988), 6.

political imaginaries and the ideas of personhood that underlay this legal agency.

Establishing the Colonial Legal System

The imposition of a legal system was integral to the colonial project as, without this, colonists would have assumed the status of immigrants and be subject to local laws.[2] Establishing legal institutions also contributed to the process of state construction. Setting up colonial courts and ensuring that they were seen as the final arbiters of justice was part of the process of establishing the ascendancy of state institutions and projecting state authority across space.[3] However, in establishing a new legal system, colonial authorities had to deal with numerous practical issues such as drawing up laws, staffing legal institutions with qualified personnel and ensuring their smooth operation. The important challenge of incorporating the 'colonized' population and bringing them to recognise the new legal institutions also had to be dealt with. In addition, the content and the administration of the law were often the source of significant friction within the settler society.

One of the first steps taken towards establishing the legal system in Southern Rhodesia was the BSAC Administrator's decision in 1890 that Roman-Dutch law, which was applicable in the Cape Colony, would also apply to the new protectorate.[4] This was followed by steps to create formal judicial structures in 1891, when magistrates were appointed in Mashonaland. However, these magistrates were only authorised to exercise criminal and civil jurisdiction over Europeans, and could only hear cases involving Africans where this was deemed 'necessary in the interests of peace or for the prevention or punishment of acts of violence to persons or property.'[5] The promulgation of the 1894 Matabeleland Order in Council initiated a number of steps to establish the legal system on a firmer basis such as extending magistrates' jurisdiction to all residents in the colony regardless of race.

---

[2] Rene Maunier cited in E. Saada, 'The Empire of Law: Dignity, Prestige, and Domination in the "Colonial Situation"', *French Politics, Culture and Society*, 20 (2002), 105.

[3] Hansen and Stepputat, 'Introduction: States of Imagination', 5–6.

[4] C. Palley, *The Constitutional History and Law of Southern Rhodesia, 1888–1965* (Oxford, 1966), 493.

[5] Ibid., 513.

However, their sentencing powers were limited to fines of up to £25, a maximum imprisonment term of three months, and up to 15 strokes.[6]

The 1894 Matabeleland Order in Council also provided for the establishment of the Matabeleland High Court which had jurisdiction over all the inhabitants of the colony. This court was later reconstituted as the Southern Rhodesia High Court by means of the 1898 Order in Council. Appeals from the High Court were heard in the Cape Supreme Court in South Africa, which was subsequently reconstituted as the Appellate Division of the Union of South Africa. The final court of appeal for Southern Rhodesia was the Judicial Committee of the Privy Council in Britain, and this remained the case until the late 1960s when the Rhodesian Front-led government unilaterally declared independence from Britain.[7]

In the early years, High Court judges were appointed by the BSAC, subject to the approval of the British Secretary of State.[8] The first judge, Sir Joseph Vintcent, was appointed in 1894, followed by John Philip Fairbairn Watermeyer in 1896. The Southern Rhodesia High Court bench continued to have two judges until 1933, when William Musgrave Hopley was appointed. However, by 1964, the number of judges sitting in the High Court had increased to nine.[9] Whereas the first few judges had been hired from outside Southern Rhodesia, over time the majority came to be selected from within the colony's legal fraternity. Significantly, many of those who were appointed to the bench had previously held the position of Minister of Justice or Attorney-General.[10] By the 1960s, four of Southern Rhodesia's Chief Justices had served as Minister of Justice. This practice, in which individuals who had held political office or served as senior members in the executive were subsequently appointed to head the judiciary, introduced a systemic bias within the judiciary. This became especially clear from the 1960s, when large numbers of overtly political cases started coming before the courts.

---

[6] Report of the Courts of Inquiry Commission, Government of Rhodesia, Salisbury, 26–7. In 1942 the maximum sentence and fine were raised to six months and £50, respectively.
[7] Courts of Inquiry Commission, 9.
[8] Ibid, 5.
[9] Ibid.
[10] Palley, *The Constitutional History*, 549.

An important feature of the legal system which was brought to the fore by the operation of the jury system was the embedded nature of ideas about racial difference. Jury trials in Southern Rhodesia had been introduced by the 1899 Juries Ordinance which stipulated that all criminal trials in the High Court were to be tried before a jury of nine European men.[11] Between 1899 and 1908, there were 'several scandalous verdicts' involving 'unjustified acquittals of Europeans charged with offences against Africans and some baseless convictions of Africans charged with offences against European women.'[12] The Special Juries Ordinance of 1912 was an attempt to deal with this problem of overt racial bias in the system. According to the law, a special jury of five men who were chosen by the Governor and approved by the Legislative Assembly, would serve as jurors in cases of serious interracial crimes such as murder, culpable homicide, rape or robbery.[13] Despite this reform, jurors still 'tended to be swayed by white public opinion in their appraisal of cases that inflamed feelings against Africans.'[14]

Jury trials for Africans were later abandoned in 1927 at the behest of the Native Affairs Department (NAD). However, this did not signify a decline in the influence of ideas about race in the administration of justice. The change was in fact justified on such grounds. As part of their attempts to establish themselves as the sole 'experts' on all matters relating to Africans, NAD officials maintained that jury trials were not suited to cases involving Africans. This, they argued, was because 'European jurors had little or no knowledge of African custom or way of life' and that, 'few had any conception of the working of the African mind.'[15] As a result, the Criminal Trials (High Court) Act of 1927 abolished jury trials for Africans and stipulated that they should be tried by a judge assisted by two assessors, whose key qualifications often consisted of having served in the NAD for a long period. By contrast, the Act gave non-Africans the choice of being tried by a jury or by a judge and two assessors.[16]

---

[11] Courts of Inquiry Commission, 31.

[12] Ibid.

[13] Ibid., 32. See also Palley, *The Constitutional History*, 524.

[14] M. C. Steele, 'The Foundations of a "Native" Policy: Southern Rhodesia, 1923–1933', (PhD Thesis, Simon Fraser University, 1972), 129.

[15] Courts of Inquiry Commission, 32.

[16] Ibid., 33.

Another key feature of the Southern Rhodesian legal system was the perennial tension between the officials from the NAD and the Law Department. Native Commissioners (NCs), who came under the NAD, were primarily administrative officers but had also been granted judicial powers over all inhabitants of Southern Rhodesia in 1899.[17] The fact that they had both executive and judicial powers, combined with their patronizing and racist views about Africans, contributed to their tendency to cultivate personalised forms of authority in their districts.[18] This brought them into conflict with Law Department officials who saw it as their duty to ensure that there was strict adherence to due process in the administration of the law.[19] It should be pointed out, however, that Law Department officials were committed to a minimalist idea of the rule of law which had two key features. First, the idea that the exercise of power had to be governed by law, and the second, that law was supposed to be administered according to set rules and procedures. As will be clear in the rest of this book, Law Department officials were much more flexible when it came to other aspects of a more elaborate idea of the rule of law, such as the independence of the judiciary, the equal application of laws regardless of race, or, indeed, the need for law to be just in a substantive sense.[20] Importantly, tensions between the NAD and the Law Department continued to be a feature of the legal system throughout the period of settler rule.

Soon after the occupation of Southern Rhodesia, a legal profession began to emerge in order to meet the demand for legal services from the growing mining, agriculture and commercial sectors in the colony. Many members of the nascent profession had migrated from South Africa, and, consequently, it took on many of the features of the South African legal profession. This was particularly evident in its structure, its commitment to formalism, and its efforts to restrict entry on the grounds of gender and race.[21] As in South Africa, the local

---

[17] Ibid., 20. This practice was abolished in 1962.

[18] A. Shutt, '"The Natives are getting out of hand": Legislating Manners, Insolence and Contemptuous Behaviour in Southern Rhodesia, c. 1910–1963', *JSAS*, 33 (2007).

[19] Ibid., 656–7. For a discussion of similar tensions in Kenya and South Africa see Shadle, 'Changing Traditions' and I. Evans, *Bureaucracy and Race: Native Administration in South Africa* (Los Angeles, 1997).

[20] D. H. Cole, '"An Unqualified Human Good": E. P. Thompson and the Rule of Law', *Journal of Law and Society* 28 (2001), 185.

[21] See M. Chanock, 'The Lawyer's Self: Sketches on Establishing a Professional Identity in South Africa 1900–1925', *Law in Context Special Issue*, 16 (1999).

legal profession was a divided one which consisted of advocates and attorneys.[22] Although attorneys could appear in the lower courts and be approached by clients directly, they could not appear before the High Court. By contrast, advocates could appear in the High Court but were barred from being approached by clients directly, and had to be briefed by an attorney. However, as Claire Palley notes, there was little justification for such specialisation in the profession, given the small size of the population that could afford lawyers' services even as late as the 1960s.[23] This 'division of juridical labour' was, in large part, an effort by lawyers to control the supply and, by extension, the cost of legal services in the colony.

Another means by which the legal fraternity sought to control the supply of legal services was by policing entry into the profession. The process of becoming an attorney involved a period of attachment to a law firm as an 'articled clerk', and the length of the attachment varied depending on whether one had a law degree or prior legal experience as an advocate.[24] This period of clerkship was followed by a three-part Attorney's Admission Exam, and individuals who wanted to work as notary publics or conveyancers had to sit for additional exams. To be admitted to the Southern Rhodesian Bar as an advocate, one had to have qualified as a barrister in Britain or South Africa, or attained a law degree in either of the two countries. After completing their pupillage, aspiring advocates had to pass exams in local statute law, as well as Roman-Dutch law in the case of those who had studied in Britain.

For the most part, colonial officials envisioned a limited role for Africans in the administration of the law. They generally played minor roles such as interpretation or carrying out various clerical duties. Two key barriers to entry into the legal profession for the vast majority of Africans were the educational qualifications and the financial requirements for pursuing a degree in law. The few Africans who did possess the necessary educational qualifications had to contend with the

I am using formalism here to refer to the view amongst legal professionals that 'the rule of the law must be maintained as a purely legal standard devoid of an ideological content'. G. Feltoe 'Law, Ideology and Coercion in Southern Rhodesia' (University of Kent MPh Thesis, 1978), 81.

[22] Advocates and attorneys are similar to barristers and solicitors, respectively.

[23] Palley, *The Constitutional History*, 558.

[24] M. E. Currie, *The History of Gill, Godlonton and Gerrans, 1912–1980* (Harare, 1982), 39.

discriminatory nature of the profession and were unlikely to secure a place for attachment. The obstacles to gaining access to the legal profession automatically eliminated the likelihood of any African becoming a judge, not that this would have been accepted. Africans were also excluded from serving as jurors in the High Court. In 1927, legal provision was made for the High Court Judge to appoint assessors, and at times Africans could be called upon. As I show later, chiefs and headmen were only granted limited judicial authority in the late 1930s.

A central aspect in the operation of the colony's legal system was the culture of 'legalism'.[25] As alluded to earlier, this was partly due to the Law Department officials' commitment to a set of ideas about appropriate rule-bound conduct on the part of state officials. It was also about the role of law as a mode of rule for the state. Legalism, as Martin Chanock has shown in the case of South Africa, was not about constraining state action, but enabling it. It was a means of 'creating powers' and 'endowing officials with regulated ways of acting'.[26] In practice, legalism in Southern Rhodesia meant the implementation of an autocratic form of rule, that was underpinned by law and the deployment of legal language. Legalism also served the secondary purpose of legitimising state actions in the eyes of the local settler population and the metropolitan government.

Although the foundation for legalism was laid during the years of company rule, it was carried much further after 1923 when a settler government led by Charles Coghlan took over, under the Responsible Government Constitution. The achievement of Responsible Government status meant that effective power now lay in Salisbury. The government could, therefore, make and implement policy without having to defer to the Colonial Office as much as other British colonies like Nyasaland and Northern Rhodesia. Although there was a reservation clause in the Responsible Government Constitution which gave the British government the right to revoke any laws that negatively affected Africans, this power was rarely exercised. Unlike the Company Government, which was primarily focused on making profits, the new government was more responsive to settler needs. It

---

[25] I am using *legalism* here to refer to the reliance on law as a mode of rule by state officials. By contrast, I use *formalism* to describe legal professionals' approach to the law.

[26] M. Chanock, *The Making of South African Legal Culture, 1902–1936, Fear, Favour, Prejudice* (Cambridge, 2001), 22.

actively pursued the goal of promoting permanent European settlement, and made extensive use of the law in order to achieve this. This was clearest in the area of agricultural policy. Soon after attaining Responsible Government status, a much better financed Land and Agricultural Bank was set up in 1924, and in 1925 the Morris Carter Land Commission was appointed to look into the question of land distribution in the colony. Speaking to the Legislative Assembly in 1927, Coghlan declared, '... this is essentially a country where the white man has come and desires to stay, and he can only be certain of doing so if he has certain portions of the country made his exclusively.'[27] These moves culminated in the Land Apportionment Act of 1930 which allocated 49 million acres of land in the country's best agro-ecological zones to the settlers who numbered approximately 50,000 and mostly lived in urban areas. Twenty-nine million acres of land in the poorer agro-ecological zones were allocated to the African population who numbered about 1,081,000.[28]

Dealing with Indigenous Legal Systems

The establishment of the colonial legal system also raised the question about how the imposed system and the indigenous ones would relate. In Southern Rhodesia, state officials initially hoped that indigenous legal systems would gradually die away as Africans abandoned their own institutions and patronised the colonial legal system. Behind this hope was a belief in the superiority of the British legal system, and a corresponding derision for African legal systems. However, these early hopes gradually waned as state officials came up against the limitations of their administrative capacity, and the resilience of African legal systems. The Southern Rhodesian experience with respect to colonial officials' efforts to deal with the indigenous legal systems suggests that a more appropriate approach to thinking about developments in the legal arena is that of 'legal pluralism'.

From the outset, the BSAC had instructions to give 'regard' to local laws. Article 14 of the Royal Charter carried the following stipulation:

---

[27] Cited in V. E. M. Machingaidze, 'Agrarian Change from Above: The Southern Rhodesia Native Land Husbandry Act and the African Response', *The International Journal of African Historical Studies*, 24 (1991), 558–9.
[28] Ibid., 558.

In the administration of justice to the said peoples or inhabitants careful regard shall always be had to the customs and laws of the class or tribe or nation to which the parties respectively belong, especially with regard to the holding, possession, transfer and disposition of lands and goods, and the testate or intestate succession thereto, and marriage, divorce, legitimacy, and other rights of property and personal rights, but subject to any British laws which may be in force in any of the territories aforesaid and applicable to the peoples or inhabitants thereof.[29]

Under the 1894 Order in Council, the position was slightly revised to include the provision that indigenous law would apply in civil cases, as long as the law in question was not 'repugnant to natural justice or morality.'[30] However, during the first few decades of colonial occupation, officials in Southern Rhodesia were reluctant to accord African legal systems a formal place within the colonial legal sphere. As Diana Jeater notes, early colonial officials felt that: 'It was both the duty of, and the justification for white occupation of the territory to ensure that African "barbarism" gave way to white "civilisation".'[31]

The differences between African and colonial legal systems were interpreted by many colonial officials as evidence of the primitive nature of the former. One such difference was the fact that, while the colonial system was based on fixed written laws, the local systems operated on the basis of oral and more flexible 'rules'.[32] In addition, colonial courts were based on a retributive approach to justice, whereas local courts tended to operate on the basis of a restorative approach that focused on reparations and the maintenance of social harmony. Furthermore, indigenous legal systems did not divide offences into civil and criminal, as was the case with the colonial legal system. The differences also extended to court procedures and rules of evidence. Whereas colonial courts had narrow criteria with respect to acceptable evidence, and strict rules limiting public participation, local courts had a more flexible approach in both regards. Holleman noted three main

---

[29] Cited in H. F. Child, *The History and Extent of Recognition of Tribal Law in Rhodesia* (Salisbury, 1973), i. Section 4 of the May 1891 Order in Council, and Section 9 of the High Commissioner's Proclamation of June 1891 contained similar provisions.

[30] Palley, *The Constitutional History*, 505.

[31] D. Jeater, '"Their Idea of Justice Is So Peculiar", Southern Rhodesia 1890–1920', in P. Coss (ed), *The Moral World of the Law* (Cambridge, 2000), 180.

[32] Ibid.

stages in the procedure of chiefs' courts among the Shona-speaking communities he studied. The hearings began with the testimonies of the litigants, and this was followed by the audience's participation in order 'to interrogate, to volunteer information, voice opinions based on intimate knowledge of local relations and specific circumstances, and generally contribute to a searching inquiry into the cause of the dispute before them.'[33] Once the matter had been discussed exhaustively, the chief and his advisors handed down a ruling.

NCs' early resistance to the exercise of judicial powers by chiefs was also based on their suspicion of chiefs, given the central role they had played in the 1896–7 rebellions. As a result, they were wary of any policies that might shore up power of the chiefs. The 1898 Order in Council, therefore, only authorised chiefs to act as salaried 'constables' whose duties included notifying the NC of 'all crimes or offences, deaths and suspicious disappearances, prevailing diseases and epidemics' within their areas.[34] As 'Indirect Rule' was adopted in many British colonies, Southern Rhodesian officials remained opposed to giving chiefs a greater role in the administration of the colony. 'The Colonial Office doctrine of Indirect Rule, as applied to certain dependencies in Africa like Tanganyika', Steele notes, 'found considerable disfavour in governmental circles and with the European public at large. A retired N.C. warned that its introduction would turn the Colony into "a second Basutoland", pre-empting its development as a white man's country.'[35] As a result, Chiefs' responsibilities were only marginally increased with the passage of the Native Affairs Act of 1927, and its subsequent amendment in 1931.[36]

The official position was, however, different from the reality on the ground. Although chiefs had limited official duties, unofficially they continued to exercise substantial judicial authority, in some cases, with the tacit approval of NCs. This approval was partly because NCs had reconciled themselves to the fact that they were not able to try all the cases arising in their areas, in addition to carrying out all of their

---

[33] J. F. Holleman, 'Law and Anthropology: A Necessary Partnership for the Study of Legal Change in Plural Systems', *Journal of African Law*, 23 (1979), 119.

[34] Child, *The History and Extent*, 12.

[35] Steele, 'The Foundations', 75.

[36] Apprehending offenders and reporting subversive rumours were added to chiefs' responsibilities in 1927, and reporting the murder of twins and 'deaths imputed to witchcraft' were added in 1931.

other duties. They also grudgingly accepted the fact that they did not have the capacity to stop all chiefs from hearing cases, even if they had wanted to. As a result, by the late 1920s there were growing calls from NAD officials to formally grant chiefs limited civil jurisdiction. Their thinking was also influenced by the passage of the 1930 Native Authorities Ordinance in Northern Rhodesia, which gave chiefs greater powers. A proposal for chiefs to be granted limited judicial powers was duly drafted and submitted to the NAD Advisory Committee in 1931. Speaking in support of this proposal the influential NC, E. G. Howman, remarked that: 'If you get the right kind of chief he settles cases very much better than I can. He has the inside knowledge which I have not got very often ... No matter how proficient a European may become in settling native cases, I do not think he ever gets to the bottom of things.'[37]

The proposal was firmly resisted by the Law Department, and a legal opinion it produced on the subject in 1931 was categorical. 'Chiefs', it argued, 'are of course completely ignorant of rules of procedure and law. To confer statutory jurisdiction in judicial matters on unqualified persons is wrong.'[38] However, by the mid-1930s senior government officials were becoming more receptive to the idea. This was partly due to concerns about rising law and order problems in the colony, which were seen as a result of the weakening of the authority of 'traditional' officials. The proposal also found favour with the Prime Minister, Godfrey Huggins, as it sat well with his policy of greater racial segregation. Consequently, in 1937 the Native Law and Courts Act, which was based on the earlier proposal, was passed.

The legislation empowered the Governor to award warrants to chiefs and headmen's courts authorising them to exercise civil jurisdiction. In reality, the Act was not providing any new powers, but simply giving formal recognition to what was taking place on the ground. The Act also represented an acknowledgement that, despite the Southern Rhodesian state's considerable capacity, after almost five decades of colonial rule it still did not possess a monopoly of judicial authority. This move to draw 'traditional' leaders' courts into the service of the state was not accompanied by any attempt to codify indigenous laws. However, one of its consequences was the gradual incorporation of

---

[37] Cited in Steele, 'The Foundations', 85.
[38] Cited in *Southern Rhodesia Parliamentary Debates*, 28 January 1969, 620.

features of the colonial legal system into the chiefs' courts. For example, under the legislation, warranted courts of headmen and chiefs became courts of record and therefore had to keep a civil record book. Other more enterprising chiefs sought to appropriate more features of the colonial courts; however, these changes occurred at different rates in chiefs' courts around the colony.[39]

Maintaining Law and (the Social) Order

The colonial legal system was enlisted in the maintenance of 'order' in two senses. First, the legal system was deeply implicated in the creation and maintenance of a colonial social and political order that was primarily founded on racial difference. In Southern Rhodesia, as in other colonial contexts, law was used to create the society envisioned by the settler administration. Law, as Bourdieu reminds us, is an active discourse that not only names but also seeks to create the things it names.[40] It was therefore used in creating and authorising categories of persons, apportioning them with rights and duties, and allocating them positions in the colonial social hierarchy. However, this process was not simply about the deployment of the constitutive power of the law. The coercive and constitutive dimensions of the law were both marshalled, often simultaneously, to achieve this end.

The efforts to police racial difference in Southern Rhodesia were most clearly dramatised in the legislation and trials that were related to the imagined threat of 'black peril' in the early years of colonial rule.[41] Settler anxieties about perceived sexual threats against European women by African men led to the passage of the Criminal Law Amendment Ordinance of 1903, which provided for the death sentence for Africans convicted of the attempted rape of European women. In the same year, the Immorality and Indecency Suppression Ordinance was passed which criminalised sexual relations between African men and European women outside of marriage. However, sexual relations between European men and African women were not subject to similar regulation. As Diana Jeater points out, both African patriarchal ideas,

---

[39] Holleman, 'Law and Anthropology', 120.
[40] P. Bourdieu, 'The Force of Law: Towards a Sociology of the Juridical Field', *Hastings Law Journal*, 38 (1987), 838–9.
[41] See J. McCulloch, *Black Peril, White Virtue: Sexual Crime in Southern Rhodesia, 1902–1935* (Bloomington, 2000); Steele, 'The Foundations', 124–30.

as well as Victorian ideas about gender, often found expression in the laws that sought to enforce a particular racial and gendered hierarchy.[42]

Besides the dramatic and emotive cases involving inter-racial sexual relations, the laws relating to everyday activities also played a role in reproducing the colonial social and economic order. As John Comaroff points out, 'it was by means of legal instruments ... that economic rights, entitlements, and proprieties were established, that labour relations and contracts were promulgated and policed, that interests were negotiated.'[43] In Southern Rhodesia several laws were passed to enable the transfer of economic resources through land dispossession, taxation and forced labour. Often these laws were both coercive and constitutive in their operation. For instance, the draconian Master and Servants Ordinance of 1901, which made workplace 'infractions' crimes against the state, provided a regulatory framework which enabled European employers to 'control' their African employees. At the same time, by making it a crime for an African worker to disobey an instruction by a European employer, the legislation effectively authorised the colonial racial hierarchy. Similarly, the Native Pass and the Native Urban Locations Ordinances were as much about regulating labour and crime as they were about policing racial difference and reserving the urban areas for the European population.[44]

The laws governing educational policy also exhibited a similar tendency towards social engineering. As Dickson Mungazi's study of colonial educational policy shows, the Education Ordinance of 1899 and the laws that succeeded it, created an education system that would prepare Africans to take up the role of manual labourers in the colonial economy.[45] This thinking was clearly expressed by the Chief Native Commissioner (CNC) for Mashonaland in his annual report for 1905, in which he observed: 'It is cheap labour that we need in this country, and it has yet to be proved that the Native who can read and write turns out [to be] a good labourer. As far as we can

---

[42] D. Jeater, *Marriage, Power and Perversion: The Construction of a Moral Discourse in Southern Rhodesia 1894–1930* (Oxford, 1993).

[43] Comaroff, 'Colonialism, Culture and the Law', 309.

[44] McCulloch, *Black Peril, White Virtue*, 52. See also T. Yoshikuni, *African Urban Experiences in Colonial Zimbabwe: A Social History of Harare before 1925* (Harare, 2007), 41.

[45] D. Mungazi, *Colonial Education for Africans: George Stark's Policy in Zimbabwe* (New York, 1991).

determine, the native who can read and write will not work on farms and in mines. The official policy is to develop the native on lines least likely to lead to any risk of clashing with Europeans.'[46] Even seemingly minor aspects of colonial social relations such as racial etiquette were subject to legislation as NCs tried to ensure that they had the power to deal with any behaviour they considered to be insolent. As Shutt's work demonstrates, the regulation of etiquette was one of the means by which 'difference and domination were defined and refined'.[47]

The legal system also played an important role in maintaining order in the sense of preventing unrest and ensuring the safety of the settler population and their property. This was achieved, firstly, through the persistent day to day efforts by NCs to prosecute and punish Africans charged with 'crimes' related to pass laws, taxes and other regulations. 'Sentences imposed on blacks, (often for minor offences) were harsh', Chanock aptly observes, 'if one views them as being only punishment for the offence, or deterrence. But punishment and deterrence were also closely involved with the protection of white power. What had to be deterred was not simply crime, but also defiance and rebelliousness.'[48] In addition, colonial officials were constantly on the watch for 'subversive' African organisations. A key difficulty the Southern Rhodesian government faced during the interwar period was the resistance to legislation that sought to silence political dissent from groups within the settler community such as the press, missionaries and settler opposition parties. This resistance stemmed from the fact that the reservation clauses in the Responsible Government prevented the government from passing legislation that explicitly targeted Africans. As such, any legislation dealing with political dissent effectively applied to all residents of the colony, regardless of race. As a consequence, opposition parties and the press were wary that such laws would be used against them. It was therefore necessary for the government to demonstrate the existence of a threat from the African population that was significant enough to convince these groups to put aside their misgivings.

A key source of anxiety for the government during the 1920s which prompted moves to enact stronger security legislation was the

---

[46] Cited in Mungazi, *Colonial Education*, 8.
[47] Shutt, 'The Natives are Getting out of Hand', 653. See also Saada, 'The Empire of Law'.
[48] Chanock, *The Making of South African Legal Culture*, 129.

Industrial and Commercial Workers Union (ICU). The ICU was originally established in Cape Town in 1919 by Clements Kadalie, a migrant worker from Nyasaland. The Southern Rhodesia branch of the ICU was established in 1927 and soon became one of the more radical African organisations of the interwar period.[49] By 1928, the government had come to see it as a subversive group, and the Chief Native Commissioner drafted the Unrest Bill in order to provide state officials with more powers to deal with it. The Bill was modelled on the Hostility Clause contained in South Africa's Native Administration Act of 1927. Among other things, it proposed a maximum penalty of 'five years' imprisonment or a £500 fine or both, against any person who incited "natives" to commit unlawful or seditious acts or who promoted "feelings of hostility between different races in the Colony".[50] However, the Bill never made it into law owing to opposition from the press and European trade unions.[51] Nevertheless, for two and a half years, ICU meetings were attended by European CID detectives who took notes of the speeches they deemed to be 'provocative'. One result of this surveillance was the conviction of Masotsha Ndlovu on charges of criminal slander for calling the Chief Native Commissioner, C. L. Carbutt, 'a bad man and an oppressor of natives'.[52]

The calls for stronger legislation to deal with dissent amongst Africans subsided in the late 1920s. However, the economic depression of the early 1930s and the attendant agitation among Africans prompted the ICU to make efforts to recruit in the rural areas. This led to renewed efforts to pass stronger legislation to deal with 'agitators' in the form of the 1932 Prevention of Racial Discord Bill which was based on the 1928 Unrest Bill. The Bill was later withdrawn partly because the parliamentary session was shortened to allow for the Prime Minister to travel abroad. More importantly, government officials could not demonstrate a sufficient threat to sway the opinions of key sections of the settler population.

In the end, it was the activities of the Independent African Churches, in particular the Watchtower movement, which tipped the scale in the

---

[49] I. Phimister and C van Onselen, 'The Labour Movement in Zimbabwe: 1900–1945', in B. Raftopoulos and I Phimister (eds), *Keep on Knocking: A History of the Labour Movement in Zimbabwe* (Harare, 1997), 17–18.
[50] Steele, 'The Foundations', 171.
[51] Ibid.
[52] Ibid, 175.

government's favour. From the 1910s, Independent African Churches had come to be seen as a problem by colonial authorities as they often disseminated 'prophecies' that foretold the end of colonial rule, and encouraged their members to defy the colonial authorities. The Watchtower was one such religious movement. It had been introduced in Southern Rhodesia prior to World War I by migrants from Nyasaland, and over the course of the following decades, the movement was kept under surveillance. This was especially so after the 1915 Chilembwe uprising in Nyasaland, which was led by Watchtower adherents.[53] From the early 1920s, there were abortive efforts by successive CNCs to have legislation enacted to suppress the Watchtower Movement. These efforts were renewed as the Watchtower took on an anti-European stance from 1933. They were given further momentum by the 1935 riots on the Copperbelt in Northern Rhodesia, which were associated with the Watchtower, as well as the rise of local independent churches whose preachers could not be dealt with by means of deportation. A Native Preachers Bill was drafted in 1936 but was later withdrawn. The powers designed to deal with 'subversive' African preachers were instead incorporated into the Sedition Bill which was enacted the same year.[54]

The challenge in the 1920s and early 1930s had been to demonstrate a threat from the African population that was sufficient to bring members of the settler populace to agree to laws that increased state powers to deal with political dissent. The Watchtower movement had reached this threshold and, notwithstanding the opposition to the legislation in the Parliament, the passage of the Sedition Act reflected this. The passage of the Act also foreshadowed what was to come in the post-World War II period, as the settler government grappled with the 'problem' of African nationalism.

African Engagement with the Colonial Legal System

With all of the legal changes that were underway, an important question to ask is how did Africans engage with the new legal system? Studies of

[53] Phimister and van Onselen, 'The Labour Movement', p. 11. For an account of the Watchtower Movement's activities in Nyasaland and Northern Rhodesia, see K. Fields, *Revival and Rebellion in Colonial Central Africa* (Princeton, 1985).

[54] *Southern Rhodesia Parliamentary Debates*, 23 April 1936, 1027–32.

early African interactions with the legal system in Southern Rhodesia have advanced two main positions. Scholars such as Elizabeth Schmidt and Tapiwa Zimudzi have maintained that Africans were quick to make use of the colonial legal system. Schmidt, for example, argues that African women took advantage of new laws which prohibited practices such as forced marriages, child pledging and polygamy in order to rebel against patriarchal power.[55] At the same time, men took advantage of the laws to gain 'control' over their wives. She notes that:

Between October 1899 and February 1905, the native commissioner heard 345 civil cases. Of this total, 95 cases pertained to girls who refused to marry men who had paid bridewealth for them, while 65 concerned wives who had actually run away. Thus nearly half the civil cases heard by the state during this period involved men attempting to obtain the return of recalcitrant wives.[56]

Schmidt, however, argues that African women's newfound freedom was short lived due to the government's efforts to shore up the authority of chiefs during the 1920s and 1930s.

Like Schmidt, Zimudzi sees a significant degree of African agency within colonial courts. His study focuses on African women who were tried in the High Court for serious offences such as spousal murder and infanticide between 1900 and 1952. For Zimudzi, the accused women's agency took a number of forms. Many sought to exploit judges' gender stereotypes by portraying themselves as weak-minded, and having been influenced by their lovers to murder their spouses. Zimudzi notes that 'many female offenders on spousal murder cases were recommended to mercy largely on the grounds that they were intellectual simpletons whose "dullness of intellect" made it impossible for them to appreciate the gravity of the nature and consequences of their offences.'[57] In cases of infanticide, accused women initially pleaded ignorance as a mitigating factor. When this strategy became ineffective in attracting the sympathy of judges, they:

---

[55] E. Schmidt, 'Negotiated Spaces and Contested Terrain: Men, Wommen, and the Law in Colonial Zimbabwe, 1890-1939', *JSAS*, 16 (1990), 625.
[56] Ibid., 640.
[57] T. Zimudzi, 'African Women, Violent Crime and the Criminal Law in Colonial Zimbabwe, 1900–1952', *JSAS*, 30 (2004), 506.

... sought to project to colonial judges the image of 'tutored natives' who had been coerced by 'raw natives' into killing their twins. These female offenders emphasised how their efforts or suggestions to take the newborn twins to mission stations, which by then had become well-established sanctuaries for such infants, had been overcome by the determination of the 'raw natives' to kill the twins.[58]

Some accused women tried to portray themselves as motherly in order to earn judges' pity, while others resorted to intimidating witnesses who gave evidence against them.

By contrast, Jeater has argued that the early courtroom interactions between Africans and Europeans were characterised by miscommunication due to the fundamentally different legal systems they were coming from. Owing to this miscommunication, judges delivered rulings that did not conform to African litigants' conceptions of justice, and as a result Africans reverted to their own legal forums. Jeater argues that:

We all now recognize that 'what colonial officials treated as immutable customary law was itself the product of historical struggles unfolding during the colonial period.' However, what struck me, from looking at the records from Melsetter district in the 1890s and 1900s, is how little this was recognized by the participants themselves. People who trekked scores of miles to take a case to the NC did so, it seems, not because they could exploit European forms of justice but because they did not accept that it differed significantly from their own systems of justice. What the NC or the magistrate thought he had heard and understood and what the litigants had heard and understood seem to have been two separate things. There may, in fact have been far less hybridity and far more conservatism in African responses to white courts than we have generally realized.[59]

With regard to Melsetter District, she observes that 'it is remarkable how rarely local Africans used the text-based legal systems of the white courts in their struggles with each other'.[60] Extending this argument to Southern Rhodesia as a whole, Jeater argues, '... as well as maintaining their own systems of jurisprudence, Africans across the territory also

[58] Ibid., 514.
[59] Jeater, *Law, Language and Science*, 77–8.
[60] Ibid.

maintained their own judicial procedures, which remained remarkably resilient against attempts to displace them.'[61]

These studies raise a number of important issues with respect to African engagement with colonial legal systems in the early colonial period, the first being the extent to which Africans utilised the new courts. The divergence in the findings of the studies may have something to do with the different case studies that they draw on. Jeater's study focuses on Melsetter District where the Mount Silinda Mission had been active from the early colonial period. She, therefore, suggests that 'the influence of the mission on both young and old, combined with the prevalence of waged labour, meant that there was little relative advantage to be gained from drawing on text or from claims to modernity.'[62] What is unclear, however, is the extent to which these findings are generalizable to the rest of the colony. A second factor that explains the divergence is the different approaches that the studies adopt. Whereas Jeater looks at African society more generally, Zimudzi and Schmidt take the path of greater disaggregation and examine the ways different categories of African women engaged with the colonial courts in specific circumstances. Zimudzi, for example, focuses on criminal cases in which the African women brought before them had no option but to engage with the colonial legal system as failure to do so was costly. Schmidt also deals with individuals who had vested interests in making use of the colonial legal system. These groups may well have found colonial courts to be uncomfortably foreign, and much is likely to have been lost in translation during courtroom exchanges. Nevertheless, the actual outcomes were probably more important in shaping their decisions to use colonial courts. This is a point that Jeater acknowledges for the 1920s but perhaps not sufficiently for the earlier decades.[63]

Notwithstanding the aforementioned points, Jeater is likely to be correct regarding the occurrence of miscommunication in the early period of colonial rule and makes an important contribution to the way we think about these early legal interactions. It is worth pointing out, however, that emphasising the idea of miscommunication might stand in the way of a better understanding of the interaction between

---

[61] Ibid., 207.
[62] Ibid.
[63] Ibid., 208.

legal systems in colonial contexts. In addition, highlighting the differences between textual and oral legal systems risks missing moments
when African agency bridged the two, either through the performance of text-based archetypes or through the selective borrowing of
concepts.[64] Last, the resilience of African legal systems and ideas of
jurisprudence, and the instrumentalisation of colonial courts need not
be seen as mutually exclusive processes.

An alternative way of approaching indigenous legal systems which
incorporates both resilience and innovation is Sally Falk Moore's idea
of the 'semi-autonomous social field'. For Moore, the semi-autonomous
social field 'can generate rules and customs and symbols internally' and
has 'the means to induce or coerce compliance; but it is simultaneously
set in a larger social matrix which can, and does affect and invade it,
sometimes at the invitation of persons inside it, sometimes at its own
instance.'[65] An important question with respect to African engagement
with colonial law is therefore how to account for the development of
African legal consciousness. Zimudzi suggests that:

By the time the High Court of Southern Rhodesia was established, African
women had already had eight years of court experience in colonial civil
and criminal courts. Throughout the half-century considered here, they dis-
played increasing boldness and agency in the High Court. The legal consciousness of African women charged with spousal murder manifested itself
in numerous ways, often showing their awareness of those openings in the
colonial legal system that could work in their favour.[66]

He is perhaps overstating the point in arguing that between 1890
and 1898 Africans had developed sufficient legal consciousness to
make use of colonial courts. This is particularly so when one considers the fact that the Magistrate's courts were only granted jurisdiction over Africans in 1894. However, Zimudzi's larger point remains
valid: the increased use of colonial courts led to greater awareness
amongst Africans of their procedures, the underlying jurisprudence
and the opportunities to make use of them for personal ends. This
increased experience with colonial courts worked in conjunction with

---

[64] See Peterson, 'Morality Plays'.
[65] S. Falk Moore, 'Law and Social Change: The Semi-Autonomous Social Field as
an Appropriate Subject of Study', *Law and Society Review*, 4 (1973), 720.
[66] Zimudzi, 'African Women', 508.

the exchange of information within social networks, as well as the role of African intermediaries such as court clerks and interpreters.[67]

The second key issue the debate on early African interactions with the colonial legal system raises has to do with why Africans made use of these courts. For the most part, scholars have emphasised calculation or opportunism. This, for example, is implicit in the study by Schmidt. Similarly, Holleman underscores the opportunities that the contrasts between the colonial and indigenous legal systems offered for 'forum shopping'. After conducting fieldwork in four different areas in Mashonaland during the 1940s, he observed disapprovingly:

I saw the kind of situations in which there was sufficient difference between various jurisdictions to make it worthwhile for litigants to shop around for the kind of law that would be profitable to them. Tanner and others have called this "the selective use of legal systems" but this kind of competition does not enhance the certainty of law and is unlikely to promote the cause of justice.[68]

An additional result he noted was the undermining of chiefs' courts which manifested itself in '... the sorry spectacle of a chief and litigant threatening one another to call in the strong arm of District Administration to see that justice be done, while the public watched with a mixture of amusement, bewilderment and scorn.' Holleman adds that: 'Such scenes were not a rarity in the later 'forties and early 'fifties, but one of the symptoms of the growing tension between tradition and innovation on the intersections of disparate legal cultures and competitive legal jurisdictions.'[69]

Although these observations about the opportunities that jurisdictional competition availed for the instrumentalisation of the law are valid, there was something else of importance that was under way. The colonial period had unleashed a number of processes that led to new conceptions of goods, persons and relationships amongst Africans.[70] The increasing levels of education and the spread of Christianity fostered new ways of thinking about the self, both in relation to others

---

[67] See B. N. Lawrence, et al. (eds), *Intermediaries, Interpreters, and Clerks: African Employees in the Making of Colonial Africa* (Madison, 2006).

[68] Holleman, 'Law and Anthropology', 120.

[69] Ibid., 121.

[70] S. E. Merry, 'Law and Colonialism', *Law and Society Review* 25 (1991), 892.

and to the state. In addition, rural to urban migration brought Africans into contact with new ideas and into new spaces which allowed for 'self-fashioning'. The courts also mediated the process of social change by introducing and enforcing new social and economic ideas related to debt, gender relations and marriage.[71] Much as they had wanted to, colonial officials were not able to control the formation of African subjectivities.

These new subjectivities were increasingly evident in African associational life. From the 1920s, new associations were forming around different issues of common concern, formulating critiques of colonial policies, and making demands of the colonial government. For example, elitist associations of the 1920s such as the Rhodesian Bantu Voters Association, made claims for the right to vote and invoked arguments about British justice and 'equal rights for all civilized men'.[72] Labour organisations like the ICU offered fairly radical critiques of the unequal distribution of wealth in the colony, deplored the constant harassment of workers by the authorities, and demanded better working and living conditions for Africans.[73] Under the leadership of Charles Mzingeli, the Reformed Industrial and Commercial Workers Union (RICU) fought for Africans' rights of access to the city and made claims for an 'imperial working class citizenship' for African workers from the 1940s.[74] The appeals to the law by Africans and their mobilisation of legal discourse, especially in cases involving the state, were thus about more than just opportunism. They reflected shifting ideas of personhood, emergent political imaginaries and alternative visions of the colony's social and political order.

Conclusion

By World War II, Southern Rhodesia had an established legal system that was central, both to the constitution of the state and the assertion

---

[71] See, for example, R. Smith, '"Money Breaks Blood Ties": Chiefs' Courts and the Transition from Lineage Debt to Commercial Debt in Sipolilo District', *JSAS*, 24 (1998).

[72] M. West, *The Rise of the African Middle Class: Colonial Zimbabwe* (Indianapolis, 2002), 127.

[73] Ibid., 134–40.

[74] T. Scarnecchia, *The Urban Roots of Democracy and Political Violence in Zimbabwe: Harare and Highfield, 1940–1964* (Rochester, 2008).

of its power. The establishment of these legal institutions had been central to state construction, aiding as it did the efforts to project state authority across space. However, law was also a source of division within the colonial state. Its content and the administration were the cause of constant friction between the NAD officials, who wanted to exercise a form of personal rule in their districts, and Law Department officials, who insisted on rule-bound conduct. An important feature of the colonial legal system was the embedded nature of ideas about racial difference. From the early years of colonial rule, state officials took the position that Africans would have a very limited role in the administration of the law, and their legal systems were to have no formal place in the colonial legal sphere. Theirs was to be the role of grateful recipients of the gift of 'civilised' law. However, colonial officials were ultimately forced to acknowledge the limits of their authority, and in 1937 chiefs and headmen were formally granted jurisdiction over civil cases amongst Africans. African responses to the establishment of the colonial legal system were far from passive. From the early years of colonial rule, there was growing recourse to colonial laws and courts by different social groups in order to pursue their respective interests. At one level, these uses of the law were calculated and opportunistic, and reflected the increasingly sophisticated legal consciousness of African litigants. At another level, they were a reflection of the underlying political imaginaries, ideas about personhood and alternative visions of the Southern Rhodesian social and political order that animated African litigants. These developments provide the necessary context for understanding the struggles about the law and by means of the law during the post-World War II period that are the focus of the rest of this book.

2 | Customising Justice and Constructing Subjects: State, 'Customary Law' and Chiefs' Courts, 1950–1980

Introduction

In contrast to other British colonies in Africa which adopted 'Indirect Rule' in the 1920s and 1930s, Southern Rhodesian authorities had largely resisted the drive to grant chiefs a significant amount of power in the day-to-day administration of Africans. However, in the early 1960s the question of drawing chiefs and their courts more firmly into the service of the state began to receive serious consideration. In March 1961, the Robinson Commission recommended that urgent attention be given to the task of 'giving the people the justice they feel meets the norms of their society'.[1] Following the Robinson Commission's report, Working Party 'C' was appointed to look into ways of augmenting the powers of chiefs' courts. The working party's recommendations formed the basis for the African Law and Tribal Courts Act of 1969 which gave chiefs limited criminal jurisdiction. Following the passage of the Act, the Ministry of Internal Affairs (MIA) made vigorous efforts to get chiefs around the country to begin exercising these new powers.

This chapter examines the role played by 'customary law' in constituting state power between 1950 and 1980. It focuses on this belated turn to 'custom' by Rhodesian authorities and argues that it was meant to deal with the state's crisis of legitimacy that was triggered by the implementation of the Native Land Husbandry Act (NLHA) of 1951, and the political threat posed by the rise of African nationalism. The move was not concerned with elaborating or codifying African 'customary law'. Its key aim was to assign chiefs sufficient powers to enforce unpopular government policies. Ironically, these were the rigid and fixed regulations rooted in the 'technical development' framework of the 1950s, and had little to do with African custom. The move also

---

[1] NAZ S2827/1/19, Report of the Working Party 'C' Chiefs Courts, 13 March 1962, paragraph 7.

exhibited the settler government's ambition to constitute a particular type of colonial subject. In a clear departure from the 'high modernist' language of the NLHA, and the efforts to transform Africans into proletariats and farmers, from the 1960s the government sought to discursively construct them as ethnicised, custom-bound subjects who were undeserving of the full rights of citizenship in the colonial polity.[2] This approach to the administration of justice was founded on an evolutionary paradigm to which many NAD officials subscribed. This paradigm sought to connect law, justice and punishment, on the one hand, to race and stages of 'civilisation', on the other. Africans, this paradigm held, were not as far along the 'civilisation' continuum as Europeans. Therefore, severe forms of physical punishment were more appropriate in dealing with them than 'rehabilitative' forms of justice. However, the state's designs were actively contested by Africans who invoked the law in a different way and asserted themselves as rights-bearing citizens.

The State and Chiefs' Courts in the 1950s

The question of whether to grant chiefs greater judicial powers had long been a contentious one within the Southern Rhodesian state. On the one hand, the Law Department had long maintained that chiefs did not have the expertise to exercise such power. On the other, the NAD felt that granting chiefs limited criminal jurisdiction would free its officials – who faced increasingly onerous demands – to focus on other aspects of administering the African areas. The decision to grant official recognition to chiefs' arbitration of civil cases in 1937 was a reluctant compromise for Law Department officials, whose acceptance of this measure had more to do with the fact that it removed some judicial powers from NAD officials.[3] However, NAD officials saw this as a first step towards giving chiefs criminal jurisdiction. Up to the 1950s these branches of government remained at odds over the question of granting chiefs greater judicial powers. However, the Ministry of Justice retained the final say in such matters, and the official status of chiefs' courts remained that of arbitration forums for civil disputes among Africans.

---

[2] Comaroff, 'Governmentality, Materiality'.
[3] Jeater, *Law, Language and Science*, 207.

The debates over chiefs' powers in the 1950s were set against the backdrop of important economic, social and political changes in Southern Rhodesia and in the region. Locally, a key concern was the growing influence of a body of political ideas about rights-bearing citizenship, national self-determination and majority rule among Africans. These ideas came to dominate nationalist political discourse and fuelled increasing African political militancy.[4] The Southern Rhodesia African National Congress statement of principles, policy and programme produced in 1957, for example, professed to recognize '… the rights of all who are citizens of the country, whether African, European, Coloured or Asian, to retain permanently the fullest of citizenship.'[5] From the early 1950s, organisations such as the Benjamin Burombo-led British African Workers' Voice Association, had started to take their message to the rural areas and were actively trying to recruit chiefs.[6] These developments made NAD officials uneasy, especially given the significant unrest that the NLHA was causing in rural Southern Rhodesia.

Drafted in the context of the post-World War II manufacturing boom, the Native Land Husbandry Act was in part a response to the industrial demand for 'stabilised' labour.[7] The state, therefore, sought to put an end to the migrant labour system, and transform Africans into either proletariats or farmers. The Act also sought to undertake an ambitious restructuring of African agriculture that was founded on a belief in technical planning. Southern Rhodesian officials disregarded the role of land expropriation in causing land pressure and falling productivity in African reserves. Instead, it took the view that falling productivity was the result of laziness and destructive agricultural methods. Consequently, state intervention based on technical planning was deemed necessary.[8] Technical experts made several prescriptions

---

[4] This language was regularly employed in the 1960s and 1970s by the *Zimbabwe News* and *Zimbabwe Review* which were published by the Zimbabwe African National Union (ZANU) and the Zimbabwe African People's Union (ZAPU), respectively.

[5] 'Southern Rhodesia African National Congress: Statement of Principles, Policy and Programme, Salisbury, 1957', in C. Nyangoni and G. Nyandoro (eds), *Zimbabwe Independence Movements: Select Documents* (London, 1979), 3.

[6] S2796/2/1 Assemblies of Chiefs General, Minutes of the Gwelo Chiefs' Assembly, 28 October 1951. See also A. K. H. Weinrich, *Chiefs and Councils in Rhodesia: Transition from Patriarchal to Bureaucratic Power* (Columbia, 1971).

[7] Alexander, *The Unsettled Land*, 44–62.

[8] Ibid., 44.

that were supposed to improve African agriculture. These related to field size, limits on household livestock holdings, reordering of settlement patterns and labour intensive soil conservation measures.

In theory, these prescriptions were supposed to lead to greater agricultural productivity. However, in reality, the NLHA was a dismal failure, and efforts to enforce policies such as destocking or the labour-intensive contour ridging were met with violent resistance. Rural discontent was further stoked by the fact that there was insufficient arable land to give to all those who wanted it, and significant numbers of unemployed migrant labourers and young men lost their farming rights. This led to a serious crisis of legitimacy for the state and fuelled a rise in nationalist agitation in the rural areas.[9] Colonial officials' concerns about rural unrest were exacerbated by the increasing challenges to colonial rule in other parts of the continent. Not only did they fear that the more vocal African nationalist groups in Northern Rhodesia and Nyasaland might 'incite' the local population, but the spectre of Mau Mau loomed large in their minds. At the same time, the independence of countries such as the Belgian Congo was a source of great concern.

For many NAD officials, chiefs were an important part of the answer to these problems. In order to outflank the political organisations that were articulating African grievances, the NAD sought to present chiefs as the 'authentic' representatives of Africans and instituted Provincial Chiefs' Assemblies. Opening the first Chiefs' Assembly in Midlands Province, the CNC L. Powys-Jones, remarked:

Now some of these [African political] organisations say they represent and know the opinion of all the people, but it is not always right that they do. Some just talk for themselves and know nothing about other people and that is why we started these Assemblies of Chiefs in each province and they are going to meet twice a year. It is the chiefs who are the eyes and ears of the Native Commissioners and the Government. If people have any troubles they should go to their Chief, not to any Association in a town.[10]

The irony in the CNC's words was that, while he was trying to present chiefs as the authentic representatives of Africans, in the same breath

---

[9] Ibid.
[10] NAZ S2796/2/1, Assemblies of Chiefs General, Minutes of the Midlands Chiefs' Assembly, 28 October 1951.

he was calling them the 'eyes and the ears' of the colonial administration. The assemblies were supposed to be forums where the government consulted with chiefs and informed them about new policies. However, the government officials were not really committed to a consultative approach to African administration, and their attitude towards chiefs during assemblies was often patronising.[11] Nevertheless, the assemblies did provide a forum for chiefs to deliberate and voice their concerns about state policies such as destocking under the NLHA, and the limit on *roora* (bride wealth) imposed by the 1950 Native Marriage Act.

Often these concerns were dismissed by NAD officials. However, where chiefs' interests coincided with those of NAD officials, such matters were taken up with their superiors in Salisbury. One such instance was the call made by Matabeleland chiefs for more judicial powers and their specific proposals about the methods of punishment that should be practised. A sore point for the chiefs in Matabeleland was the issue of stock theft, and this came up as the first item for discussion during the 1952 Assembly. The outcome of the deliberations was a resolution that tried to fuse the principles of restorative justice with the colonial state's retributive approach to punishment. The resolution, which was proposed by Chief Sitauze of Beitbridge and supported by all thirty-seven chiefs present, made the following request:

That government introduce immediate legislation on the following lines:-

(a) The provision of work colonies or like institutions where prisoners convicted of stock theft or other kinds of theft causing loss or damage to the owner of the property should be put to work after serving the term of imprisonment imposed.
(b) The earnings of persons thus committed should, by suitable arrangement, be paid to the injured party until his claim is satisfied.
(c) The persons sentenced to perform labour on the basis suggested, should remain as prisoners and be subject to all the penalties applicable to prisoners undergoing ordinary prison sentences.[12]

The second resolution was proposed by Chief Kayisa Ndiweni. He requested that, '… the powers of chiefs be restored; that their duties

---

[11] See Ibid., Minutes of the Midlands Chiefs' Assembly, 28 June 1954.
[12] NAZ S2796/2/4, Assemblies of Chiefs Matabeleland 1951 June- 1958 December, Minutes of the Matabeleland Chiefs' Assembly, 29 August 1952.

and powers be clearly and precisely defined; that they be given limited criminal jurisdiction; and that all these matters should be contained in written form and every Chief supplied with a copy.'[13]

Although the Provincial Native Commissioner (PNC) for Matabeleland supported both resolutions, he was particularly keen on the one relating to the punishment of theft. Writing to the Secretary of Native Affairs, he opined:

This to my mind is the sanest resolution yet submitted. The Natives can learn nothing from us about the treatment suitable for criminals – particularly thieves. I should, for example, like to see Native Tribunals dealing with the Housebreakers and those who specialise in thefts from cars. I wager there would pretty soon be an end to a sorry business. Quite candidly, hardened thieves simply laugh at our punishments. I hope this resolution will receive early and careful consideration.[14]

Implicit in the PNC's letter was the view that Africans were accustomed to, and required, more severe methods of punishment than incarceration. As David Killingray and Stephen Pierce show, this view was not unique to Southern Rhodesia.[15]

The PNC's letter was forwarded to the Secretary for Justice who was not persuaded by the argument that more severe punishments would be more effective. In light of the history of disagreements between the Ministry of Justice and NAD officials, the ensuing exchange between the officials from the two departments is not surprising.[16] The Secretary for Justice responded with a lengthy letter that delved into the nineteenth-century debates over penal practices in England.[17] In it, the Secretary argued that the historical experience pointed to the need for rehabilitative measures, not the more retributive ones suggested by NAD officials or the restorative measures suggested by chiefs. However, NAD officials remained unconvinced by the Secretary

---

[13] Ibid.
[14] NAZ S2796/2/4, PNC Matabeleland to Secretary for Native Affairs, 9 December 1952.
[15] See Killingray, 'The "Rod of Empire', 201–216; Pierce, 'Punishment and the Political Body', 206–21.
[16] See Shutt, 'Legislating Manners', 656–58, and Jeater, *Law, Language and Science*, 205–13.
[17] NAZ S2796/2/4, Secretary for Justice to Secretary of Native Affairs, 8 January 1953.

for Justice's reasoning and maintained that more severe punishments were the appropriate approach to administering Africans. The NC for Filabusi, for example, felt that 'a more concrete reply' was necessary and wrote emphatically to the PNC for Matabeleland South: 'If I may be allowed to draw swords with the Secretary of Justice, can the pious hopes and abstract principles expressed be appreciated by the native in this country or can his phychology [*sic*] be compared with that of the English. It is notorious that sentences in England today and under the Colonial system are far more savage than they are in Southern Rhodesia. I feel the chiefs are justified in being alarmed at our weak sentences.'[18] The PNC added his voice to these concerns and observed: 'The British have been somewhat arrogant in their assumption that their legal system becessarily [*sic*] meets the needs of other races. We imposed on the inhabitants of this colony a body of law but we seem never to have questioned its suitability in practice.'[19]

Further representations by NAD officials on the matter were futile. Consequently, the Matabeleland NCs resorted to making a request that corporal punishment be approved as a sentence for cattle theft.[20] However, this request did not receive favourable consideration either. Two years later, the PNC noted with concern: 'There is evidence of very considerable frustration that despite resolutions at previous Assemblies the Chiefs are still as they were. They attach the utmost importance to this as the minutes amply demonstrate. I do hope some tangible results will be produced soon, otherwise I fear the Assemblies will fail . . . '[21]

For their part, chiefs continued to demand greater powers. In addition, they complained about the fact that the system of appeals allowed people to disregard their rulings. During the Midlands Assembly of 1951, Chief Chivese complained that '[c]hiefs have certain judicial powers, but they are in many cases ignored by the people, who go direct to the Native Commissioner. They despise the Chiefs

[18] NAZ S2796/2/4, NC Filabusi, to PNC, Matabeleland South, 29th January 1953.
[19] Ibid., PNC, Matabeleland South, to Secretary for Native Affairs, 3 February 1953.
[20] Ibid., Secretary for Native Affairs to the Secretary, Law Department, 26 November 1953.
[21] Ibid., PNC Matabeleland to Secretary for Native Affairs, 10 May 1955.

because they can ignore their judgements.'[22] At the 1952 Midlands Assembly, Chief Neshano raised a similar concern in pointing out, 'When people come to chiefs with their complaints and chiefs give a judgement they are invariably disgraced in front of these people by the Native Commissioner who gives a different judgement.'[23] For Chief Ngungumbane, the answer to the problem of 'troublemakers' who defied the NLHA lay in chiefs being granted the powers to remove these 'unwanted elements' from their areas. This met with the support of the chiefs and led to a resolution that 'whenever anyone is troublesome or incorrigible he should be sent away from the kraal and it is his business to find other accommodation . . .'[24]

The picture that emerges from the deliberations in the Chiefs' Assemblies during the 1950s is not one of an institution of chieftaincy that had a stable base of authority. Rather, chiefs were fully aware of the progressive erosion of their authority and prestige during the colonial period, as well as their inability to enforce their rulings. They, therefore, looked to the government for a wider range of coercive powers couched as custom. Chiefs also expressed a desire to appropriate the symbols and forms of the colonial legal system in order to shore up their own legal authority. At the 1952 Midlands Assembly, for example, Chief Ndanga made the following request: 'I would like to have a courtroom at the kraal, for on rainy days it is impossible to hold court and this causes inconvenience; we also need a gaol for detaining people; a clerk is also necessary … I suggest that law books be translated into our own language to enable us to try cases properly.'[25] At the 1954 Chiefs' Assembly in Matabeleland, Chief Nqoya proposed that the Native Law and Courts Act be amended to enable them to execute their judgements by collecting any money or property due.[26]

By the end of the 1950s NAD calls for chiefs to be assigned more powers had acquired a greater urgency, due to the social and political unrest being experienced in Southern Rhodesia. NAD officials thus engaged in heated debates with Justice Ministry officials and mobilised

[22] NAZ S2796/2/1, Assemblies of Chiefs General, Minutes of the Midlands Chiefs' Assembly, 28 October 1951.
[23] Ibid., 27–28 September 1952.
[24] Ibid.
[25] Ibid.
[26] NAZ S2796/2/4, Minutes of the Matabeleland Chiefs' Assembly, 26 May 1954.

an evolutionary paradigm to support their claims. At the same time chiefs were also making claims for greater powers. What was especially evident in these claims was a desire to appropriate the forms and symbols of state law in order to augment their own authority. Despite this pressure, up to the end of the 1950s the Justice Ministry was unwilling to budge. However, in the 1960s the NAD gained the upper hand in this debate.

Constructing the Ethnicised, Custom-bound Subject

In the early 1960s, the position of the NAD was strengthened by the findings of a series of commissions, and this culminated in the 1969 African Law and Tribal Courts Act which provided chiefs with limited criminal jurisdiction. The Act was part of the broader shift in the state's approach to African administration from the early 1960s, which Jocelyn Alexander has shown was a response to the disastrous effects of the NLHA on state authority in the rural areas.[27] It was in the context of this rural crisis, the spread of nationalism, and regional developments that the aforementioned commissions were appointed. Commissions, as Ann Stoler points out, were technologies of rule which did much to produce the realities they claimed to only record.[28] 'By the time most commissions had run their course (or spawned their follow-up generation)', she notes, 'they could be credited with having defined "turning points," justifications for intervention, and, not least, expert knowledge.'[29] The first commission was the Mangwende Commission, which was appointed on the twenty-seventh of October 1960.[30] It was tasked with investigating the unrest in the Mangwende chieftaincy that had been sparked by the opposition to the NLHA and the clashes between Chief Mangwende and the NC. Among other things, the Commission recommended that the implementation of the NLHA in the Mangwende reserve be immediately suspended and that more land be provided for grazing and farming purposes. A key

---

[27] Alexander, *The Unsettled Land*, 63–82.
[28] A. L. Stoler, 'Colonial Archives and the Arts of Governance', *Archival Science*, 2 (2002), 103–7.
[29] Ibid., 104.
[30] G. C. Passmore, *The National Policy of Community Development in Rhodesia: With Special Reference to Local Government in the African Rural Areas* (Salisbury, 1972), 75.

conclusion reached by the Commission was that there was a need for a 'restructuring of the Administrative approach' in African areas.[31]

The question about how to restructure African administration was taken up by the Robinson Commission, which focused on the administrative and judicial functions of the Native Affairs and District Court departments.[32] Following its consultations, it recommended far-reaching changes in the structure of local government in Southern Rhodesia. It further recommended that judicial powers be taken away from Native Commissioners and be assigned to the District Courts Department. Regarding chiefs' courts, it stressed that '[t]he important thing is to give the people the justice they feel meets the norms of their society'.[33] The Working Party 'C' was in turn tasked with investigating how this could be done, and giving recommendations on how chiefs' status could be enhanced.[34] In her assessment of the failure of technical development and the subsequent shift to community development, Alexander has shown that this 'required that Africans be reconceptualised once again as communal, bound by irrational beliefs and so incapable of modernisation.'[35] A similar process of 'othering' was at work in the Working Party 'C's efforts to elevate chiefs' courts.

The Working Party was led by H. R. G. Howman, a long-serving senior NAD official, whose family members had served in the NAD since the early decades of colonial rule. He was therefore considered an expert in African administration. In all, four of the seven members of the Working Party were NAD officials, the others being the PNC for Gwelo N. L. Boast, as well as N. L. Dacomb and N. J. Brendon, the NCs for Bulawayo and Sinoia, respectively. The Justice Ministry was represented by the Attorney General E. W. G. Jarvis, and an Undersecretary, A. M. Bruce-Brand. The last member of the Working Party was B. J. M. Foggin, who served as the secretary. As with most colonial enquiries on matters of custom, chiefs were the main group who were consulted by Working Party 'C'. It was therefore not surprising that the version of custom they gave affirmed their demands for more judicial powers.

[31] Ibid., 79.
[32] Ibid.
[33] NAZ S2827/1/19 Report of the Working Party 'C' Chiefs Courts, paragraph 7.
[34] Working Party 'C' was one of four working parties set up under the Robinson Commission.
[35] Alexander, *The Unsettled Land*, 63.

Unlike the provincial Chiefs' Assemblies of the 1950s, Working Party 'C' officials showed more respect for the views of chiefs. However, it was clear that Howman, who led many of the meetings, was trying to steer the chiefs in a particular direction on a number of issues. The exchanges between Howman and the chiefs during the consultation meetings highlighted the fact that what was happening was not a genuine search for African legal ideas and practices, but a negotiation between government officials and chiefs over the extent and nature of authority they could exercise. Chiefs were particularly opposed to Howman's insistence on the 'right of election' or allowing African litigants to choose the court they wanted to try their cases. They also objected to the proposal that it be possible to appeal against chiefs' rulings in a higher court. During the consultation meeting with the Council of Chiefs, Chief Myinga of Nkai argued that during pre-colonial times: 'The chief was a personality in his own right and nobody had the right to query the chief's right to do things. The only person who could take a complaint direct to the king would be the chief. It was the chief's duty to settle these matters and then make a report to the king.'[36] Chief Shumba of Fort Victoria was far more strident in his views:

I want this word 'choosing' to be obliterated because I want people to be united because they are all African. All these people are under my control and I would want to try all matters arising because if I as chief fail then they can appeal to that court of appeal which we are going to form, and that is final. I even want to try criminal cases. Even though the man may be convicted I still want to try him when he comes out of jail and I would make him pay.[37]

Chief Sigola similarly felt that the 'right of election' was not consistent with African customs and posed a rhetorical question to Howman: 'Why do you say that we can adjudicate according to our own native custom when you give to us with one hand and take away with the other[?].'[38]

---

[36] NAZ S2824/11, Minutes of the Working Party 'C' consultation with the Council of Chiefs, 12 October 1961.

[37] Ibid.

[38] Ibid.

Howman's efforts to change chiefs' minds by pointing out that commercial disputes between businessmen might involve intricate matters
of law did not help matters. Instead, it touched a raw nerve with some
chiefs who objected to the idea that wealthy business people could circumvent their chiefs. Chief Kayisa's contribution to the debate went to
the core of chiefs' concerns with the idea of the 'right of election' and
the exclusion of particular social groups from their jurisdiction *viz* the
impact this had on chiefs' prestige. He explained: 'What increases a
chief's prestige is that even the business people with troubles take them
to the chief. And if the case is too difficult for the chief, it is up to the
chief to give permission to take it to another court. Even a European
situated in the chief's area should also report in the first place to the
chief when he has any difficulty.'[39]

The final report of Working Party 'C' took little note of the basis
for chiefs' objections. Instead, it was couched in a language of cultural difference. It prefaced its recommendations with a section entitled 'Indigenous law and the community' which presented Africans as
essentially communal and resistant to change. 'Life in a tribe', it began,

... has certain features which throw a light on the operations of a tribal
customary system and it must be stressed that whatever legal enactments
and structures may be superimposed, tribal life ... has a remarkable way
of persisting and even flouting the external system imposed by the ordinary
law of the State.[40]

It went on to highlight the 'communal' nature of African society pointing out that 'In a normal communally minded society a number of
individuals who feel themselves united, normally by kinship bond,
participate in disputes as a single unit. They are benefitted or injured
together.'[41] On these grounds the Working Party 'C' concurred with
the Robinson Commission and argued that it was necessary to give
Africans 'the justice that meets the norms of their society'. Ironically,
these 'norms' were to be defined by state appointed 'experts' not chiefs
or the 'Africans' themselves.

Drawing on the work of anthropologists such as J. F. Holleman and
Max Gluckman, the report went on to describe the process of dispute

[39] Ibid.
[40] NAZ S2827/1/19, Report of the Working Party 'C', 2.
[41] Ibid.

resolution in chiefs' courts in idealised terms. It made the following observation:

The chief is the tribal community in action, the headman the ward community in action, and neither acts alone. It is the assessors or counsellors ("abatonisi" or "wachinda") of the chief or the headman who conduct the proceedings, they digest the evidence, probe witnesses, measure behaviour against the recognised code of behaviour and finally, as Holleman puts it, "the solution emerges as the common product of many minds and the chief's decision is as undramatic and uneventful as a full stop after a long paragraph." He, the chief, may not even be present, or be there for only part of the time, but the formality of the "cutting of the case" is always done in his name.[42]

At least two things are worth noting in the Working Party's statement. The first is the contrast it bore with what had actually come out of the consultation with chiefs. Far from describing this romanticised state of affairs, the chiefs had highlighted the increasing disregard for their decisions, and the tensions between them and other social groups such as the youth and wealthy business people.

Secondly, the 1950s tradition of anthropological writings by Gluckman and Holleman which the Working Party decided to draw on was a curious choice. In justifying the creation of homelands, the South African authorities had preferred to draw on an older anthropological tradition, the 1920s writings of Bronislaw Malinowski that took as granted the existence of separate homogenous 'tribal' societies.[43] The work of Gluckman and others, however, challenged colonial stereotypes that presented African societies as irrational, primitive and homogenous. Gluckman's work on the Barotse, for example, argued that African legal systems, like European systems, met Weberian standards of rationality.[44] The Rhodesian authorities' appropriation of this anthropological writing was strategic in that it enabled them to support the proposal to elevate chiefs' courts with academic arguments. At the same time, these writings did not unsettle the notions

---

[42] Ibid., 11.
[43] B. Oomen, *Chiefs in South Africa: Law, Power and Culture in the Post-Apartheid Era* (Oxford, 2005).
[44] M. Gluckman, *The Judicial Process among the Barotse of Northern Rhodesia* (Manchester, 1955).

of cultural difference which undergirded the state's new approach to African administration. State officials could thus argue that African legal practices were 'rational', but they were not 'modern'. As such, Africans remained cultural 'others' who were to be treated as such.

In the government's designs, chiefs' courts were to play a role in the effort to 'distance the state from its coercive role and to legitimise authority over people and land in customary guise'.[45] The Working Party's reasoning was that, since chiefs already meted out punishment for offences against the communal welfare, such as incest, cutting down fruit trees and setting fires irresponsibly, they could be called upon to enforce new categories of offences.[46] The report explained the thinking in the following terms:

We believe that these traditionally recognised offences against the communal welfare could be expanded to cover such injurious actions as digging mice out of a dam wall or contour ridge, grazing stock in a prohibited paddock or cutting fences, if African courts could be empowered to try such cases as civil matters and impose damages. We consider that this 'injury to the community' aspect could, at the wish of the people, be extended to many violations of by-laws made by Native Councils and Tribal Land Authorities without at the same time precluding recourse to prosecution in the criminal courts in a proper case.[47]

By trying to pass off deeply unpopular state policies that were rooted in the NLHA as 'wrongs against the communal welfare' to be enforced by chiefs, the state hoped to become, to paraphrase Karen Fields, a consumer of legitimacy generated in the customary sphere.[48]

All in all, Working Party 'C' made a total of twenty-five recommendations on augmenting the powers of chiefs and elevating the role of their courts. These recommendations formed the basis of the African Law and Tribal Courts Bill which was tabled in Parliament in 1969. In presenting the Bill, the Minister of Internal Affairs went to great lengths to counter the long-held stereotypes about African 'customary' law within the settler population. Much like Working Party 'C', he spoke in glowing terms about 'customary law' in an attempt to mask the

---

[45] Alexander, *The Unsettled Land*, 63.
[46] NAZ S2827/1/19 Report of the Working Party 'C', 10.
[47] Ibid., 11.
[48] Fields, *Revival and Rebellion*, 31.

underlying process of constructing Africans as ethnicised, custom-bound subjects and establishing institutions that would treat them as such. He argued that the negative stereotypes about African custom were influenced by early travellers who chose to report 'the newsy, sensational episodes of life' while failing to acknowledge the everyday workings of the indigenous legal system which, he argued,

… in its search for the truth, in its weighing of evidence, in its judgements of conduct, in its decisions as to who was acting as he ought to act in a reasonable manner, in its concern to keep order in the community – in all these basic problems a system of law, more notable for its fundamental similarity with the Western legal system than in contradiction, was and still is in operation.[49]

Invoking Eugen Ehrlich's classic work on the sociology of law, the Minister declared that his Bill sought to recognize this 'living law' that had remained resilient despite 'non-recognition, discouragement, neglect and even prohibition in some respects'.[50]

Although some African Members of Parliament (MPs) welcomed the legislation, seeing it as according chiefs their rightful status, a number were apprehensive about it. These MPs often spoke on behalf of the African middle class, and not in defence of the interests of the majority of 'ordinary' Africans in the rural areas. Nevertheless, their contributions reveal two main points. First, that some Africans imagined themselves as rights-bearing citizens and consciously opposed the state's attempt to treat them as custom-bound subjects. Second, their statements bore testimony to the role of education and interaction with colonial courts in shaping African legal consciousness and ideas of personhood. Chigogo, the MP for Gokwe, was amongst those who had concerns about the implications of the Act for the educated elite. He opined:

Today you have the University here where you produce African doctors, where you produce African lawyers and all sorts of graduates, not speaking about the numerous secondary schools we have the whole country wide. [*sic*] I wonder if you will agree with me to say that such an African, having

---

[49] *Rhodesia Parliamentary Debates*, 28 January 1969, 618.
[50] Ibid., 622. See E. Ehrlich, 'The Sociology of Law' *Harvard Law Review*, 36 (1922).

left the University of Rhodesia, having acquired knowledge of the legal systems, although this man is an African he goes into the Tribal Trust Land and here this individual is taken before the chief's court or chief's *dare*, or whatever the name may be, and he is going to be flatly told because the Minister has formulated such type of a legislation that the man has no right of appeal, I look very far, far from the District Commissioner's office or from the provincial commissioner's office to the highest courts we have in this country which we have become acquainted with for the last 70 years since the Europeans came into this country.[51]

Speaking on a personal note he declared,

I would find it very difficult myself, personally, if I went before the chief's *dare* and I was charged in the tribal court. Maybe I will be out of this Parliament, having known the system ..., how the rights of men are contained in this House and dished to the rulers of this country. Surely I will conflict with the chiefs and his *Indunas* at this *dare* because I will claim to know my rights. But because I happen to be an African, because the Minister's department has chosen to frame the law in such a way that I must be muzzled, I must not open my mouth; I must have no rights so I have to go to be punished like a sheep.[52]

As I show in the next section, it was not just members of the educated elite who refused to be 'muzzled' or 'go to be punished like a sheep'.

For all his rhetoric about the virtues of African legal systems and the government's efforts to recognise these, the Minister was in fact proposing an authoritarian piece of legislation that had little to do with African legal ideas and practices. This comes out clearly in the provision that dealt with corporal punishment. Under the 1969 legislation, the Minister sought to widen the use of bodily punishment by empowering chiefs to administer it on juveniles in public, and without judicial or medical supervision. In effect, the state was responding to rising political agitation amongst African youth by resorting to corporeal technologies. What is more, the administration of this bodily punishment would take the form of a public spectacle, making it both a means of control and a performance of power.[53]

---

[51] *Rhodesia Parliamentary Debates*, 31 January 1969, 843.

[52] Ibid., 844.

[53] See M. Foucault, *Discipline and Punish: The Birth of the Modern Prison* (London, 1977), chapter 2.

The legislation tabled by the Minister was thus not aimed at elaborating or codifying African 'customary law'. Its objective was to enable the government to draw on the legitimacy of 'traditional' leaders' legal authority and exploit its authoritarian potential.[54] As a result, the African Law and Tribal Courts Act passed in 1969 went very far in augmenting the powers of chiefs, if only on paper. Section 13 of the Act granted Chiefs the power to 'impose a moderate correction of whipping, not exceeding eight strokes' on young men who 'ha[d] not attained the apparent age of nineteen years'.[55] In civil cases, appeal from their courts was limited to the provincial Tribal Appeal Courts made up of three chiefs. However, in criminal cases, the Act allowed for convicted individuals to take their appeals to the magistrate's court though, in reality, every effort was made to frustrate such steps. Section 19 (1) gave chiefs the powers to evict 'problem makers' from their areas.

Chiefs' courts were also protected by a strict contempt provision which defined contempt in very wide terms, and provided for a fairly severe maximum punishment of £50 or six months in prison. District Commissioners' intervention in the operation of chiefs' courts was limited to administrative matters, and lawyers were barred from appearing in these courts.[56] The fact that the Act empowered chiefs to try 'offences' under a wide range of laws also indicates the government's objectives of making chiefs do the heavy lifting with respect to enforcing state policies in the rural areas. The laws included the African Affairs Act, African Beer Act, African Councils Act, Tribal Trust Lands Act, Natural Resources Act, African Cattle Marketing Act, Tribal Trust Land Forest Produce Act and the African Land Husbandry Act. The irony underlying all these measures, however, lay in the fact that very little of what chiefs were supposed to enforce was in any sense based on African custom, real or imagined. Many of these were statutes and regulations rooted in 1950s technical development.

---

[54] For a discussion of colonial states' efforts to 'marshal the authoritarian possibilities' of African culture, see Mamdani, *Citizen and Subject*.

[55] African Law and Tribal Courts Act 1969.

[56] The title Native Commissioner was changed to District Commissioner in 1962.

Implementing the African Law and Tribal Courts Act

From 1970, when the Act became operational, the Ministry of Internal Affairs (MIA) set about issuing 'traditional' leaders with warrants that authorised them to exercise civil and/or criminal jurisdiction.[57] However, the state faced a number of obstacles. Chief amongst these was the reluctance of 'traditional' leaders to exercise these powers, and the refusal of their followers to submit to them. An increasingly important factor in the 1970s was the pressure being exerted on chiefs by the ZANU and ZAPU guerrilla armies that had begun waging a war against the Rhodesian state in the mid-1960s. Although the late 1960s had witnessed a lull in the military clashes, the early 1970s saw intensified fighting and increased aggression towards chiefs and others who were perceived to be 'sell outs'. Chiefs were thus caught between a government that sought to use them to enforce unpopular policies, and guerrillas who threatened them with violence if they did. As a consequence, after five years, only 117 out of 252 chiefs had warranted courts and many of those chiefs that did receive warrants were hesitant to exercise their increased judicial powers.[58]

A by-product of the moves to draw chiefs' courts into the service of the state was that the courts gradually began to take on many of the features of state courts, especially with regard to procedures and the generation of paperwork. This was partly the result of pressure by the Justice Ministry officials for close supervision of chiefs' courts, and MIA officials' fear that decisions by chiefs' courts might be quashed on procedural grounds. The Secretary for Internal Affairs (SIA), R. J. Powell, therefore, circulated a checklist to all DCs and PCs in January of 1975 for use by all chief's courts in order to ensure that the procedures they followed '... satisfied the requirements of justice'.[59] Due to the importance that proper court procedures began to assume, court clerks came to be viewed as important to the operations of chiefs' courts. In some cases, however, the state's insistence on the observance of procedures was a source of tension between the chief and his assessors on the one hand, and the clerk on the other. Such was the case

---

[57] The MIA was the reconstituted Native Affairs Department.

[58] NAZ S2930, Vol. 1 African Law and Tribal Courts, Tribal Courts of Chiefs Mid-March 1975, 19 March 1975.

[59] NAZ S3700/103/1, African Law and Tribal Courts Act, SIA R. J. Powell to All PCs and DCs, 20 January 1975.

Figure 2.1 Chief's Court in 1973

in Chief Chibi's court where the chief and his assessors were angered by the fact that the clerk, to them a mere child, insisted on instructing them on how to run the court.[60] In other areas, however, the adoption of the forms and symbols of state courts was welcomed. This symbolic appropriation was a sign of progress and endowed chiefs' courts with a measure of prestige and authority.[61] Significantly, this indicated that a two-way process of appropriation was at play. As the state sought to borrow the authority of 'traditional' courts, chiefs were also actively trying to appropriate the symbols of state law in order to bolster their legitimacy.

In practice, the fortunes of chiefs' courts varied widely over time and space. Some chiefs, like Dakamela of Nkai district, were able to assert their power through their courts up to the mid-1970s. Although Dakamela was reluctant to implement conservation policies, he had

---

[60] NAZ S3700/103/2, Tribal Courts: Court Clerks, Training: Allowances, DC Chibi to PC Victoria, 24 October 1972.
[61] Interview with Reuben Ndanga, Ndanga Township, 18 April 2011.

Figure 2.2 Tribal Appeal Court in 1974

no qualms about enforcing council rate payments.[62] In the second half of 1973, Dakamela's court heard 17 civil cases and handed down judgements that amounted to R$440 and 25 cattle.[63] During the same period, his court had also heard 102 criminal cases, all of which dealt with African Council rate defaulters. During one of the trials, the court refused to accept the absence of the actual defaulters as an acceptable excuse and placed the guardians, parents and wives of the defaulters on trial in their stead. The plea recorded in the transcript was: 'We do accept the $2 rate and cost incurred by the said Council.' Three individuals who attempted to object to the process were charged with contempt, and one of the three appeared before the court in handcuffs.[64]

---

[62] For more on Chief Dakamela's relations with the government, see J. Alexander, J. McGregor and T. Ranger, *Violence and Memory, One Hundred Years in the 'Dark Forests' of Matabeleland* (Oxford, 2000), 129–31.

[63] NAZ-S3700/103/4/2, District Commissioners' Court Rules, Report: Chief Dakamela's Tribal Court for the period 1 July 1973 to 31 December 1973, Nkai District.

[64] NAZ-Bulawayo, Local Government District Nkai, Chief Dakamela's Court, Criminal Case No. 6/73.

In the end all of the accused were ordered to pay the outstanding rate of R$2-00 as well as court fees.

It is unclear from the available evidence how successful the court was in enforcing the judgement. However, a 1971 comment by the DC for Nkai that Dakamela enjoyed 'terrific respect in the district, albeit as a dictator' suggests that his court may well have been able to enforce its rulings. In addition, in 1975 he was appointed as a District Authority and granted emergency powers 'to counter terrorist activities'. These authorised him to effect arrests without a warrant, to issue summary judgement and to administer immediate punishment to individuals he deemed to be causing hostility towards him.[65] It should be added though, that Dakamela's actions ultimately incurred him the wrath of ZIPRA guerrillas, and in the late 1970s he was forced to flee his home and live in the Dakamela sub-office under the protection of government paramilitary forces.[66]

In other areas several factors militated against the operation of chiefs' courts in the way that the state had intended. Among the Tonga, for example, chiefs had not exercised the degree of authority required to make the state's policy work.[67] In parts of Manicaland, chiefs were reluctant to exercise the powers accorded to them in the new legislation, realising the risks this posed to their own legitimacy.[68] As Alexander notes, reliance on chiefs was further hindered by the fact that state officials often found themselves entangled in disputes between different leading houses vying for the chieftaincy.[69] In addition, chiefs often had their own agendas that were distinct from those of the government. Consequently, it was not uncommon for chiefs who had once been in alliance with district officials, to transfer their loyalties to the nationalists. In addition, the war also meant that chiefs' judicial powers were progressively eroded by both state and non-state judicial forums. Norma Kriger's study of the experiences of the guerrilla war in Mutoko shows, for example, how chiefs' judicial powers were eroded by the imposition of martial law on the one hand, and the

[65] Alexander et al., *Violence and Memory*, 130.
[66] Ibid., 150.
[67] NAZ S3700/40 Tribal Land Authorities, DC Binga to PC Matabeleland North, 23 April 1975.
[68] Ibid., DC Melsetter, J. R. Peters, to PC Manicaland, 21 November 1974.
[69] Alexander, *The Unsettled Land*, 83–99.

ZANU-related people's committees which began to take over the task of adjudicating disputes and enforcing law and order, on the other.[70]

In trying to rely on chiefs and their courts, the Rhodesian state failed, or refused, to recognise the inherent limitations of this strategy. As Fields correctly points out, 'Not all commands may be legitimately issued even by a legitimate ruler.'[71] Working Party 'C' had been overly optimistic in thinking that unpopular state policies could be made acceptable by giving chiefs the task of enforcing them. In addition, as Thomas Spear's points out, there were inherent limits to the strategy of 'inventing' tradition.[72] Not only did the legitimacy of 'traditional' leaders have to be maintained, but the policies implemented had to resonate with people's values. The Rhodesian government largely disregarded these limitations and sought, in overt ways, to manipulate the institution of chieftaincy and use chiefs to implement deeply unpopular policies. Consequently, not only was it unsuccessful in legitimising itself through chiefs, it also delegitimised those chiefs who tried to do its bidding and made them targets for guerrilla attacks.

Chief Ndanga was one of the many chiefs who tried to walk the fine line between staying in good books with the MIA and not incurring the wrath of the guerrillas. From his appointment in 1958, he had managed to cultivate a fairly comfortable working relationship with the government. During the early 1960s he was elected to the Council of Chiefs and, along with twenty-nine other chiefs, he went on the 1964 overseas tour organised by the Rhodesian Front government. In 1969 his court was included in the pilot group of courts that were to be warranted under the African Law and Tribal Courts Act, and his son Reuben Ndanga was sent for training as a court clerk.[73] Like Dakamela, Chief Ndanga was appointed as a District Authority in October 1975. However, as the war intensified in the late 1970s and guerrillas began operating in Ndanga and the neighbouring Bikita district, he and other 'traditional' leaders became reluctant to be associated with government policies. This comes out clearly in the October 1977 minutes of the DC's monthly meetings with headmen and chiefs

---

[70] N. J. Kriger, *Zimbabwe's Guerrilla War: Peasant Voices* (Cambridge, 1992), 199.

[71] Fields, *Revival and Rebellion*, 64.

[72] T. Spear, 'Neo-Traditionalism and the Limits of Invention in British Colonial Africa', *JAH*, 44 (2003), 3–27.

[73] Interview with Ndanga, 18 April 2011.

Figure 2.3 An anti-chiefs sign encountered by the Pearce Commission in 1972

Figure 2.4 An anti-chiefs placard during a demonstration against the Pearce Commission proposals in 1972

which record that: 'The tribal leaders had many excuses why it was difficult to report even finding out where terrorists are operating. The Member I/C pointed out that he was very busy fighting the war without much help from the Tribal leaders ... It was quite evident that all the Tribal leaders are frightened of the result of terrorism and they found it easier to sit on the fence. It is highly recommended that these meetings be discontinued.'[74]

The chiefs and headmen's fear was not unfounded as is attested to by the experience of Headman Muroyiwa. In explaining his absence from two consecutive meetings, Muroyiwa recounted his ordeal at the hands of the guerrillas at the February 1978 meeting. The minutes for the meeting record that,

[74] NAZ-Masvingo, Local Government District Administration Chiefs and Headmen: CHK & HM 14 1975-1982, Minutes of DC Ndanga's meeting with Chiefs and Headmen, October 1977.

On the 12th December, 1977 he was abducted by a group of terrorists and taken to Hozwi Plateau where another group of terrorists set about beating him with a log. The reason they gave was that he was too progressive and that he always had too much to say in the past at TLA meetings, also that he was the District Commissioner's stooge. He was beaten 30 times until he fainted and collapsed. The women at this unknown kraal poured buckets of water over him shouting 'you are going to kill our headman'. He was then told if he reported this incident to the District Commissioner that they would kill him and leave him to rot in his yard and that no funeral services would be permitted.[75]

Headman Muroyiwa's misfortunes did not end with this encounter with the guerrillas. He was later arrested by the BSAP and detained under Martial Law regulations on suspicion of assisting guerrillas and being involved in stock theft.[76] Muroyiwa was not the only one to have a violent encounter with the guerrillas. Two of the four chiefs in Ndanga district, Nyakunuwa and Bota, were killed by the guerrillas for allegedly reporting their movements to the authorities.

Chief Ndanga appears to have tried to tone down his cooperation with the administration and, for example, ceased his involvement in the District Show. However, this decision is likely to have been influenced more by the instinct of self-preservation, than by political conviction. After being visited at his homestead by guerrillas, Ndanga chose to build rapport with them and would, on occasion, slaughter a cow for them.[77] As a result of his cooperation with the guerrillas, he was able to continue running his court despite the presence of ZANU committees in his area. However, the guerrillas did appoint two people, Runochinya Chikato and Simon Musuka, to sit on the court, and guerrillas would sometimes turn up to witness hearings in the court.[78] Chief Ndanga's relations with the guerrillas ultimately brought him under the government's suspicion and, as a result, he was arrested and detained for six months. Through the assistance of Dr Simon Mazorodze, who had worked at Ndanga hospital, he was able to secure legal representation from an African lawyer, Wilson Sandura, and was ultimately released. After his release he became unwilling to attract any attention from the

---

[75] Ibid., Minutes of DC Ndanga's meeting with Chiefs and Headmen, 3 February 1978.
[76] Ibid., DC Ndanga to PC Victoria, 13 December 1979.
[77] Interview with Ndanga, 18 April 2011.
[78] Ibid.

Rhodesian security forces and even forbade the all-night church meetings of the Zion Christian Church in his household. However, what is clear is that, where his court was concerned, it was the guerrillas who ultimately managed to exert influence.

The Rhodesian government's intention to make use of chiefs' courts was also frustrated by the resistance that came from 'ordinary' Africans in rural Rhodesia. As highlighted earlier, the new strategy involved legally inscribing the status of ethnicised, custom-bound subjects on Africans and setting up institutions that would treat them as such. On the ground, however, 'ordinary' Africans resisted being treated in this way. Instead of simply complying with orders given by 'traditional' rulers or administrative officials, Africans sought legal counsel where they felt that their rights were being violated. That Africans should respond in this way is explained by a number of factors. As alluded to by MP Chigogo's speech in Parliament, the long period of engagement with the colonial legal system gradually began to shape African ideas about personhood. Processes unleashed by colonisation such as rural to urban migration also had an important impact. Urban areas were spaces for self-fashioning and the adoption of new ideas and notions about personhood which included rights-bearing citizenship.[79] This process was further reinforced by the body of political ideas that was gaining currency in the post-World War II period. The overall impact of these processes was to reshape the way Africans saw themselves in relation to the state, and to 'traditional' leaders.

Consequently, local authorities, such as the DC, chiefs and headmen, were confronted with 'ordinary' African villagers who refused to simply 'obey and comply' with their orders. On a number of occasions this resistance found its way into the legal arena as Africans who had been convicted by chief's courts appealed the decisions in higher courts. It is difficult to quantify the extent to which such struggles between state officials and Africans found their way into the legal arena. This is partly due to the unavailability of the records of the Court of Appeal for African Civil Cases and Magistrate's Courts for the 1960s and 1970s, where such appeals would have been lodged. However, as the war intensified, there was a substantial rise in the numbers of Africans who sought legal assistance in locating and/or defending their relatives, as well as suing the Rhodesian security forces

[79] Jeater, *Marriage, Power and Perversion.*

for assault and destruction of property.[80] Another challenge is that, unless the matter went to court, and many did not, the dispute would leave very few traces in the archival record. In addition, pursuing disputes in the legal arena often required resources which Africans in the rural areas did not always have. However, this makes the cases of those who did decide to devote substantial amounts of money to consult lawyers all the more interesting. Invariably, DCs were greatly offended when lawyers intervened and did their best to ensure that such legal action was unsuccessful. Nevertheless, the importance of these cases lies less in their success and more in the way they provide a window into the legal consciousness of 'ordinary' Africans, as well as the political imaginaries that drove them to seek recourse in the law.

When faced with legal resistance, state officials often responded by trying to close up any legal avenues available for Africans to challenge them. For example, after a successful appeal by Beaven Manyuchi against a ruling by a chief who had no warrant, the SIA was concerned about the precedent it set and its potential broader impact. He thus wrote, with a note of urgency, to the PC of Manicaland, pointing out that 'The situation it was sought to prevent has in fact arisen. May all District Commissioners please be urged to establish Courts with all convenient speed to avoid otherwise valid judgements being upset for lack of the necessary warrant.'[81] The detailed records that were compiled by the MIA about cases brought against its officials by Africans show that such cases were taken seriously by the colonial officials. One such case detailed the lengthy legal struggle between Mqibelo Dube and local authorities in Gokwe who were trying to evict him. In response, Dube secured the services of the Bulawayo law firm, Ben Baron and Partners, and was able to press the government into awarding him $1,500 in settlement for the assault and destruction of his property by the Tribal Land Authority.[82]

---

[80] The International Defence and Aid Fund files contain hundreds of cases in which Africans took legal action against the Rhodesian government. See NAZ MS587/4, Untitled, and NAZ MS591/2/4, Legal Sheridan.

[81] NAZ S3700/103/1, African Law and Tribal Courts Act: Policy Procedure, N. A. Hunt for SIA to PC Manicaland, 19 June 1975.

[82] See G. H. Karekwaivanane, '"It shall be the duty of every African to obey and comply promptly": Negotiating State Authority in the Legal Arena 1965–1980', *JSAS*, 37 (2011), 333–49.

Similarly, in Mrewa, a man named Driver approached the Salisbury law firm Stumbles and Rowe to assist him in challenging the efforts by Chief Nyajena to evict him from his area.[83] Driver refused to recognise the authority of the chief and chose instead to defend his rights to reside, cultivate and graze his livestock in the area. The MIA's internal correspondence shows that the DC for Mrewa was clearly annoyed at the fact that Driver had chosen to defy the chief and seek legal counsel. In a letter to his superior, the PC for Mashonaland South, the DC wrote: 'The tribal authority have [sic] withdrawn the above-named's cultivation and grazing rights and have no intention of returning them, furthermore they are not obliged to give the Attorneys any reasons.'[84] He went on: 'With reference to his rights to reside, these have not as yet been withdrawn but as soon as Head Office warrants Chief Njajina's Court he intends serving a removal order on Driver, however please simply advise the Attorneys that the DC Mrewa states that his rights to reside have not been withdrawn. The removal order will come as an unpleasant surprise to them and will put an end to this trouble maker.'

In Inyanga, the efforts by the state to remove the Tangwena people from their ancestral lands also provoked a legal response. Wonesayi responded to their harassment by the government – which included physical violence, the destruction of their homes, confiscation of their cattle and the detention of their children – by suing the Ministers of Justice, Law and Order and of Internal Affairs. Wonesayi was successful in his suit and an appeal by the Ministers was dismissed.[85] After unsuccessfully trying to resist the eviction in the courts, Chief Tangwena resorted to taking the matter up with Queen Elizabeth II. In a letter that critiqued the repressive nature of the law in Southern Rhodesia, he wrote: 'I am informing you what is happening in this country of Chief Tangwena, people are suffering terribly they are having their huts destroyed by your children of this country, the government of Rhodesia which is destroying the richness of Chief Tangwena. Is that the law? To rob someone's richness without a reason? ... When you will have read this you must put this in papers so that everybody

---

[83] NAZ S3700/43, TTL Authorities Disputes 1973–1976. Stumbles and Rowe to PC Mashonaland South, 17 January 1973.
[84] Ibid., DC Mrewa to PC Mashonaland South, 4 June 1973.
[85] 'Notes on Cases: Smith N. O. and Lardner Burke N. O. vs. Wonesayi', *Rhodesian Law Journal*, 12 (1972), 150.

Figure 2.5 The eviction of the Tangwena people in September 1969

reads and know whether this is law which is being done by this Rhodesian government.'[86]

Africans were not always successful in their legal encounters with the state as the two following recounted disputes show. Both disputes had to do with efforts by local authorities to enforce the unpopular policy of digging contour ridges and were handled by A. J. A. Peck, a Salisbury-based lawyer. Neither of them went before the courts; however, they appear in the archival record largely because Peck protested in writing to the Ministry of Internal Affairs, about the way he and his clients had been treated by the Mrewa Police and DC, D. W. Walters. The dispute arose out of the headman's attempt to punish two village heads, M. Munwa and N. Chimbangu, for not completing their contour ridges in the set time.[87] Although both men had dug some of the required ridges, they had not completed all of them partly due to the labour-intensive nature of the work. The headman, who had not completed digging his own contour ridges, imposed a fine of R$3 which Munwa and Chimbangu refused to pay. As a result of their

---

[86] British National Archives (hereafter BNA) FCO36/741, Tangwena Dispute, Chief Rekayi Tangwena to Queen Elizabeth, 18 February 1972.
[87] NAZ S3700/43, TTL Authorities: Disputes 1973 May–1976 April, A. J. A. Peck to Minister of Internal Affairs, 26 May 1972.

defiance, they were arrested and detained in Mrewa from 4 to 13 May 1972. After their release, the two men still would not pay the fine, and instead travelled to Salisbury to seek legal advice from Peck. Due to the hostile reception he had been given by Walters and the police in Mrewa while handling a previous case, Peck decided to take the matter up with the Minister of Internal Affairs.

In a lengthy letter to the Minister, which he copied to the Secretary of the Law Society and the Commissioner of Police, Peck detailed the ill-treatment that he and his clients had been subjected to at the hands of the Mrewa officials in both cases.[88] In the previous case, Peck had been consulted by a group of residents of Pfungwe Tribal Trust Land who included Munyarara, Ndowa, Chidzimura, Dzika, Matambura and Mukango. The group had three concerns about the way the policy of digging contour ridges was being enforced in their area. In the first instance, they objected to the fact that they were being made to pay for the pegging of their land while other areas had not been asked to do so. They also felt that the time allocated for the digging of contour ridges was insufficient. In addition, they had been told that those who had not completed the contouring of their land would not be allowed to plough it. Peck telephoned Walters to raise these concerns and had a less than amicable conversation with him. This was largely because the Walters viewed the involvement of a lawyer in the matter as an affront to his authority as the District Commissioner.[89]

Following his conversation with Walters, Peck wrote a letter summarising the exchange, and sent one copy to the DC and another to his clients addressed to Munyarara. Upon discovering that the letter for Peck's clients had arrived, Walters summoned Munyarara to his office on the 14th of September 1971 and compelled him to collect his letter and read it aloud. After doing so, he confiscated the letter and instructed Munyarara to remain at his homestead awaiting arrest. Instead of complying, Munyarara travelled to Salisbury to inform Peck about the incident. In response, Peck secured an appointment with the SIA on 18 September and registered his complaints about the conduct of the Mrewa DC. While he was in Mrewa the next day on other business, Peck was surprised to find five of his clients under arrest

[88] Ibid.
[89] Ibid.

'for going to see an attorney'. His account of the events that followed gives a clear sense of the attitude of local administrative officials to Africans who sought legal recourse:

A meeting was held that afternoon at which the District Officer (Mr Nicolle) and the Member in Charge (Mr Walters) indeed "apologised" to my clients, but this did not stop –

a) The Member in Charge declaring "I am sorry, but I must over-rule you, Mr Peck", and interrogated them.
b) The Member in Charge telling my clients that they should always go to see "the proper authorities", which I regarded as gross impertinence, and I as much as said so.
c) My clients being lectured as though they were naughty children. (My letter was returned to me in the course of the meeting.)

Quite frankly, words fail me. No wonder there is so often trouble in Mrewa! Here a group of tribesmen behaves in the most reasonable and responsible way they <u>could</u> behave, by consulting an attorney to put forward enquiries on their behalf in a sane and reasonable fashion. I will reserve my comments as to how the attorney himself was treated, but they themselves were treated like common criminals. If this is how they (and their attorney) are treated, little wonder they hesitate to make enquiries from the "proper authorities"![90]

Walters' response to Peck's letter was unapologetic, and he made it clear that he considered himself, and not the law, to be the final authority in Mrewa. Regarding the dispute involving Munyarara and others he explained:

All went well until Rhodes & Founders [holiday] in July when many of the town workers returned for that week end. Hereafter, a group of tribesmen consulted Mr Peck and raised queries which he has listed under (a) (b) & (c) on page 2 of his letter. When I spoke to Mr Peck on the telephone on 19th July 1971 I told him that I had already answered those queries directly to the kraal heads at the meeting in June 1971. I said that if tribesmen wished further explanations they should come to see me instead of "running off to Salisbury to see an Attorney" and I wish to stress here that I stand by this

---

[90] NAZ S3700/43, Peck to Minister of Internal Affairs, 26 May 1972. (Emphasis in original)

comment. I am the Administrator responsible for the Mrewa district and I am always prepared to give tribesmen a hearing if they wish to raise complaints or ask for explanations of policy.[91]

Walters' statement was reminiscent of the opposition that had been expressed by chiefs to appeals against their rulings, and indicated the personalised way in which he sought to construct his authority. Dismissing Peck's objections, Walters concluded his letter by asserting: 'Finally I wish to say that I intend to continue administering this district as I have done in the past and I have no doubt that Mr Peck or others of his ilk will always have complaints such as this or try to discredit our administration. My only annoyance over this business is that I have had to spend the whole morning of Sunday 11th May 1972, writing this report when I could have been enjoying 18 holes of golf.'[92] In this he had the support of his superior A. D. B. Yardley, the PC for Mashonaland South, who remarked, 'I too resent the tone of this [Peck's] letter and also take strong exception to the remarks made about the work of a dedicated District Commissioner on my team who has been under considerable pressure in recent months.'[93]

The DC's comment that 'Mr Peck or others of his ilk will always have complaints such as this or try to discredit our Administration' was misleading. Peck had graduated from Oxford with a degree in politics, philosophy and economics before taking up a legal career in Southern Rhodesia. In the 1960s, he had ventured into politics and stood for a seat in Parliament as an independent candidate. In the course of the 1960s he had also written a series of books commenting on the dispute between Britain and Rhodesia over the Unilateral Declaration of Independence of 1965. His 1966 book was entitled *Rhodesia Accuses*, taking its inspiration from Emile Zola's letter *J'accuse*. The book celebrated Cecil John Rhodes' 'vision' for Africa and accused Britain of betraying it and yielding to communism by calling for majority rule in Rhodesia.[94] Although Peck was not a Rhodesian Front supporter, he was neither a nationalist lawyer like Leo Baron, nor a 'liberal' one like Hardwicke Holderness. The last words of his letter to the Minister suggest his possible motives. He wrote:

[91] Ibid., DC Mrewa to PC Mashonaland South, 13 June 1972.
[92] Ibid.
[93] Ibid., PC Mashonaland South to SIA, June 1972.
[94] A. J. A. Peck, *Rhodesia Accuses* (Salisbury, 1966).

May I request, Sir, that the present matter receive reasonable, careful and prompt consideration, and that I may be advised of developments in this matter? You will appreciate that I have acted with restraint, I have in fact done nothing at all for nine months, and have refrained from adopting any of the courses open to me. It is simply that I have been consulted again in virtually the same matter. This is not the first time I have been treated in this somewhat high-handed fashion at Mrewa. I regret that I owe a duty to my clients and to my profession to ensure that it does not continue.[95]

What drove Peck was an ideal of how the law was supposed to be administered and therein lay the source of his outrage at the practices of the DC of Mrewa. Like the Justice Ministry officials who had long criticised the practices of administrative officials, his was a commitment to due process. It should be added, however, that his next letter was more temperate, beginning as it did with the words: 'On my perusing my own letter again, it does strike me that my letter may be misunderstood in one or two points . . .'[96]

Conclusion

When the Robinson Commission recommended that Africans be provided with 'a justice that met the norms of their society', it was in fact talking about a 'justice' that met the needs of a settler government that was faced with a deep crisis of legitimacy and rising African nationalism. This was a 'justice' that was founded on notions of racial and cultural difference, which sought to treat Africans as ethnicised, custom-bound subjects, as opposed to rights-bearing citizens. As this chapter has shown, these efforts were unsuccessful for a number of reasons. State officials had overestimated the ability of the institution of chieftaincy to lend legitimacy to unpopular land use policies. In addition, chiefs proved to be less pliable than had been hoped for. Not only did they have their own agendas which did not necessarily coincide with those of the government, they were also keenly aware of the threat to their lives, let alone their legitimacy, should they try to implement unpopular land-use policies under customary guise. As a consequence, it was ultimately the guerrillas, not the state, that

---

[95] NAZ S3700/43, Peck to Minister of Internal Affairs, 26 May 1972.
[96] NAZ S3700/43, Peck to Minister of Internal Affairs, 19 June 1972.

exerted influence on chiefs' courts. Another reason for the failure of the strategy was the resistance from 'ordinary' individuals in the rural areas who refused to comply with the directives of local authorities. Notwithstanding their harassment by state officials and the expense involved, they persisted in seeking legal advice about how they might check the state's intrusions in their lives. At one level, these were efforts by Africans to instrumentalise the law. At another, their actions signified an attempt to assert themselves as rights-bearing citizens. In the next chapter I turn to the sphere of politics and examine the state's efforts to use the law to deal with African nationalism and the responses this evoked from Africans.

3 | *Legislating Against Dissent: Law, Race and Politics, 1950–1964*

Introduction

Aside from the crisis of state legitimacy in the rural areas caused by the Native Land Husbandry Act, the post-World War II period witnessed the rise of African nationalism in Southern Rhodesia. A central feature of the government's response to this was the enactment of a series of repressive laws that were designed to quell African political dissent. Much of the scholarly literature that focuses on legal developments between 1950 and 1964 has tended to treat the passage of the Law and Order (Maintenance) Act in 1960 as the key starting point.[1] This has not been without justification; nevertheless, it has had the effect of occluding the decade between 1950 and 1960 during which several repressive Acts were passed, and during which government officials and legislators debated amongst themselves what actions they could legitimately take without betraying British legal traditions. These debates provide a window onto the shifts in settler opinions about the relationship between law and the legitimate exercise of state power and how these shifts in turn shaped state practice. In addition, they shed light on how the law and ideas about racial difference were enlisted by the state in its effort to deal with African nationalism.

This chapter examines the legal response by the colonial state to African nationalism between 1950 and 1964, paying particular attention to the debates about the relationship between the law and the legitimate exercise of state power. However, legislating against African political dissent was not the end of the story. It invariably led to arrests and prosecutions, which in turn provoked a diverse set of responses from Africans. As such, the chapter explores African nationalists' engagement with the government in the legal arena. In particular, it looks at how

---

[1] See Feltoe 'Law, Ideology and Coercion', and C. Palley, 'Law and the Unequal Society: Discriminatory Legislation in Rhodesia under the Rhodesian Front from 1963 to 1969, Part 1', *Race and Class*, 12 (1970).

they made use of the law instrumentally and discursively. In so doing, it sheds light on the place of law within the nationalist movement.

The Rise of Nationalist Politics

From 1945 Southern Rhodesia witnessed a surge in African political militancy characterised by workers' strikes, urban riots, rural unrest and a general increase in confrontations between Africans and colonial authorities.[2] This militancy was fuelled by, among other things, a body of political ideas which were gaining currency during this period. These ideas about national self-determination, universal human rights, majority rule and rights-bearing citizenship formed the basis for critiques of colonial rule. In addition, Africans from different backgrounds made claims for full citizenship and challenged the colonial government to live up to its rhetoric about 'civilisation' and 'British justice'. World War II was particularly important in exposing the double standards of empire. Although African soldiers had fought to defend the rights of Europeans to self-determination in the face of Fascism and Nazism, they were denied those same rights when they returned home.[3] In 1944 Lance Corporal Masiye, a World War II veteran, wrote a letter to the *Bantu Mirror* which read in part:

It must be a shameless sort of ruler who exploits people under his thraldom at ease and yet he never dreams of their release nor allows them to have privileges to race for comparative human rights. The African has served his rulers with admirable devotedness. What is he to receive for this? A continual exclusion from human rights? If so, our rulers must be quite shameless to blame the enemy for his brutality and assumed racial superiority.[4]

This strategy of challenging the government on the basis of its own claims was also used by labour and political leaders in their engagements with officials.

---

[2] For a detailed account of the rise of mass nationalism, see West, *The Rise of an African Middle Class*, and Scarnecchia, *The Urban Roots*.

[3] A. S. Mlambo, 'From the Second World War to UDI, 1940–1965', in B. Raftopoulos and A. S. Mlambo (eds), *Becoming Zimbabwe: A History from the Pre-colonial Period to 2008* (Harare, 2009), 78–80. See also C. Banana (ed), *Turmoil and Tenacity: Zimbabwe, 1890–1990*, (Harare, 1989).

[4] Cited in Mlambo, 'From the Second World War to UDI', 79.

The intellectual currents of the period also inspired the formation of a number of organisations that sought to improve the living conditions of Africans in the urban areas. During the early 1950s, the Reformed Industrial and Commercial Workers Union (RICU), under the leadership of Charles Mzingeli, was at the forefront of attempting to address the grievances of Africans living in the urban areas. As Timothy Scarnecchia shows, Mzingeli's energies were devoted to fighting for 'the rights of access of township residents to the city'. At the same time, he urged them 'to gain more education in order to obtain greater respect so that they could in turn make greater claims to an imperial working-class citizenship'.[5] RICU was also involved in campaigning against the harassment associated with the implementation of the Native (Urban Areas) Accommodation and Registration Act of 1946, and in making calls for the government to address the rising cost of living.[6] However, by the mid-1950s, RICU's dominance in township politics was being challenged by a number of organisations.[7] One such organisation, that would go on to play a central role in the rise of mass nationalism in Southern Rhodesia, was the Salisbury City Youth League (CYL).

The CYL was formed in August 1955 by young men who resented their exclusion from the opportunities being availed to African elites during the 1950s under the banner of 'racial partnership'.[8] Under the leadership of James Chikerema, Edson Sithole, George Nyandoro and Maurice Nyagumbo, the CYL opposed the elitism that underpinned the policy of 'racial partnership' and adopted a more confrontational approach than RICU in engaging the government.[9] The CYL got involved in opposition to the Native Land Husbandry Act (NLHA) of 1951, and helped villagers to institute lawsuits against DCs who overstepped their authority in enforcing the NLHA. As Nathan Shamuyarira notes, 'In the Weya case they took it to the point of

---

[5] Scarnecchia, *The Urban Roots*, pp. 12–13. Scarnecchia uses the term 'imperial working class citizenship' to distinguish African workers' claims to citizenship from 'the more elitist view of "Imperial citizenship" that was marked by attaining European attributes of civility and wealth.' *The Urban Roots*, 169, footnote 1.

[6] Ibid., 52.

[7] B. Raftopoulos, 'Nationalism and Labour in Salisbury 1953–1965', *JSAS*, 21 (1995), 88.

[8] West, *The Rise of an African Middle Class*, 204.

[9] N. Shamuyarira, *Crisis in Rhodesia* (New York, 1966), 41.

summoning Sir Edgar Whitehead, who had become premier by then, to appear in court on a charge of destroying tribesmen's crops.'[10]

An important moment in the CYL's life was the September 1956 Bus Boycott against rising bus fares and the general cost of living in Salisbury. However, the success of the boycott was tarnished by violent attacks against the young women of Carter Hostel who were accused of defying the boycott. These events, Scarnecchia correctly notes, marked 'a turning point in both nationalist politics and also in the role of women in politics.'[11] Whereas Mzingeli's brand of township politics had been focused on defending community interests and had recognised the important role of women in this endeavour, the new politics championed by the CYL was characterised by violence and intolerance, and reversed the progress towards greater gender equality in township politics. In 1957, the CYL was transformed into the Southern Rhodesian African National Congress (SRANC), and this ushered in the era of mass nationalism in Southern Rhodesia.[12] Nationalism was also developing in the rural areas of Southern Rhodesia but was not simply the result of its importation from the urban areas. Over time, different communities gradually began to view the solution to their problems as being the overhaul of the colonial state, as opposed to specific policies or legislation.[13] This gave rise to what Alexander, McGregor and Ranger have referred to as 'local nationalism' which was fuelled by local grievances, had a local social base and drew on local sources of legitimation.[14]

Unlike the working class and the peasantry, members of the African middle class were late to embrace nationalism. This was largely because many of them had either bought into the 1950s project of 'racial partnership' or sought to take advantage of the opportunities it availed for personal advancement. The idea of 'racial partnership' had been promoted by Godfrey Huggins' administration, partly as a way of allaying African concerns about the plans to form the Federation of Rhodesia and Nyasaland, which came into being in 1953. However, from the outset, Huggins assured the European electorate that the kind of partnership he was referring to was that between 'a horse and

---

[10] Ibid.. 42.
[11] Scarnecchia, *The Urban Roots*, 85.
[12] Ibid., 207.
[13] Alexander et al., *Violence and Memory*, 83–7.
[14] Ibid., 87.

its rider'. The second, and more important, goal behind 'racial part-nership' was to co-opt the African middle class through inter-racial organisations and use them as a buffer against the 'masses'.

Multi-racialism was taken up enthusiastically by the 'liberal' wing of the settler population in the 1950s. As Michael West notes, the Southern Rhodesian 'liberals' were a 'a small minority, [of] mainly post-war white collar immigrants from Britain, [who] had an alter-nate vision of racial partnership in which the African elite would be gradually incorporated into the white-dominated civil society.'[15] Nevertheless, they shared a number of traits with the hard-liners on the right of settler society. Both groups aimed to preserve settler priv-ilege in Southern Rhodesia, were ethnocentric in their assumptions about the superiority of western civilisation, and were paternalistic in their attitude towards Africans. Their key point of difference, however, lay in how they thought settler privilege should be preserved.

Whereas the hard-liners' position was that no effort should be spared in clamping down on African politics, the liberals feared that increased repression would most likely lead to a severe backlash, thereby imperilling the future of all settlers in Southern Rhodesia. Instead, they advocated for educated Africans to be accepted into the ranks of the 'civilised' so that they could act as a bulwark against pol-itical pressure from the rest of the African population. 'Liberal' organi-sations such as the Inter-Racial Association (IRA) and the Capricorn Africa Society (CAS) thrived during the 1950s as African elites eagerly joined them. However, by the late 1950s it had become clear to many of them that 'racial partnership' had delivered few tangible benefits. The final straw for many of African elites was the removal of Garfield Todd from office by his cabinet on the grounds that he was too liberal. It should be said, though, that this charge exaggerated the liberal cre-dentials of Todd's administration. West is closer to the truth in observ-ing that, 'Although liberal in his use of the stick, Todd, in contrast to the white ultra-diehards, also saw the need for the carrot. In essence, his policy was to apply the one to the African working class (as evi-denced by his response to the strikes over which he presided), while offering the other to the black elite (as seen in his proposal to enfran-chise teachers and nurses).'[16]

---

[15] West, *The Rise of an African Middle Class*, 192–93.
[16] Ibid., 213.

Upon taking up office, the new Prime Minister, Edgar Whitehead, was faced with increasing unrest from an agitated African population whose demands had shifted from calling for reforms to colonial policies, to demanding a transfer of power. From 1959, the pace of political events picked up significantly. A month-long state of emergency was declared in February and then renewed in March. In addition, a series of new laws designed to quell African political militancy were passed. During this period, the SRANC was banned and hundreds of its leaders were detained.[17] Those detainees who were deemed to be less of a threat were soon released, but others like Nyagumbo and Chikerema, who were considered to be a serious threat, remained incarcerated for the next four years.

Despite these measures by the Whitehead administration, political agitation continued to intensify in the rural and urban areas; in January 1960, a new party, the National Democratic Party (NDP), was formed under the leadership of Michael Mawema, Moton Malianga, Enos Nkala and Sketchley Samkange.[18] In an attempt to clamp down on the continued political unrest, the government arrested Mawema, Samkange and Leopold Takawira, who was the chairperson of the NDP's Harari branch. However, these arrests provoked further unrest in Salisbury, which later spread to Gwelo and Bulawayo. In Bulawayo, the unrest manifested itself in the Zhii riots of 24 and 25 July during which 11 Africans were shot dead by the police.[19] As a result, the NDP was banned in 1961, as was the Zimbabwe African People's Union (ZAPU) which succeeded it, and the Zimbabwe African National Union (ZANU) which broke off from ZAPU in 1963. Despite these attempts to suppress African nationalism, the early 1960s continued to be characterised by increasingly violent confrontations between Africans and state officials in both rural and urban areas.[20]

---

[17] J. McCracken, 'In the Shadow of Mau Mau: Detainees and Detention Camps during Nyasaland's State of Emergency', *JSAS*, 37 (2011), 538.

[18] T. Ranger, *Are We Not Also Men? The Samkange Family and African Politics in Zimbabwe, 1920–1964* (London, 1995).

[19] Ibid., 186–89.

[20] There were also violent confrontations amongst Africans, especially after the formation of ZANU.

Law, Politics and Race

At the beginning of 1950 the main piece of legislation that dealt with political dissent in Southern Rhodesia was the Sedition Act of 1936. However, by 1960 no less than six pieces of legislation had been passed by the Parliament. These were the Subversive Activities Act of 1950, the Public Order Act of 1955, the Unlawful Organisations and the Preventive Detention Acts of 1959, and last, the Law and Order (Maintenance) Act and the Emergency Powers Act, both passed in 1960. In their efforts to come to terms with the rise of nationalism and devise a response to it, settler officials drew liberally on a range of colonial tropes about Africans. These were used to justify the increasingly repressive turn in the legislation, and the continued refusal to grant Africans full citizenship and the right of self-determination.

The Subversive Activities Act of 1950 arose out of a recommendation by the Hudson Commission of Enquiry into the 1948 general strike. In its final report, the Commission highlighted the fact that Southern Rhodesia had no legislation in place to deal with riots and advised that steps be taken to rectify this. Another factor that weighed on the minds of the drafters of the legislation was the Cold War and the fear of communist agents infiltrating the colony and causing unrest. The resultant legislation was modelled on South Africa's Riotous Assemblies Act of 1914; however, its scope was widened to provide for the control of the movement of people spreading 'subversive propaganda' and 'subversive materials'. In presenting the Bill to Parliament, the Minister of Justice and Internal Affairs, Julius Greenfield, played up the threat of communist agents who, he argued 'employ insidious methods of propaganda which has a certain appeal to ignorant minds, and it is unnecessary for me to stress what volatile material we have in this country which might fall prey to propaganda of this sort. It is propaganda which is particularly dangerous with ignorant uneducated people.'[21] By constructing the African population in this way, the Minister sought to counter the argument that the solution to the political problems lay in improving the living conditions of the African population. For such a population, he maintained, it was 'not sufficient merely to improve living conditions without at the same time protecting them from subversive doctrines of this description.'[22]

---

[21] *Southern Rhodesia Parliamentary Debates*, 2 June 1950, 1905.
[22] Ibid., 1907.

However, support for the Bill in Parliament was not unanimous, and at the heart of the debate that ensued was the question of the relationship between law and the legitimate exercise of state power. Two of the Bill's most vocal opponents were Laurence Keller and William Eastwood, the MPs for Raylton and Bulawayo District, respectively. Both men were members of the Rhodesia Labour Party and feared that the legislation would be used to clamp down on settler opposition parties like theirs. Keller, therefore, condemned the legislation in very strong terms: 'Let me say immediately we deprecate tyranny or brutality or fear. We do not stand for that sort of thing, but this Bill itself is going to endeavour to maintain control over the people of this country through fear of punishment, fear of the penalties contained in this Bill.'[23] He added, 'It places too much power in the hands of Government and in the hands of the hon. Minister who is not always entirely responsible. You cannot legislate against doctrines, creeds and ideas.'[24]

For Eastwood, a serious problem with the legislation was that it went against British legal traditions. He observed sarcastically,

I appreciate the Minister's difficulty because being well versed in law, I presume he must know about the Magna Carta and the Petition of Rights and about *Habeus Corpus* and about the Combination Acts. He must be so well versed in all the instruments which have finally been put on the Statute Book of Great Britain and for which men have fought and given their lives over a period of centuries. I cannot believe that with that background he can feel very sincere and earnest about a Bill of this nature.[25]

By invoking the notion of British legal traditions, Eastwood and other opponents of the Bill were not making a case for the extension of equal rights to Africans. Rather, they were expressing a concern similar to that of the nineteenth century 'moralising imperialists' who saw British legal traditions as the hallmark of its civilisation.[26] They therefore maintained that the empire had to be run according to these standards, and that failure to do so delegitimised it. Although Eastwood's rhetorical

---

[23] *Southern Rhodesia Parliamentary Debates*, 13 June 1950, 2011.
[24] Ibid., 2019.
[25] Ibid., 2034–5.
[26] R. W. Kostal, *A Jurisprudence of Power – Victorian Empire and the Rule of Law* (Oxford, 2005), 474.

strategy of invoking British legal traditions had a long history in the British empire, it was not always a persuasive argument within settler populations. This was partly because there was no single interpretation about what exactly the core of that heritage was, or what adherence to it meant in practical terms. In his study of interracial murders in the British empire, Martin Wiener shows how contested the idea of 'rule of law' was in colonial contexts. On the one hand, members of the 'colonised' took it to mean 'the same law for all British subjects'. On the other, settlers interpreted it as '"the Englishman's Birthright" of rights against Government, including trial by a jury of his peers'.[27]

In Southern Rhodesia, a similar tension existed within the settler community over what respect for British legal traditions meant in practical terms. For Eastwood and others, it meant remaining true to the traditions in which law constrained government action, and settlers retained rights which protected them against the arbitrary use of power by the state. However, for their opponents it meant protecting the settler society from the perceived threat posed to it by communist *agents provocateurs* and their African followers. One such proponent, Neville Barret, the MP for Marandellas, rejected the claim that British legal traditions had been violated, and argued instead that critics of the Bill needed to understand the 'exceptional' circumstances of Southern Rhodesia *viz* the presence of a large African population. The proposed legislation, he argued,

… has been threshed out and gone into from all angles and has been altered and as a result we have arrived at something which to my mind is entirely reasonable and compatible with our British observations of justice. When one is considering this question in a country where there is an entirely European population, there might be a different approach … But what we have to remember in this country is that we are in the midst of central Africa and we are surrounded by a very large native population, uneducated and easily influenced . . .[28]

George Munro, the MP for Gatooma, took the argument further in arguing that the legislation was not just compatible with British legal traditions but it in fact defended them. The Bill, he argued, would '…

---

[27] M. Wiener, *An Empire on Trial: Race, Murder, and Justice under British Rule, 1870–1935* (Cambridge, 2009), 230–1.
[28] *Southern Rhodesia Parliamentary Debates*, 13 June 1950, 2027.

prevent a certain class of people who are taking advantage of <u>our</u> liberties and <u>our</u> privileges from depriving the people of those privileges and liberties and therefore subjecting them to absolute slavery and degradation. This Bill is really a shield to <u>our</u> present liberties and <u>our</u> freedom.'[29] Although Munro argued the Bill was about defending liberties, the subtext of his statement revealed that it was in fact about excluding Africans from enjoying the same liberties enjoyed by settlers.

Several African organisations such as RICU, the African National Congress, and the Federation of Bulawayo Trade Unions realised this and mocked the state's democratic pretensions.[30] Nevertheless, the Bill was passed and subsequently used to ban several publications such as the book *Nehru on Africa*, as well as all publications of the World Federation of Trade Unions (WFTU) and the Pan African Trade Union Congress. In 1953, Joshua Nkomo, a trade unionist who would later lead ZAPU, was arrested and charged under the Act, and the following year, the legislation was used by the Todd administration to quell the strike at the Wankie Colliery.[31]

The debate over the 1955 Public Order Bill again revealed the centrality of race in the way African political militancy was understood, and how responses to it were rationalised. The key opponents of the Bill in this instance were not latter-day 'moralising imperialists', but 'liberals'. The legislation had been drafted in the wake of the Mau Mau revolt in Kenya, as well as the 1953 Cholo disturbances in Malawi; therefore, it reflected an anxiety on the part of state officials to avoid a similar occurrence in Southern Rhodesia. This, it was hoped, would be achieved by criminalising an even longer list of political acts than that of 1950. These included marching in formation without permission, carrying a flag or wearing a uniform associated with a political party, 'suggesting that it was desirable for someone to die', and being in the leadership of an organisation 'prepared to use force to achieve political aims'. In an apparent reference to events in Kenya, consenting to take an oath, administering one or being present at an oath-taking ceremony were also made illegal. Much to the ire of Rhodesian journalists, publishing a false rumour was also made a criminal offence.

---

[29] Ibid., 2031. (Emphasis added)
[30] West, *The Rise of an African Middle Class*, 178–179.
[31] J. Nkomo, *Nkomo: The Story of My Life* (London, 1984), 57–61.

The Bill also gave state functionaries greater powers to control riots and all gatherings deemed unlawful by the government.

As he introduced the Bill to the House, the Minister of Justice and Internal Affairs, Albert Stumbles, was conscious of the public outcry the proposed legislation had already caused. His speech was therefore carefully crafted to pre-empt any objections. 'The provisions which it is decided to introduce in this Bill', he argued, 'are English in the main, from the United Kingdom, and very, very old, many of them. They have stood the test of time and they have remained on the Statute Book.'[32] Drawing on the ideas of the English philosopher Edmund Burke he reminded the Parliament that '… it was Burke, that famous politician, that famous statesman, who once said that the only liberty which is valuable is a liberty connected with order. – [HON MEMBERS: Hear, hear.] – And we must not confuse liberty with licence. Take away our laws, take away our order, and where is our liberty, Mr Speaker? It is gone; completely gone.'[33]

The Minister also invoked the spectre of Mau Mau by quoting a letter from a man who had lived in Kenya during the 1950s, which claimed that '… if the then Government had brought in such a Bill as this when it was first warned about Mau Mau in 1947, the emergency would probably not have arisen.'[34] The Minister's scaremongering was not enough to persuade European journalists to set aside their concerns that the provisions on publishing false rumours would be used to target them. The *Rhodesia Herald*, for example, pointed out that 'Even if some curtailment is necessary to prevent freedom degenerating into licence it does not seem to us that this Bill gives sufficient protection to innocent and responsible persons acting in what they are convinced is in the public interest.'[35] Criticism of the Bill also came from the 'liberals' who felt that the legislation not only betrayed British legal traditions, but also undermined the efforts to preserve settler privilege in Southern Rhodesia. The Inter-Racial Association dismissed the Bill in its entirety arguing that the proposed legislation was undemocratic, and that the existing legislation already provided sufficient powers for the Minister to deal with unrest.[36]

[32] *Southern Rhodesia Parliamentary Debates*, 29 July 1955, 1427.
[33] Ibid., 1426.
[34] Ibid., 1430.
[35] *Rhodesia Herald*, 18 July 1955.
[36] *Southern Rhodesia Parliamentary Debates*, 29 July 1955, 1449–50.

Hardwicke Holderness, a prominent Salisbury lawyer and a leading 'liberal' politician, was particularly opposed to the Bill. He disagreed with the thinking that criminalisation was the solution to African political unrest.[37] For him the nationalist movement was an inevitable reality; therefore, the best course of action was to try to channel it in a different direction. As such, he argued that 'We must accept [nationalism] as a dynamic force, but we must not make the mistake of assuming that everybody who has a nationalist feeling necessarily has an anti-European feeling, or an anti-British feeling.'[38] He went on:

… with the development of our country and the uprooting of the African people you have a whole section of people who are politically conscious, and, as I once said before are, for lack of a better phrase, knocking at the door of Western civilisation. That being the position, we must accept it, and we must try to take positive measures, we must find ways and means of integrating these people into Western civilisation, and we must in fact find an inter-racial nationalism.[39]

For a while, these ideas had attracted the African elite. However, there were few takers amongst the audience that Holderness was addressing in the Southern Rhodesian Parliament.

Holderness' contribution drew fire from the hard-liners in Parliament. For Harry Reedman, the MP for Braeside, it was not a question of Europeans ushering Africans into 'western civilisation', but one of them instilling discipline in Africans as a parent would do to impatient children. 'I would say Mr Speaker', he observed:

… that there is a slow emergence from primitive life to civilized behaviour with the white or any race. At some stage there is a clamouring for self-expression, and a reluctance to complete the apprenticeship. By that, Mr Speaker, I mean that it is not uncommon to consider the adolescence of a person, or the adolescence of a nation, when one is full of inspiration and wanting to jump fences, as being that time that discipline, that parental discipline, is so very necessary.[40]

---

[37] Ibid., 2 August 1955, 1496.
[38] Ibid., 1498.
[39] Ibid.
[40] *Southern Rhodesia Parliamentary Debates*, 2 August 1955, 1520.

Despite their disagreement, both Reedman and Holderness' arguments were founded on an evolutionary paradigm in which Africans figured as less 'civilised', and in need of European custodianship.

A notable contribution to the debate was the brief unguarded speech by the Minister of Native Affairs, Patrick Fletcher, which went to the heart of the matter in explaining the necessity of the legislation before the House. He dispensed with appeals to lofty ideas and plainly pointed out that such legislation was central to maintaining the social and political status quo in Southern Rhodesia:

Without belittling the importance of this measure, a thought has gone through my mind. What a wonderful opportunity this Bill would offer to a fifth form scholar in debate, attacking it on the academic and unrealistic basis of repugnancy; repugnant to our ideas of freedom and democracy; repugnant to our way of life – of course it is repugnant. Just as repugnant as are whippings, prisons and gallows, but those devices are essential supports of our social order … It is so easy for a measure of this kind to be attacked by people with their feet off the ground. We hear fatuous argument that although the United Kingdom has powers of this kind they are relics of the past and no Government of the United Kingdom of Great Britain would dare to attempt to take powers like these. That no Government in the United Kingdom of Great Britain would attempt to use such powers. The fact remains that Governments have come and Governments have gone in the United Kingdom of Great Britain and still these powers remain.[41]

Fletcher's views were very much in keeping with the long-held view within the Native Affairs Department (NAD) that authoritarian measures were the most appropriate when dealing with Africans.

The trend towards more repressive legislation persisted, and in March 1959 the new Minister of Justice and Internal Affairs, Reginald Knight, tabled two new pieces of legislation aimed at dealing with African political nationalism: the Preventive Detention and the Unlawful Organisations Bills. Amongst other things, the two Bills sought to empower the state to issue detention orders and to proscribe organisations without having to rely on the declaration of a state of emergency. In October 1960, amidst growing urban unrest, the Minister of Justice was again before Parliament with a new Bill, and expressed the hope that 'through its more comprehensive

---

[41] Ibid., 1535–6.

provisions, through the more severe penalties provided, it will enable the Government more effectively and firmly to discharge its responsibilities for the maintenance of law and order in the colony.'[42] The Bill was the Law and Order (Maintenance) Act, which the sitting Federal Chief Justice, Robert Tredgold, described as an 'anthology of horrors' and elected to resign rather than enforce it.[43] The same year saw the passing into law of the Emergency Powers Act. In the years that followed, the extensive powers provided for by these two Acts were used to proscribe African political parties and prosecute and/or detain their leaders and supporters on a huge scale.

It is worth noting that the actions of the Southern Rhodesian government were taken in response to both local and regional events. The passing of the 1955 Public Order Act, for example, was done in conjunction with the other members of the Federation of Rhodesia and Nyasaland, as was the declaration of the state of emergency in 1959. There were, however, differences in Southern Rhodesia's approach in dealing with political dissent as compared with that of Nyasaland and Kenya.[44] A key difference related to how political militancy was constructed by the colonial state and how this informed its response. In Kenya, African political militancy was viewed through a 'medical' lens and officials took the view that it stemmed from a psychological disorder. As David Anderson shows, Kenyan officials 'diagnosed' Mau Mau as a 'mind destroying disease' arising from the Kikuyu's inability to cope with civilisation.[45] The grievances of the Kikuyu were thus denied validity, and the colonial state exonerated itself from any blame in the war. This understanding of Mau Mau fed directly into the solutions that Kenyan officials proposed. If Mau Mau was an illness, it followed that the Kikuyu had to be cured. Consequently, tens of thousands of detainees were put through the 'pipeline', a multi-stage process of 'rehabilitation', and release was only granted once one had confessed and recanted the Mau Mau oath.

The situation in Nyasaland bore some similarities to that in Kenya though there was a marked difference in terms of scale. Nyasaland's colonial authorities secured the services of John Pinney, a District

---

[42] *Southern Rhodesia Parliamentary Debates*, 27 October 1960, 2517.
[43] R. Tredgold, *The Rhodesia That Was My Life* (London, 1968), 229.
[44] J. Alexander, 'Nationalism and Self-government in Rhodesian Detention: Gonakudzingwa, 1964–1974', *JSAS*, 37 (2011), 553.
[45] Anderson, *Histories of the Hanged*, 280.

Officer previously based in Kenya, to assist in dealing with the political disturbances.[46] John McCracken notes: 'As in Kenya, [Pinney] started with the assumption that political militancy was a disease that could be cured only through a combination of confession and hard work: "a desire for release must be inculcated in the detainee and this can be best achieved by subjecting him to strict discipline and getting him to work." '[47] By contrast, in Southern Rhodesia, the 'disease theory' did not take root as a way of interpreting African political militancy. During much of the 1950s, settler rhetoric constructed Africans involved in political unrest as children or simpletons who were being misled by communist *agents provocateurs* into disrupting law and order in the colony. This view enabled the state to deny the validity of African grievances and gave credence to its chosen response of criminalising political dissent and imposing more severe sentences as a deterrent. The early treatment of detainees in Southern Rhodesia was particularly distinct from that in Kenya and Nyasaland. Jocelyn Alexander notes that during the late 1950s and early 1960s 'detainees were legally recognised as distinct from criminals by right of the fact that they had not been convicted of an offence … ' What is more, the 'state accepted that it had obligations to the maintenance of detainees' businesses, properties and dependents through the provision of allowances and a range of other material and administrative support.'[48]

However, the coming of the Rhodesian Front (RF) into power in 1963 led to a shift in the way political dissent was viewed and dealt with. The RF arose out of a coalition of right-wing settler groups and two of its key aims were to ensure 'the Government of Southern Rhodesian would remain in responsible hands', as well as 'the permanent establishment of the European' in the colony.[49] As a result, it took an uncompromising stance when it came to dealing with any threats to continued settler rule. This was clear in the way they dealt with detained African nationalists. As Alexander points out: 'In contrast to its predecessor, the Rhodesian Front did not view detainees as citizens temporarily deprived of their rights in the interests of security. It constructed detainees as something considerably worse than convicted

---

[46] J. McCracken, 'In the Shadow of Mau Mau: Detainees and Detention Camps during Nyasaland's State of Emergency', *JSAS* , 37 (2011), 544.

[47] Ibid.

[48] Alexander, 'Nationalism and Self-government', 553.

[49] P. Godwin and I. Hancock, "*Rhodesians Never Die*": *The Impact of War and Political Change on White Rhodesia c. 1970–1980* (Oxford, 1993), 57.

criminals, referring to them as violent thugs and terrorists, miscreants who had placed themselves outside society and so – quite literally – deserved to be isolated in the "bush"'.[50]

The laws that had been passed by the Whitehead administration served as the foundation on which the RF immediately set about expanding the already substantial powers of the state. Between 1960 and the late 1970s, the Law and Order (Maintenance) Act was amended twelve times, while the Emergency Powers Act was amended thirty-two times.[51] These amendments were concerned as much with the expansion of state powers as they were with providing for more severe punishments for 'offenders'. Perhaps the most infamous of the amendments to the Law and Order (Maintenance) Act was the 1963 'hanging clause' which introduced a mandatory death sentence for individuals found guilty of using petrol bombs. It also provided for the administration of corporal punishment, in addition to imprisonment, for those convicted of political offences, on the grounds that imprisonment on its own was not a sufficient deterrent for Africans.

The strident language used by the proponents of the 1963 amendment to justify the mandatory death sentence for individuals convicted of using petrol bombs vividly captures the new shift in the way that the RF constructed African nationalist supporters. Although they had previously been portrayed as children requiring a firm disciplining hand, they were now discursively constructed as animals that needed to be killed. Clearly influenced by the Mau Mau rebellion and the language used to describe it, J. A. Newington, the MP for Hillcrest, asserted that '... Mau Mau and even this petrol bombing is merely an expression of tribal bestiality.'[52] He maintained that

... in the peculiar circumstances of our environment we are at a disadvantage. It is easy to ensure the rule of law is maintained where people are prepared to live according to the rule of law, where it is a natural progression, where they have been used to it over the centuries. Here the vast majority have no real understanding of what democracy means and I think it is true to say they only obey the law because of the penalties imposed. The greater the severity in many cases the greater the obedience.[53]

[50] Alexander, 'Nationalism and Self-government', 554.
[51] Cited in Alexander, *The Unsettled Land*, 82. See also Munochiveyi, *Prisoners of Rhodesia*, 70–1.
[52] *Southern Rhodesia Parliamentary Debates*, 26 February 1963, 590.
[53] Ibid.

Echoing these sentiments, Col. George Hartley, the MP for Victoria and a former director of the Salisbury Native Administration Department, declared,

If a mad dog is loose in the community the whole community as a rule rises to shoot it down. – [MR GAUNT: Hear, hear.] – They do this from one desire and that is to protect society from that class of offender. – [MR GAUNT: Or rabid animal.] – I believe that drastic measures of a similar sort should be introduced to deal with the mad dog who throws a petrol bomb. – [HON. MEMBERS: Hear, hear.][54]

The fervour of the advocates for capital punishment was evident both in the exclamations of approval in Parliament and in their insistence that there be no room for judicial discretion in the matter.

Among the few members of Parliament who opposed the amendment were the African MPs who had been elected to Parliament after the adoption of 1961 Constitution which set aside fifteen seats in Parliament for Africans. C. Hlabangana, for example, asserted: 'Unless and until the voice of the African today is heard when he claims his right, no death sentence, no severe penalty will ever stop him from achieving his end and this is one of those bills which will lead to an Act that will, in the long run, aggravate the situation instead of bettering it.'[55] These objections went unheeded, and the Bill was passed into law. However, this was not to be the final word on the matter, as the debate over the political questions facing the Southern Rhodesian body politic would be reconvened in courtrooms across the country.

Courtroom Encounters

The arrest and prosecution of Africans for political offences began fairly early in the 1950s. However, the annual figures rose significantly in the late 1950s, and in 1964 as many as 4,435 Africans were arrested and 2,017 of those were prosecuted.[56] These numerous political trials served a number of functions. In the first instance, they were instruments that facilitated the state's desire to apprehend and

---

[54] Ibid., 607.
[55] Ibid., 26 February 1963, 531.
[56] Feltoe, 'Law, Ideology and Coercion', Appendix B- Criminal Offenders.

punish those it deemed its political enemies.[57] At another level, they were performances in which state power was ritualised and presented as unquestionable.[58] These performances were also meant to authorise the official narrative about African politics. As Paul Gready points out, the political trial 'reconstructs and rewrites events as they are perceived by the government, and reproduces for the public the image of a society threatened by people and organisations who seeks its violent destruction, thereby serving to justify actions taken by the state against political opponents'.[59] However, an analysis of the political trials in Southern Rhodesia shows that state designs were actively challenged and at times subverted.

Up to the mid-1960s, many nationalists responded to prosecution by investing a great deal of energy and resources in putting up legal defences. Although they were critical of the repressive laws and the actions of the state, by and large nationalists still recognised the legitimacy of the courts and looked to them to deliver just outcomes. Their defences were structured according to the stipulations of Rhodesian law, and they generally conformed to the niceties of the Rhodesian courts. However, to interpret these actions as being founded on a naïve and misplaced faith in the legal system misses the fact that they were also expressions of an imaginary of rights-bearing citizenship.[60] In addition, nationalists won their cases on a number of occasions, especially in the higher courts. Furthermore, the importance of political trials went beyond the opportunity they provided for nationalists to defend themselves legally. They were also high-profile moments of conflict with the state which could be used to gain political mileage locally and abroad. In such moments, courtrooms could be usurped and used as sites of personal performance by nationalists.

---

[57] M. Chanock, 'Writing South African Legal History: A Prospectus', *JAH*, 30 (1989), 268.

[58] D. Hay. 'Property, Authority and the Criminal Trial', in D. Hay et al. (eds), *Albion's Fatal Tree* (Middlesex, 1975), 17–63. See also J-G Deutsch, 'Celebrating Power in Everyday Life: The Administration of Law and the Public Sphere in Colonial Tanzania, 1890–1914', *Journal of Cultural Studies*, 15 (2002) and S. Verheul, 'Performing the Law: Plays of Power in Harare's Magistrates Court, Zimbabwe' (MPhil Thesis, University of Oxford, 2011).

[59] P. Gready, 'Autobiography and the "Power of Writing": Political Prison Writing in the Apartheid Era', *JSAS*, 19 (1993), 498.

[60] See Alexander, 'The Political Imaginaries'.

Part of the reason for nationalists' victories in court was the relatively rule-bound nature of the Southern Rhodesian state. This meant that up to the mid-1960s it could be prevailed upon by means of legal argument. Their chances in the courts also improved the higher up the judicial hierarchy they went. This was in large part because of the backgrounds of the officials who served in the lower courts such as magistrates and prosecutors. Many of these officials had begun their careers in the police or the railways and often had no formal legal training. In most cases, they had become prosecutors or magistrates by passing a civil service law exam.[61] In 1959, for example, only sixteen prosecutors had legal qualifications, while eighty-three prosecutors were members of the British South Africa Police. Of these eighty-three, only eleven had successfully undertaken one or both parts of the civil service lower law examination.[62] In addition, up until 1962, Native Commissioners also acted as assistant magistrates. What this meant was that the magistrate's courts were run by individuals with limited legal training, who often shared the racial prejudices of the settler community. This often found expression in the way they conducted their duties in cases about African nationalism. However, their conduct often grated against the legal sensibilities of High Court judges, which resulted in their rulings being overturned on appeal.

One of the early trials was that of Joshua Nkomo, who was charged in 1953 with bringing in a WFTU pamphlet from his trip to Britain. By his own admission, however, the 'offence' had not been a deliberate act of protest, he simply had the pamphlet in his luggage. Notable in Nkomo's account of the trial was his conscious self-identification as a 'respectable citizen' as opposed to a criminal:

I was, at first, frankly rather alarmed by having to appear in court. I was a respectable citizen, and I did not like being put on trial. So I enquired about getting a lawyer, and found that although there were law firms perfectly willing to act for me, I would have to put down £400 in cash before they started. That much money I did not have, so I decided to defend myself in person.[63]

[61] Interview with A. Masterson, Harare, 28 April 2011.
[62] *Southern Rhodesia Parliamentary Debates*, 22 April 1959.
[63] Nkomo, *Nkomo: Story of My Life*, 59.

The niceties of the courtroom were not without their attractions to Nkomo:

The presiding magistrate first put me in the dock, like any criminal. Then I requested more room to arrange my documents. The magistrate politely agreed, and allocated me the place usually occupied by defending counsel, right alongside the prosecutor. The prosecutor himself was polite too. I laughed aloud the first time he answered a point of mine by referring to me, in English barristers' style, as "My learned friend". I was tempted to return the compliment but managed to keep to the rules and not seem impertinent.[64]

At the conclusion of the trial, Nkomo was convicted but got off with a caution. However, the trial foreshadowed a key challenge that the settler administration would face in trying to deal with its political opponents through the courts: the publicity prosecution afforded them. Nkomo recalled, perhaps with some exaggeration, that 'factories had closed because so many people had taken time off to go to court: white people found their domestic servants missing, gone to Bulawayo for the trial. There had never been anything like it before. The government by putting me on trial, had helped to rally African opposition to their plans for Federation.'[65] Although Nkomo had lost in the courtroom, he had won in the court of African public opinion. In the years to come, nationalists would become adept at converting their prosecution into political capital. The individuals on trial became symbols of defiance to the settler government, and their convictions helped to portray them as 'martyrs'. In 1958, for example, Chikerema was triumphantly carried out of the courtroom by nationalist supporters after being found guilty of libel, for having accused the Minister of Native Affairs of theft during a political address.[66]

However, political trials did not always end well for nationalists or indeed lead to greater unity in the nationalist movement. Such was the case with the 1959 trial of the NDP leaders Mawema, Samkange and Takawira. The three were arrested on the 19th of July for making statements that were deemed to be subversive. Mawema was also charged with an additional offence of continuing the banned SRANC under a

[64] Ibid., 60.
[65] Ibid.
[66] Interview with T. Ranger, Oxford, 27 September 2011.

different name.[67] Israel Maisels, a prominent South African advocate, was brought in to defend the NDP leaders assisted by Chitepo. When the trial opened at the Salisbury Magistrate's Court, it attracted such huge crowds that the police struggled to control them. As a result, the trial was moved to Inkomo Barracks located a few miles outside Salisbury, where it lasted several months and gradually fell out of the spotlight.[68] Samkange and Takawira were ultimately acquitted when the prosecution failed to make its case, although Mawema remained on trial. At the same time, tensions arose within the NDP leadership over the distribution of funds as party branches outside Salisbury complained that a disproportionate share of the money was being allocated to Salisbury and was being used to pay for the legal expenses of the leadership. The dispute over funds ultimately led to Mawema's resignation from the leadership of the NDP.[69]

The trial of Mawema is also important in that it cast a light on the workings of the Southern Rhodesian legal system. The charges against him were based on security reports supposedly drawn up from the notes of the African police details who attended the NDP meetings. In reality, senior European police officers had edited the security reports and added incriminating statements in order to ensure the conviction of the NDP leadership. During the cross-examination of the state's witnesses, it soon became clear that many of the African police details did not understand much of the content of 'their' reports.[70] Part of the cross examination of Hode, one of the African police details, went as follows:

MAISELS: You are interested in subversive organisation? [sic]

HODE: Yes

MAISELS: What is meant by subversive?

HODE: Group of people.

MAISELS: What is meant by colonialism?

HODE: I did not read it.

MAISELS: Have you heard the word colonialism at these meetings?

---

[67] Ranger, *Are We Not Also Men*, 182.
[68] Ibid.
[69] Ibid., 191–3.
[70] Rhodes House Library, Terence Ranger Papers, Trial of Michael Mawema 1960.

HODE: If it was used I cannot remember.

MAISELS: What does it mean?

HODE: I don't know. I cannot explain it.

MAISELS: Tribalism. What does that mean? What was the attitude of the National Democratic Party to tribalism?

HODE: You said nationalism?

MAISELS: No, tribalism.

HODE: They did not want it.

MAISELS: What is racialism?

HODE: It is the same as tribalism. They did not want it.[71]

As the questioning went on, the magistrate was forced to remark, 'The witnesses don't seem to understand what the report is that they have signed. They don't seem to understand the report.' To which the prosecutor replied 'I am only too aware of it'. The magistrate went on to remark of Hode that: 'He is virtually refreshing his memory from something which he does not appear to comprehend and I think that criticism can be levelled at the previous witness too.' Despite the numerous irregularities in the testimony of many of the state's witnesses, when it came to handing down judgement, the magistrate changed his opinion about the evidence given by the witnesses. He dismissed the words they could not explain as editor's gloss added by a European typist and saw nothing sinister in the fact that some of the original notebooks had been lost. He, therefore, found Mawema guilty on all charges and sentenced him to four years in prison with hard labour. However, Mawema successfully appealed the conviction in the High Court.

Notwithstanding the obstacles they faced in the lower courts, there was some room for nationalists to exercise agency within the courtroom in ways that caused great anxiety amongst state officials. The Rusape trial of Nkomo, Chikerema and Nyagumbo in February 1963 clearly illustrated the possibilities that existed to exercise such agency. Nkomo and his colleagues were charged under the Law and Order (Maintenance) Act with participating in an illegal procession and for obstructing a police officer from carrying out his duties. A charge of common assault was also made against Nkomo for poking a policeman in the ribs with his ceremonial walking stick.

[71] Ibid.

Nkomo had come to the town of Rusape to speak to the Aged and Destitute People's Association in Vengere Township, and was accompanied by Nyagumbo and Chikerema who had just been released from 'restriction'.[72] The three arrived by train and were welcomed by a crowd of approximately 1,000 people who proceeded to escort the three men to the African township about a mile away. In the evening, Nkomo and his colleagues went to Abisha Mudzingwa's home in the single men's quarters where they were to have supper. Whilst they were eating, three policemen came and ordered them to leave the township on the grounds that they did not have the approval of the Township Management Board to spend the night. The policemen who appeared as state witnesses alleged that their orders had been greeted by defiant shouts of 'warrant' from inside the room. They, therefore, decided to force their way into the room and a scuffle ensued which led to the arrest and prosecution of the three men.[73] The regional magistrate, P. van Renen, came from Umtali to preside over the case, and Herbert Chitepo, who was now working as the Director of Public Prosecutions in Tanzania, flew back to lead the defence team, and was assisted by Leo Baron, a Bulawayo-based lawyer.

The amount of anxious correspondence by senior officials from different branches of the state, and the energy devoted to following the local and foreign coverage of the trial, suggests that courtrooms were important sites of struggle. From the outset, the state struggled to impose its authority inside and outside the courtroom. The small Rusape courtroom, which could only take 30 people, was filled with members of the now banned ZAPU. Outside the courtroom, hundreds of people gathered, and many wore fur hats, which were important cultural symbols of nationalist resistance.[74] A little over a decade earlier, members of the *Sofasonke* movement had similarly drawn on cultural symbols in their efforts to resist eviction from the Matopos National Park.[75] As Terence Ranger notes, in March 1949 *Sofasonke*

---

[72] 'Restriction' was the term used by Southern Rhodesian authorities to refer to the confinement of individuals who were viewed as a threat to law and order in remote areas around the country.

[73] *Rhodesia Herald*, 19 February 1963.

[74] S. Ndhlovu-Gatsheni and W. Willems 'Making Sense of Cultural Nationalism and the Politics of Commemoration under the Third Chimurenga in Zimbabwe', *JSAS*, 35 (2009), 948.

[75] T. Ranger, *Voices From the Rocks: Nature, Culture and History in the Matopos Hills of Zimbabwe* (Oxford, 1999), 153–77.

Figure 3.1 Joshua Nkomo wearing a fur hat in the early 1960s

members appeared at a hearing of the Commission of Enquiry into the Matopos Park in the Bulawayo High Court dressed in Ndebele war regalia.[76] In a similar way, Nkomo and his colleagues entered the Rusape Magistrate's Court wearing their fur hats on the first day of the trial, but the magistrate quickly ordered them to remove the hats. In the days that followed, Chikerema and Nyagumbo resorted to giving their hats to members of the crowd before they entered the court, and wearing them once more outside the courtroom. Wearing these nationalist symbols in the courtroom was important both as a performance of the nation and a challenge to the state's own symbols and rituals.

The *Rhodesia Herald*, a conservative daily newspaper that was part of the South Africa-based Argus Printing and Publishing Company, gave daily coverage of the trial. In comparison to the *African Daily*

[76] Ibid., 163.

News, which was sympathetic to the nationalists, it was less positive in its portrayal of the actions of the nationalists and clearly omitted certain events, such as the triumphant carrying of the nationalists' lawyers by the crowd. However, it gave a more detailed account of the exchanges in the court and the events outside it, and therefore provides valuable insight into the trial. The *Rhodesia Herald* described the atmosphere outside the court on the first day as follows:

Leaving the courtroom the three men were greeted by loud cheers, hand clapping and whoops from the assembled crowd which had now swelled to about 500 people. Ignoring police appeals, the crowd swept across the road and surrounded the car as it tried to back out. Two police attacker dogs were brought into action and the crowd dispersed. On their return, the accused were again acclaimed by the crowd as they entered the courtroom. At the end of Mr. Chitepo's cross-examination the three accused were remanded until tomorrow morning on existing bail of £25 and one surety of £75 each. The crowd outside the courtroom slow-clapped and cheered and the women ululated when the convoy headed by Nkomo's car, left in the direction of Umtali.[77]

The trial itself was punctuated by moments of humour, often at the expense of state officials. Nkomo, now a seasoned politician, poked fun at the proceedings, much to the delight of the nationalist supporters in the gallery. The *Rhodesia Herald* recorded the following excerpts of Nkomo's cross-examination by the prosecution:

During the proceedings Nkomo was asked by the prosecutor to demonstrate how the police had entered the room. He left the dock, closing the door behind him, and then burst into the courtroom to loud laughter and cheers from the audience … The prosecutor asked him whether it did not occur to him at any time during the progress of the gathering that he was taking part in a procession [he replied] "It did not, because short of a helicopter picking me up I could not have got out in any case."[78]

Nkomo's antics evidently had an impact on the audience's view of the proceedings. The *Rhodesia Herald's* report on the last day of the trial recorded the following incident: 'As Mr Nkomo took his place this

[77] *Rhodesia Herald*, 19 February 1963.
[78] Ibid., 22 February 1963.

morning an African man called out in the courtroom 'This is your last meeting, you had better address it now.'[79]

The lawyers representing the three also assumed great prestige in the eyes of the crowds who turned up to witness the trial. Chitepo impressed the crowd with his forensic skills and oratory. Something that is likely to have made an impression on the audience was his lengthy grilling of the European policemen, Detective Sergeant C. D. Sewell and Inspector Leamon, who participated in the arrest.[80] This questioning of white policemen by a black lawyer inverted the racial hierarchy in a way that made the magistrate very uncomfortable. Nyagumbo later recalled that the magistrate's 'attitude to our defence counsel was very startling. He would interject at nearly every question advanced to the police by the defence.'[81]

On the last day of the trial, Chitepo made a 135-minute closing address, and at the end of the trial he was carried triumphantly by the crowd. The mood of the day was captured in the following terms by the *Rhodesia Herald*:

More than 70 Africans packed the courtroom at Rusape, designed to seat 30, to hear the address at the close of the defence case today. Outside the court a crowd of about 300 Africans cheered Mr Nkomo's party across the street to an African restaurant. Women wearing hats of leopard, buck and wild cat skin danced and sang as the accused men and their colleagues packed to leave.[82]

This triumphant carrying of nationalists' lawyers highlighted the prestige that lawyers began to assume as individuals uniquely positioned to advance Africans' struggle against colonial rule. In the end, Nkomo was convicted and sentenced to six months in prison with hard labour, but immediately appealed the sentence. His conviction does not appear to have dampened the mood of the crowd. If anything, the trial seemed to recharge nationalist fervour. On the day the ruling was handed down, Baron was carried out of the court by the crowd. Importantly, by prosecuting Nkomo, the government had

---

[79] Ibid., 27 February 1963.
[80] Ibid., 20 February 1963.
[81] M. Nyagumbo, *With the People: An Autobiography from the Zimbabwean Struggle* (London, 1980), 167.
[82] *Rhodesia Herald*, 20 February 1963.

drawn attention to the nationalist cause locally and abroad, and did a much better job at it than Nkomo's address to the Aged and Destitute People's Association could have done. Furthermore, the government had failed to stamp its authority on the proceedings. For the crowds that thronged the Rusape courtroom dressed in nationalist regalia, the trial was generally not seen as a performance of state power: this was Nkomo's 'meeting'.[83]

Rethinking the 'Rules of Law'

Senior state officials soon realized that political trials were a double-edged sword. Having followed Nkomo's Rusape trial closely, G. B. Clarke, the Secretary to the Prime Minister and Cabinet, realised that the government had inadvertently given prominence to the nationalist cause and was losing the struggle to frame the trial in the media.[84] He therefore suggested that A. M. Bruce-Brand, the Secretary of Law and Order, 'give consideration to the compilation of an authoritative version of the trial. This version could then be sent to London and other Federal External Missions, to be used to put across the proper story.'[85] Although officials from the Ministry of Law and Order shared these concerns, they disagreed with the proposed solution. Bruce-Brand felt that no good could come out of such a statement given that 'any official statement would probably highlight [Nkomo's] name in the newspaper headlines, and would invite some kind of adverse comment from persons ill-disposed toward us.'[86]

Bruce-Brand's opinion is likely to have been influenced by a candid memorandum on the trial written by his deputy. It observed:

Having now had the opportunity of studying the reports submitted by Police, the Prosecutor and the Magistrate's judgement, in my opinion, it would be unwise to publicise this matter any further. My reasons for saying this are three-fold. Firstly I think the Police acted in rather a high-handed

---

[83] For accounts of similar use of the courtroom by African nationalists in South Africa, see N. Mandela, *Long Walk to Freedom* (London, 1995), 385, and A. Sachs, *Justice in South Africa* (London, 1973), 214–29.

[84] NAZ S3331/17/12/1, Bruce-Brand to Hutton-Williams, 3 April 1963.

[85] Ibid., Clarke to Bruce-Brand, 3 April 1963.

[86] Ibid., Bruce-Brand to Clarke, 24 April 1963.

manner in this case. It is obvious from the evidence available that at 9.10 pm on the night in question they were looking for trouble and got it. Personally I think anybody would have been annoyed at the way the Police acted when there were obviously no signs of trouble, and Nkomo and his companions were just sitting down having a meal. Secondly I do not like the Magistrate's judgement. It seems to me quite a lot of it is completely irrelevant and some of it even shows signs of bias. If and when the matter comes to the appeal court I can easily visualise it will be torn to shreds in no time. Thirdly, an examination of the facts of this case reveals to me, and I think probably to the outside world, that the sentence of Nkomo was rather excessive in the circumstances. All he did was to poke Superintendent Eagleton in the ribs. My own opinion is that a more appropriate sentence would have been in the region of £5 for common assault.[87]

The opinion of the Deputy Secretary was a reflection of the aforementioned tensions within the different levels of the legal system. True to his predictions, Nkomo's conviction was overturned on appeal.

Such unsuccessful prosecutions were very frustrating to state officials in the Law and Order Ministry and prompted a rethinking of the 'rules of law'.[88] This frustration was evident in a memorandum sent by the new acting Secretary for Law and Order, J. A. C. Fleming, to his Minister in January 1964. In it, he expressed his concerns about 'gaps in the law' which were emerging in the state's efforts to deal with political dissent. He was particularly annoyed by the actions of nationalists of whom he remarked:

There is no doubt that the Nationalists are making a mockery of the Courts. With regard to the Courts, I need only draw your attention to Mr Nkomo's present tactics, namely two Appeals (from Gwelo and Bulawayo) pending, not to mention calling 100 defence witnesses in his current trial at Umtali. The object of the exercise is obviously to delay proceedings, waste everybody's time and generally disrupt the smooth working of the courts; and Nkomo is not the only one adopting these tactics.[89]

---

[87] Ibid., Deputy Secretary of Law and Order to the Secretary of Law and Order, [Undated but was most likely written early in April 1963].

[88] This phrase is adapted from J. Lonsdale, 'Kenyatta's Trials: Breaking and Making and African Nationalist', in Coss, *The Moral World*, 196. I use it here to refer to the procedures and regulations that guide the administration of the law.

[89] NAZ S3332/2/2, J. A. C. Fleming to Minister of Law and Order, 11 January 1964.

What Fleming viewed as Nkomo's unacceptable 'tactics' were in fact appeals that followed on from the numerous charges that had been brought against him by the government. Between 1963 and 1964, Nkomo was tried in Gwelo, Sinoia, Nyazura, Umtali, Rusape, Salisbury and Bulawayo, largely for things he had said in political addresses. In Gwelo, for example, Nkomo had pointed out that the government had removed Africans from their land and given it to German and Italian veterans of World War II. As a result, he was charged with making a statement which, the state alleged, encouraged hostility between the races. Nkomo was tried in November 1963 and sentenced to nine months in prison.[90] In Nyazura, Nkomo was convicted for making a 'subversive' speech and was restricted to Gonakudzingwa. He, along with twenty-five other leaders of the People's Caretaker Committee who were restricted with him, subsequently challenged the legality of their restriction.[91] In the Umtali case that Fleming referred to, Nkomo had been charged with making 'untrue statements about torture by the police', and in his defence he called 100 witnesses who testified that they had indeed been tortured.

Fleming's words betrayed his irritation at the fact that nationalists had become sufficiently knowledgeable of the legal system that they could use it to frustrate government designs. However, they also signalled an important shift in the role that the law would play in the constitution of state power. 'As a result of all this nonsense that has been going on', he observed,

… it now appears that the Government (whose stated policy is to rule via the Courts and not administratively) will soon have to decide whether to continue to rule by the Courts, with amendments to such items as regards Bail, Appeals, Increasing sentences for frivolous appeals etc. etc., or whether terrorists, who take every advantage of our present legal system, should be dealt with as such in the same manner that South Africa (or Ghana) deals with subversive elements.[92]

Whereas state officials had relied on the law for its legitimating and coercive potentials, in the years that followed the balance would shift firmly towards coercion.

---

[90] *Zimbabwe Review*, 28 December 1963.
[91] E. Mlambo, *Rhodesia: Struggle for a Birthright* (London, 1972), 198–9.
[92] NAZ S3332/2/2, Fleming to Minister of Law and Order, 11 January 1964.

Conclusion

In its attempt to respond to the rise of African nationalism in the post-World War II era, the Southern Rhodesian government was forced to grapple with the question of the relationship between the law and the legitimate exercise of state power. For the majority of the settlers, it was clear that African political dissent had to be suppressed. However, the challenge was how to tap into the coercive potential of law without undermining its legitimacy in the eyes of the settler populace, metropolitan officials and Africans. In their search for an answer, colonial authorities turned to the canon of racial tropes about Africans, and argued that the normal standards of due process did not apply when dealing with less 'civilised' Africans. For much of the 1950s, Africans were discursively constructed as simpletons or errant children who were being misled by agitators. As such, they were seen as requiring firm disciplining by means of strict laws in order to deter them from 'disrupting public order'. However, with the coming of the Rhodesian Front, African nationalists and their supporters soon came to be seen as 'animals' who had to be killed, and the law was amended to correspond with this new construction.

Although there was substantial deliberation within Southern Rhodesian officialdom about African political militancy, these discussions failed to engage with the intellectual currents and political imaginaries that were animating African nationalism. Consequently, a central irony that marked the legal engagements between the state and Africans was that it was Africans who asserted themselves as rights-bearing citizens and demanded fair trials, whereas colonial officials, who saw themselves as the bearers of the 'rule of law', often subordinated due process to political expediency. As nationalists developed a more sophisticated legal consciousness and became adept at using the courts to advance their cause, political trials became high profile moments where they clashed with the government. They subverted court rituals and symbols by staging their own performances and introducing nationalist symbols. In addition, African lawyers and litigants were able to invert colonial racial hierarchies in the courts. As a result, by 1964, government officials were calling for a revision of the law in order to enable them to effectively silence political dissent. As I show in the next chapter, these proposals sat well with the Rhodesian Front administration.

4 | *Legality without Legitimacy: Law and Politics during UDI, 1965–1980*

Introduction

The Rhodesian Front's assumption of power in 1963 reflected the growing dominance of the right wing elements in Rhodesian politics, and within the party itself, the ascendance of hardliners was evident in the replacement of Winston Field by Ian Smith in 1964. One consequence of this shift to the right in settler politics was a decidedly authoritarian shift in the content and administration of the law. Soon after taking office, Smith imposed five states of emergency in various locations around Southern Rhodesia and hundreds of nationalist leaders and supporters were arrested and detained.[1] This was followed by the Unilateral Declaration of Independence (UDI) on 11 November 1965. In response, the nationalist parties ZAPU and ZANU resolved to wage a guerrilla war and began launching military attacks in Rhodesia from 1964. The Smith government dug its heels in further; consequently, the period between 1965 and 1980 was characterised by an escalating cycle of political agitation and increased repression which culminated in a bitter guerrilla war.

Studies of the turbulent last decades of settler rule in Zimbabwe have paid detailed attention to a diverse range of 'struggles within the struggle', from those related to land and labour to those involving religion and ethnicity, as well as those around gender and generation.[2] However, the legal dimension of these struggles remains understudied,

---

[1] E. Mlambo, *Rhodesia: Struggle for a Birthright*, 209.
[2] See M. Sithole, *Zimbabwe: Struggles Within the Struggle, 1957–1980* (Harare, 1999); N. Kriger, *Zimbabwe's Guerrilla War: Peasant Voices* (Cambridge, 1995); N Bhebe and T. Ranger (eds), *Society in Zimbabwe's Liberation War* (Harare, 1996); B. Raftopoulos and T. Yoshikuni (eds), *Sites of Struggle: Essays in Zimbabwe's Urban History* (Harare, 2001); N. Bhebe and T. Ranger (eds), *Soldiers in Zimbabwe's Liberation War* (Harare, 1995); J. Nhongo-Simbanegavi, *For Better or for Worse: Women and ZANLA in Zimbabwe's Liberation Struggle* (Harare, 2000).

and in most cases, law serves only as a backdrop against which other struggles are examined. The few scholars that do focus on law and politics such as Geoffrey Feltoe and Claire Palley have, for the most part, highlighted the increasingly repressive nature of Rhodesian laws.[3] However, these studies do not show how Africans responded to this legal repression, and in doing so, they miss an important dimension of the legal developments during UDI. There are, however, more recent studies such as those by Jocelyn Alexander and Munyaradzi Munochiveyi that are taking a new look at legal and penal institutions as important sites of struggle.[4] This chapter builds on these studies and focuses on the struggles between the state and Africans about the law, and by means of the law between 1965 and 1980.

Administering the Law During UDI

As we have seen, between 1950 and 1964, there had been vigorous debates within the state as officials grappled with the question about how the coercive capacity of law could be harnessed to deal with rising African nationalism without sacrificing its legitimating capacity. By 1964 there was growing frustration among officials in the Ministry of Law and Order, who were calling for more powers to deal with the 'problem' of African nationalism. In response to these calls, the Rhodesian Front began to engineer a decisive shift in the balance of the role of law away from legitimation and towards coercion, whereas the task of legitimising the state increasingly fell to 'traditional' leaders. The trend towards a legalistic authoritarianism was further strengthened by the intensification of the guerrilla war from the early 1970s.

Two key features characterised the administration of the law during this period. The first was the extensive employment of what Giorgio Agamben has called the 'state of exception'. For Agamben the state of exception involved the 'suspension of the judicial order', and amongst its essential features included the extension of military power into the civil sphere, the suspension of the constitution or constitutional norms and 'the provisional abolition of the distinction amongst legislative, executive and judicial powers'.[5] Important in Agamben's analysis of the

---

[3] Feltoe 'Law, Ideology and Coercion' and Palley, 'Law and the Unequal Society'.
[4] See Alexander, 'Nationalism and Self-government', and Munochiveyi, *Prisoners of Rhodesia*.
[5] G. Agamben, *State of Exception* (Chicago, 2005), 6.

Figure 4.1 Ian Smith announcing the Unilateral Declaration of Independence in 1965

state of exception is 'its tendency to become a lasting practice of government.'[6] During UDI, there was a clear expansion of executive power into the legislative domain, and the military progressively extended its authority over civilians. At the same time, there was a drastic narrowing of what few civil liberties had existed for Africans. In addition, as Luise White shows, the 1969 constitution 'all but stripped Africans of access to the institutions of representative government.'[7] However, the state of exception in Rhodesia was not a complete 'suspension of the judicial order' or 'an emptiness of law' as per Agamben's formulation.[8] Rather, it sat somewhat uneasily with the second feature of the administration of the law: a commitment to legalism.

[6] Ibid., 7.
[7] White, *Unpopular Sovereignty*, 206.
[8] Ibid., 6.

For Max Weber, the importance of legalism in aiding state legitimacy lay in the fact that it gave the impression that the arbitrary exercise of state power was constrained by law.[9] Although this legitimating function of legalism had been important prior to 1965, this was less so during the UDI period. Chanock's insights on the role of legalism in South Africa are instructive in trying to understand its function in Rhodesia during the UDI period. 'Legitimation', he argues, 'requires an audience with a potential to applaud, but the great majority of the population always watched with hostility.'[10] He thus proposes that 'We must instead develop our explanation around the core notion that legalism exists because it is instrumentally effective, more of a mechanism than an ideology.' Seen from this perspective, 'trials are primarily instruments – a continuation of and a climax to the long processes of detention, interrogation and torture – to investigate, strip, divide, disillusion and punish opposition.'[11] Legalism served a similar instrumental function in the Rhodesian political sphere. In addition, the adherence to legalism enabled the Smith administration to criminalise Africans' political dissent while ignoring their social, political and economic grievances. However, as in South Africa, the legalism of the Rhodesian state went hand in hand with numerous covert forms of illegality perpetrated by state officials; by the 1970s, cases of abduction, torture, killings of Africans and the destruction of property by government agents had become commonplace.[12]

In 1966 Desmond Lardner-Burke, the new Minister of Law and Order, defended the Rhodesian government's repressive use of the law by invoking the 'state of exception' argument. 'A fundamental truth', he argued, 'is that the rule of law only operates when there is tranquillity. When there is any chaos, it is impossible to apply the rule of law.'[13] In supporting this position, he quoted the following statement made by Thomas Jefferson during the American War of Independence:

---

[9] D. M. Trubek, 'Max Weber on Law and the Rise of Capitalism', *Wisconsin Law Review*, 720 (1972), 736–9.
[10] Chanock, 'Writing South African Legal History', 267.
[11] Ibid., 268.
[12] See R. Abel, *Politics by Other Means: Law in the Struggle against Apartheid, 1980–1994* (New York, 1995), 539.
[13] D. Lardner-Burke, *Rhodesia: The Story of Crisis* (London, 1966), 57.

A strict observance of the written law is doubtless one of the high duties of a good citizen, but it is not the highest. The laws of necessity, of self-preservation, of saving our country when in danger are of higher obligation. To lose our country by a scrupulous adherence to written law would be to lose law itself, with life, liberty, property and all those who are enjoying them with us; thus absurdly sacrificing the end for the means.

That Lardner-Burke should quote Jefferson is not surprising, the wording of the Rhodesian declaration of independence was itself closely modelled on the American Declaration of Independence.[14]

The argument about the need for exceptional measures to deal with African nationalism continued to be a feature of official discourse about law during UDI. During the presentation of the Indemnity Bill in 1975, which protected government forces from legal action for a range of actions taken in the course of their duties, Lardner-Burke, who was by then the Minister of Justice, again employed this language. He began by affirming the primacy of the law and the importance of the courts in protecting the rights of individual citizens. However, this was followed by an important qualification:

But an inherent right reposes in every State to use all means at its disposal to defend itself when its existence is at stake: when the force upon which the constitution is based is itself challenged. Under such circumstances, the State may be compelled by necessity to disregard for a time the ordinary safeguards of liberty in defence of liberty itself.[15]

As Agamben shows, the arguments being made by Lardner Burke had long been used by governments that sought to justify the employment of exceptional measures. What is more, the question of 'necessity' on which the decision turned was always a subjective judgement.[16] What is of particular importance here, however, is the fact that this statement was coming from the Ministry of Justice which had previously taken pride in its strict adherence to due process. It therefore signalled a deeper institutional shift within the state and the cementing of the 'state of exception' as a feature of Rhodesian statecraft.

---

[14] See a copy of the UDI proclamation at http://upload.wikimedia.org/wikipedia/en/7/75/Rho-udi.jpg

[15] *Rhodesia Parliamentary Debates*, 28 August 1975, 1438.

[16] Agamben, *State of Exception*, 13.

Figure 4.2 Minister of Law and Order, Desmond Lardner-Burke

Guided by this thinking, the Rhodesian Front proceeded to make significant changes to the content of the law and its administration, and where existing legislation proved to be inconvenient or inadequate for government purposes, it was amended. As Feltoe observes, 'government by executive regulation became the order of the day. Ministerial action in this area required no explanation and was not subject to scrutiny. The Parliamentary institution was to a large extent rendered redundant as emergency powers exercisable at the instance of executive members became widespread.'[17] The principles of due process were progressively undermined under the pretext of 'preserving law and order', and fundamental practices such as ensuring prisoners' right to legal representation and a fair trial, as well as the presumption of innocence were increasingly disregarded. In addition, the burden of proof

---

[17] Feltoe, 'Law, Ideology and Coercion', 50.

was shifted onto the accused, and judicial discretion was progressively eroded by legislation that provided for mandatory sentences. The torture of individuals arrested for political offences became routine, and legal action against the state for abuses perpetrated by its agents was blocked by the 1976 Indemnity and Compensation Act.[18]

Detention without trial and large-scale imprisonment became important tools for the state; as a result, many prominent ZAPU and ZANU leaders spent close to a decade in detention.[19] Although they were periodically brought before a Detainees Review Tribunal, their applications for release were repeatedly rejected, and they were only freed in 1974 thanks to the Détente negotiations.[20] In addition to detention, thousands of Africans were hauled before the courts and charged with contravening the Law and Order (Maintenance) Act, and the numerous regulations gazetted under the Emergency Powers Act. These two Acts criminalised virtually all forms of political protest, from wearing party regalia to participating in the armed struggle. As the backlog in the courts grew, the jurisdiction of magistrates' courts was expanded and new courts were created.[21]

From the late 1960s, a degree of secrecy came to surround political trials as *in camera* hearings became common place. The ban imposed on reporting details of the trials was partly intended to prevent nationalists from acquiring potentially useful information about the fortunes of their units in the battlefield. It was also driven by the government's desire to keep the settler community from knowing the true extent of the guerrilla war for fear that this would lead to increased emigration. In addition, it wanted to prevent the release of any information that might be viewed negatively abroad. One consequence of this secrecy was that it undermined the effectiveness of courtroom performances by accused individuals.

There were other instances, however, when the government desired maximum visibility for trials. This was particularly so with the Special Courts, which were created in 1976 through the Emergency Powers

---

[18] Ibid.
[19] For a detailed account of experiences of detention in Rhodesia, see Munochiveyi, *Prisoners of Rhodesia;* and Alexander, 'Nationalism and Self-Government'.
[20] These were negotiations between the Rhodesian government and the nationalists that had been advocated for by Kenneth Kaunda and John Vorster, the leaders of Zambia and South Africa, respectively.
[21] NAZ MS591/2/4, Legal Sheridan, Lazarus and Sarif to Bernard Sheridan and Company, 22 August 1975.

(Criminal Trials) Regulations.[22] These were mobile courts that were convened in the areas where guerrillas were operating. The practical objective of these courts was to expedite the hearing of the numerous cases around the country involving people charged with contravening the security legislation. However, they also served the purpose of performing and re-asserting state power in areas where the state's sovereignty was increasingly being challenged by the guerrillas who were themselves setting up quasi-judicial structures. An important component of the trials was the audience of villagers from the surrounding areas who were frogmarched to witness civilians or captured guerrillas being tried. According to the International Defence and Aid Fund (IDAF), during the first month these courts handed down death sentences to at least eleven guerrillas in trials held in different parts of Rhodesia.[23] These severe sentences which were handed down in full view of the public were meant to deter any villagers who might be inclined to assist the guerrillas. In addition, '… the new courts [we]re being used as a psychological weapon to terrorise local villagers into collaborating with the security forces.'[24]

The use of capital punishment was another key feature of the Rhodesian government's attempt to deal with political dissent during the UDI period. The mandatory death sentence had been introduced by Parliament in 1963, guided by the thinking that the greater the severity of the punishment, the greater the deterrence, and throughout the 1960s and 1970s the list of acts punishable by a mandatory death sentence was progressively expanded. Acts such as recruiting for the guerrilla armies, attempting to leave the country for training, assisting guerrillas, or failing to report their presence were amongst the many that were punishable by death. However, capital punishment proved to be much more complicated to implement than had been anticipated, because it soon became clear that the death sentence was not an effective deterrent for guerrillas. Indeed, some Rhodesian Parliamentarians began to express concerns that it might in fact be pushing guerrillas to fight to the death.[25] A second challenge inherent in the use of

---

[22] Feltoe, 'Law, Coercion and Ideology', 60.
[23] NAZ MS591/2/7, Ian Smith's Hostages, Geneva Press Conference October 1976, IDAF Notes on the Zimbabwe Situation. IDAF was actively involved in providing assistance to individuals arrested or detained for political reasons.
[24] Ibid.
[25] *Zimbabwe News*, 6 July 1968.

capital punishment was that it usually took several years for cases to go through the full process of trial and appeals.

The first execution of political prisoners in Rhodesia was conducted on the sixth of March 1968, when three ZANU activists, James Dlamini, Victor Mlambo and Duly Shadreck, were hanged.[26] The three had been arrested in 1965 for petrol bombing a car that was driven by Pieter Oberholzer, a European reservist who subsequently died of his burns. In the intervening period, the case had gone from court to court as the defendants appealed the sentence.[27] The process of appeals ultimately came to an end in 1968 when the Appellate Division of the Rhodesian High Court rejected both the defendants' application to appeal to the Judicial Committee of the Privy Council, and the royal reprieve issued by Queen Elizabeth II.[28] The three were executed on the sixth of March, followed by another two African activists on the eleventh.

The executions of Dlamini and his colleagues played the dual function of punishing the government's political enemies and asserting Rhodesia's independence from Britain.[29] However, the international uproar that followed and the difficulties in controlling the meaning ascribed to the executions forced the Rhodesian government to reconsider the value of such brazenness. Domestically, nationalist newsletters seized on the executions and made efforts to interpret them for their constituencies. The March 1968 issue of the *Zimbabwe News* published a letter that was said to have been written by James Dlamini to his parents and used it to portray him as a martyr. The letter read in part:

Our lawyers have tried all they could to have our lives spared. They appealed to the British Queen who authorised a reprieve, but it all failed. Now, it's all right, father, because I know I die for my people. Many, like me, have sacrificed their lives throughout the world so that their people may live freely in their own countries. Your conscience and mine are clear, dear father, for I die not as a thief or a lover of riches. I die for the liberty of my country and

[26] *Zimbabwe News*, March 1968.
[27] Interview with Ken Reagan, Harare, 13 April 2011. Reagan was one of the lawyers who represented the captured guerrillas. See also White, *Unpopular Sovereignty*, p. 152.
[28] Mlambo, *Rhodesia*, 207–8.
[29] NAZ MS591/2/7, Ian Smith's Hostages.

Figure 4.3 Salisbury High Court

people. My comrades and I will be remembered in the pages of history, not as criminals, but as champions of the cause of our people. So don't let my death trouble you; because I chose this road myself and I die without any doubt as to the justice and worth of this noble cause.[30]

It is not possible to determine the authenticity of the letter. However, what is clear is that the newsletter sought to use the 'last words of a condemned man' in order to neutralise the government's intended message of deterrence, and re-cast his death as the ultimate sacrifice for the liberty of the nation.[31]

As the Rhodesian authorities worked towards a settlement with the British government during the early 1970s, a greater degree of caution came to characterise their approach to executions. In the context of these diplomatic efforts, it was not executions, but rather commutations

---

[30] *Zimbabwe News*, 16 March 1968.
[31] Foucault, *Discipline and Punish*, 59–69. See also S. Hynd, 'Killing the Condemned: The Practice and Process of Capital Punishment in British Africa, 1900–1950s', *JAH*, 49 (2000).

of death sentences that served the Smith regime's political interests as they could be used as diplomatic levers. This, however, was not a premeditated choreography of 'majesty' and 'mercy', but a shift that was tied to the conflicting political imperatives of the moment.[32] By 1972, a total of 225 people had been sentenced to death by Rhodesian courts since 1965, and of these, 7 sentences had been quashed and 22 had been commuted to imprisonment.[33] On 14 September that year, the government released a statement indicating that President Clifford Dupont had commuted the sentences of 54 of the 59 individuals on death row to life imprisonment.[34] As the conversations between Ian Smith and the British Secretary of State revealed, the RF hoped that the commutations would defuse the tense political atmosphere in Rhodesia that prevailed during the Pearce Commission's consultations.[35]

However, from April 1975 executions became shrouded in secrecy, as the government tried to manage the local and external political ramifications.[36] Given the ongoing negotiations with the nationalists, the RF recognised that publicising executions might prove to be very costly in diplomatic terms. It is unclear how many people were actually executed by the Rhodesian government during this period. However, the figures compiled by Marie Chihambakwe from the High Court records on death sentences for the 1970s show that executions did indeed continue in secret. In 1975, thirty-six individuals on death row were executed, while forty death sentences were handed down, and the following year another twenty-seven were executed while twenty-eight

---

[32] Hay, 'Property, Authority'.

[33] *Rhodesia Herald*, 14 June 1972. These figures were provided by the Minister of Justice to the Parliament. The Minister did not say how many had been executed.

[34] *Rhodesia Herald*, 14 September 1972. The remaining four whose sentences were not commuted had been convicted of brutal murders. It was therefore felt that their sentences should not be commuted.

[35] BNA FCO36/1273, Commutation of Death Sentences in Southern Rhodesia, P. R. A. Mansfield to Mr Le Quesne, 23 February 1972. The Pearce Commission was tasked with investigating whether Africans accepted the prospective agreement between the Rhodesian and the British governments for independence on the basis of the 1969 constitution. The said constitution did not provide for universal suffrage or the realistic prospect of majority rule. As a result, it provoked significant political agitation amongst Africans along with campaigns for the rejection of the proposed agreement.

[36] NAZ MS591/2/7, Ian Smith's Hostages.

Table 4.1 *Rhodesia High Court Capital Punishment Statistics,*
1970–1979

Year	Total High Court death sentences	Executions carried out	Commuted sentences	Other outcomes – release, sentence altered on appeal
1970	23	–	19	4
1971	24	3	16	5
1972	9	4	3	2
1973	30	24	3	3
1974	33	27	5	1
1975	40	36	2	2
1976	28	27	–	1
1977	22	15	4	3
1978	31	18	8	5
1979	37	9	24	4

Source: Adapted from Chihambakwe, 'Study of Zimbabwean Cases', 42.

more death sentences were handed down.[37] However, these figures do not include cases that were heard in the Special Courts and the Special Courts Martial. They are therefore likely to be lower than the actual figures of death sentences and executions.

Nationalist and Guerrilla Critiques of the Law

An important consequence of the authoritarian shift in the law under the Rhodesian Front outlined earlier was the loss of legitimacy for the Rhodesian legal system, particularly amongst nationalists and guerrillas. Eshmael Mlambo traces this loss of legitimacy to the Unilateral Declaration of Independence in 1965.[38] Although the UDI certainly

[37] M. Chihambakwe, 'Study of Zimbabwean Cases on the Death Penalty, Part 1', *Legal Forum*, 1 (1990), 42. The individuals who were executed were those whose appeals had run their full course, not those who were sentenced that year.
[38] Mlambo, *Rhodesia*, 196–7.

strengthened nationalist antipathy towards the courts, it is possible to detect a growing feeling amongst nationalists, prior to 1965, that the courts were neither legitimate nor an effective means of pursuing their cause. In his presidential address at ZANU's 1964 inaugural congress in Gwelo, Ndabaningi Sithole observed that

The white minority made laws are indeed inherently unjust in relation to the majority who do not have the vote, and since the so-called courts administer such laws, it is not wrong to say that such courts are in fact rubber stamps of injustice. This is why many of our people cannot find justice in these courts. The legislature and the courts reflect minority and not majority interests.[39]

The nationalist newsletters that were published in exile, such as ZANU's *Zimbabwe News* and ZAPU's *Zimbabwe Review*, also provided a platform for similar critiques of the law. Some of the key contributors to these newsletters were African journalists such as Nathan Shamuyarira and Saul Gwakuba Ndlovu, both of whom had worked for the *African Daily News* before it was banned in 1964. In the early 1960s, the newsletters regularly reported on the prosecution and detention of nationalist leaders and activists, and criticised the state's persecution of its political opponents. However, over time, their criticism of repressive laws developed into critiques that unmasked the legalistic pretences of the Rhodesian legal system and often challenged the legitimacy of the state, which they routinely derided as 'fascist' or 'evil'.[40]

Several articles carried in the newsletters drew on alternative ideas about the law and its legitimacy in their critiques, and one example was the article carried by the September 1968 issue of the *Zimbabwe News* entitled 'What in Hell is Justice'. The article discussed the High Court's dismissal of Baron and Madzimbamuto's legal challenges to the constitutionality of the Rhodesian state after UDI. In doing so, the court

---

[39] Cited in Nyangoni and Nyandoro, *Zimbabwe Independence Movements*, 77–8.

[40] See *Zimbabwe Review*, 12 December 1963. African nationalists were not alone in recognising the similarities between the Rhodesian Front's actions and Fascism. Elaine Windrich notes that the *Rhodesia Herald* carried several letters from members of the settler population which made similar observations. See E. Windrich, 'Rhodesian Censorship: The Role of the Media in the Making of a One-party State', *African Affairs*, 78 (1979), 525.

effectively provided judicial endorsement to the unilateral declaration of independence.[41] Drawing on Marxist ideas, the writer dismissed the comments made by 'British legal commentators' that the Rhodesian judges had forgotten British legal traditions. Instead, he argued that, '… the important thing to remember is that there has never existed such a thing as abstract "justice". Laws have always been created to serve the interests of the powerful. Thus, in capitalist countries, "justice" is there to guarantee the supremacy of the ruling cliques just as socialist justice in, say, China is there to look after the interests of the working class and peasants. In Rhodesia Judge Beadle at least understands his assignment.'[42]

Another article entitled 'Prostitution of Justice' argued that: 'The Smith fascist clique has always used magistrates' courts as tools for oppressing the African population. Every case which smacked of resistance by Africans has always been decided in favour of the regime.'[43] It rejected the few instances in which nationalists won in court as an effort by magistrates 'to put on the appearance of impartiality on [their] judgement without giving the slightest concession to the forces of justice.' The 1969 trial of the ZANU leader Ndabaningi Sithole on charges of plotting to assassinate Smith and two of his Ministers, Lardner Burke and Jack Howman, also provoked sharp criticism. An article carried in the *Zimbabwe News* observed: 'While the Portuguese use devices such as time bombs to murder their revolutionary adversaries, the Rhodesian fascists are employing the semi-legal method of fascist legality to achieve a similar end. For that is the only difference – a difference of style – between the dastardly murder this week of Edwardo Mondlane by agents of Portuguese colonialism and the planned hanging of Ndabaningi Sithole and company.'[44]

Similar critiques of the Rhodesian legal system were increasingly articulated in the courts by captured ZIPRA and ZANLA guerrillas. Instead of enlisting the services of lawyers and staging legal defences, as had been the case with nationalist leaders in the early 1960s, many chose to use the dock as a platform to challenge the legitimacy of the Smith regime.[45] Rather than answer the charges put to them by the

---

[41] See White, *Unpopular Sovereignty*, 119–23.
[42] *Zimbabwe News*, 14 September 1968.
[43] *Zimbabwe News*, 3 March 1968.
[44] *Zimbabwe News*, 8 February 1969.
[45] Not all guerrillas chose the path of defiance. In the 1968 case of *Regina v. Esironi Fani, Langton Chakusa, Gladman Gurapira and Joburg Mabutu,*

prosecution, they sought to place the government on trial. For many guerrillas, the legal system and the state had completely lost legitimacy; as such, they refused to participate in what they viewed as a charade. As Pierre Bourdieu points out, 'To join the game, to accept the law for the resolution of conflict, is tacitly to adopt a mode of expression and discussion implying the renunciation of physical violence and of elementary forms of symbolic violence, such as insults. It is above all to recognize the specific requirements of the juridical construction of the issue.'[46] It was this constraining effect of the judicial process that the guerrillas rejected.

The trial of Thomas Mutete Makoni, Jonathan Maradza, Amidio Chingura and Joseph Muyambo in 1968 illustrates the new strategies adopted in the courts by guerrillas.[47] The four had entered Rhodesia from Zambia in 1968 and hid their arms at a homestead in Mrewa. The arms were subsequently discovered by the police acting on information provided by a friend of the four, leading to their prosecution. During the trial, Makoni and his colleagues chose not to retain legal counsel or to call any witnesses in their defence, and they refused to conform their testimonies to the stipulations of the Rhodesian legal system.[48] In addition, they resisted the government's efforts to frame their actions within a discourse of crime and terror. The following is an excerpt of the exchanges between Makoni, Justice Lewis and the prosecutor Mr Glaum, when Makoni was asked to plead.

LEWIS, J: Please put the indictment to the accused, Mr Interpreter.

INTERPRETER: The first accused, my Lord, there is nothing at all among the weapons that I did not bring with me.

LEWIS, J: Let me be clear about that. He says there is nothing in this list of arms and ammunition that he did not bring with him, is that right?

ACCUSED 1: In other words I admit being in possession of these things.

---

the accused guerrillas engaged lawyers and upon conviction they appealed the ruling.

[46] Bourdieu, 'The Force of Law', 831.

[47] NAZ S3385, Salisbury High Court Criminal Cases 11496–11502, *Regina v. Makoni et al.*

[48] The lorry driver who gave them a lift into Rhodesia and the friend who subsequently reported them to the authorities were also tried. The driver was charged with failing to report the presence of 'terrorists', and the friend was charged as an accomplice. By contrast, these two chose to secure legal representation and went on to appeal their convictions.

LEWIS, J: Well, the main charge, Mr Interpreter, alleges that he had possession of these weapons wrongfully and unlawfully and with intent to endanger the maintenance of law and order in Rhodesia. What does he say about that?

ACCUSED 1: According to my knowledge, my lord, I knew that I was doing nothing wrong.

LEWIS, J: Mr Glaum it seems to me that there is a plea of not guilty on count 1 and guilty to the alternative charge.

MR GLAUM: I think that is correct, yes, except possibly if he says he was doing nothing wrong he might deny that his possession is unlawful.

LEWIS, J: Just clarify that, Mr Interpreter. He has admitted being in possession of these arms, ammunition, weapons of war as set out in both the main and the alternative counts of the indictment. In regard to the alternative count, does he allege that he had lawful authority or reasonable excuse for the possession of these arms and ammunition?

ACCUSED 1: Yes, my Lord

LEWIS, J: Well, what excuse does he allege?

ACCUSED 1: The reason being that these arms will never be laid down until such a time as the country will have been released and handed over to the black man.

LEWIS, J: Yes. Well, the legislature does not regard that as a lawful excuse; lawful authority or reasonable excuse means lawful permission to have possession of these weapons. I think that must be a plea of guilty on the second, alternative count.

MR GLAUM: Yes

Lewis' disregard for the political grievances behind the actions of the four, and his insistence on what he called 'lawful' excuse, authority and permission were part of the typical response of Rhodesian judges who heard these overtly political cases. This rigid commitment to formalism was often a fig leaf beneath which many judges sought to conceal their solidarity with the Smith regime, and Justice Lewis was no exception in this respect. He was born in London in 1917 and later moved to Rhodesia, where his family became part of the Rhodesian political establishment. His father had been a Minister of Justice in Godfrey Huggins' cabinet before serving as Chief Justice.[49] Lewis himself had

[49] C. Palley, 'The Judicial Process: UDI and The Southern Rhodesian Judiciary', *The Modern Law Review*, 1 (1967), 265.

studied at Rhodes University in South Africa and Oxford University, then returned to Rhodesia to practice law as a member of the bar until 1960, when he was appointed as a judge. He had been amongst the judges who heard the Madzimbamuto case, and during the trial he:

… interrupted counsel on a number of occasions and the language in which these interventions were couched indicated that the judge was strongly "Rhodesian," was critical of the British government, was critical of the Africans and African government, and felt a personal responsibility for maintaining the workings and financial machinery of present Rhodesian society.[50]

Another judge who made little effort to hide his RF sympathies and was known to berate Africans accused of political offences from the bench was Justice Hector Macdonald. There were a few judges, such as Justices Fieldsend and Dendy Young, who followed former Chief Justice Robert Tredgold's example and resigned in protest. However, the majority of Rhodesian judges ruled in favour of the state in these political cases and helped to prop up the settler regime.

Ideally, the rigid application of formal legal rationality by judges aided governments by depoliticising political trials and facilitating the elimination of their political opponents by imprisonment. In addition, this strategy would also discredit accused individuals by portraying them to their own supporters as ordinary criminals.[51] However, in Rhodesia, these efforts were actively contested. During their trial Makoni and his colleagues consciously resisted the efforts to depoliticize the case and brand them as criminals. On being asked what he had to say in his defence, Makoni rejected the authority of the Rhodesian government to try him:

I am surprised to learn that I am being charged with the crime of entering Rhodesia carrying arms when Rhodesia is in fact my own country. I am also surprised to find that I am facing trial in this court. When a person has fought with someone, it would not be expected that one of the parties in the fight will try the other. It is equally surprising to learn that I am being

[50] Ibid., 266.
[51] Feltoe, 'Law Ideology and Coercion', 52.

accused of having entered the country with arms without permission to do so. I do not know who is the true owner of this country?[52]

He went on to explain the political grievances that had led him to take up arms against the Rhodesian government. However, Justice Lewis was keen to narrow the scope of the case and responded, 'Yes. Well you have made a political speech and you have had your say. Do you wish to deal with the merits of this case, that is to say do you wish to put forward any defence based on the fact that you didn't have the intention to endanger the maintenance of law and order in this country?'[53] Feeling constrained by the judge's efforts to limit his testimony, Muyambo addressed the Judge in frustration: 'I cannot understand your lordship's attitude. When we referred to politics why did you take it upon yourself to try political issues? This is purely a political dispute. You consented to try it why can't you listen to it?'

In his final statement to the court, Makoni made a defiant assertion of the illegitimacy of the Rhodesian laws, the courts and the very state itself:

My lord, I do not know if your lordship appreciates the words you addressed to us during the course of the trial and whether you abide by them. This is what I have got to remind you: You said this court has been constituted and it is independent of any governmental influence. The present Government is an unlawful Government, and yet if you are not depending on the laws which are promulgated from time to time by that unlawful government, why do you associate yourself with an unlawful entity and conduct the court with the law promulgated by an unlawful body.

I am not accusing you in your personal capacity. I am accusing the Government of this oppressive law. This government knows fully well that it does not belong to Zimbabwe. This country shall ever be called Zimbabwe. If the Government is interested in calling this country Rhodesia, or if it is interested in the name Rhodesia, it should transfer the name Rhodesia to Holland and declare Holland to be Rhodesia.

---

[52] *Regina v. Makoni et al.* See also the defiant testimony of Nelson Mandela and his co-accused in the Rivonia Trial in N. Mandela, *Long Walk to Freedom* (London, 1995), 439. For the full transcript of Mandela's famous speech, see Nelson R. Mandela, Statement to the court during the Rivonia Trial, 20 April 1964, www.aluka.org/action/showMetadata?doi=10.5555/AL.SFF .DOCUMENT.rivon0001, accessed 10/6/2012.
[53] Ibid.

I know that your lordship is about to pronounce the death sentence upon me now. I still maintain that I have not been lawfully tried. Had I been tried in a country outside Rhodesia I should know for certain that it was a legal sentence. The judge and assessors are white people, the people who we came to fight, and they are the people that say they are lawfully trying me. I wonder where a black man is, why isn't a black man among the members of the court?

I am going to tell you this High Court, Smith and his regulations and all his new laws that he has promulgated in this country – to hell with him, let him leave this country with them. That is all, my lord.[54]

What is clear from Makoni and his colleagues' statements in the court was that they were challenging not only the repressive laws, but the way the law was made and administered in Rhodesia. Like many guerrillas, he dismissed the courts on the grounds that they were biased and were playing a part in holding up the Smith regime. Whereas judges emphasised a procedural conception of justice, the guerrillas insisted on a substantive one. His final address to the courts also challenged the legitimacy of the existence of minority rule and racial dominance in Rhodesia. Makoni and his colleagues were ultimately sentenced to death and unsurprisingly, they did not appeal the ruling.

The use of the dock as a platform from which to critique the Rhodesian government by Makoni and his colleagues was by no means unique. The *Zimbabwe News* and the *Zimbabwe Review* regularly carried articles which recounted the defiant testimony of guerrillas and took full advantage of their propaganda value.[55] Often, these trials were held up as evidence of the oppressiveness of the Smith regime, and the defiant testimonies of guerrillas were celebrated as examples of bravery. The reporting of these trials by nationalist newsletters had the additional significance that it was part of the effort to interpret these trials for their African readers as well as the international community. In March 1968, the *Zimbabwe News* carried an article entitled 'They Told It like It Is' which celebrated the defiance of nine 'Chimurenga fighters' tried in the Salisbury High Court. The

---

[54] Ibid. The references to the judge as 'My Lord' are likely to have been added during translation or transcription.

[55] For other accounts of courtroom defiance by guerrillas, see NAZ-MS591 Ian Smith's Hostages: Political Prisoners in Rhodesia, *International Defence and Aid Fund Fact Paper*, Special Issue, October 1976, 5; Munochiveyi, *Prisoners of Rhodesia*, chapter 3; and Mlambo, *Rhodesia*, 206–7.

leader of the group, Comrade Mutangamberi, is reported to have said 'I came to fight. Even at this moment as I sit quietly, I am planning and scheming to kill.'[56] Another article entitled 'Freedom Fighters in an Enemy Court' carried in the May 1968 issue similarly celebrated the menacing statements of defiance made by three guerrillas tried in the Bulawayo High Court.[57]

Evidently, by the late 1960s, nationalists and guerrillas in Rhodesia no longer recognised the legitimacy of the legal system. The laws and the courts that administered them were dismissed as tools for the repression of Africans by an illegitimate settler government. If the capacity of the law to legitimise state power lay in its ability to give the impression that it was impartial and constrained the exercise of state power, as well as instil a sense of awe, then the by the late 1960s, the law was no longer able to legitimise the Rhodesian state in the eyes of the nationalists and guerrillas. As coercion became the government's primary objective, what remained was legality without legitimacy.

Civilians in the Rhodesian Courts

The defiant rejection of the Rhodesian legal system by the national-ists and guerrillas discussed earlier was only one form of response by Africans to the repressive nature of the legal system during UDI. Civilian engagements with the government in the courts often took a different form.[58] Their experiences in the Rhodesian courts bring to the fore the repressiveness of the Smith regime, as well as the fact that these legal encounters were between unequally matched parties. The courts, it should be borne in mind, were part of what Taylor Sherman has described as wider 'coercive networks', and the coercive function they played in this larger network comes out very clearly in the experi-ences of civilians who were charged with political offences.[59]

---

[56] *Zimbabwe News*, 16 March 1968.
[57] *Zimbabwe News*, 11 May 1968.
[58] I am using the word *civilian* to refer to Africans who did not fall into the categories of senior nationalist leaders or guerrilla fighters.
[59] T. C. Sherman, 'Tensions of Colonial Punishment: Perspectives on Recent Development in the Study of Coercive Networks in Asia, Africa and the Caribbean', *History Compass*, 7 (2009), 669. She uses the phrase 'coercive networks' to refer to the chain of institutions and coercive practices that were geared towards maintaining colonial rule.

A distinctive feature of the 1970s was the increase in the number of civilians who were charged under the Law and Order (Maintenance) Act for offences punishable by lengthy imprisonment or death. As the guerrilla war intensified in part due to the support of civilians living in the rural areas, the state responded by targeting them. This trend was confirmed in a letter by the law firm Winterton, Holmes and Hill in 1976 which observed that: 'An increase in the number of arrests [reported] by both ANC factions is apparent, from a monthly average of 60 to one of 207. A large proportion of these come from Tribal Trust Lands adjacent to the Operational Area and, in a few cases, it has been learned that subjects have been convicted and sentenced for failing to report the presence, and the feeding and harbouring of terrorists.'[60]

Some of the people charged in such cases were local party members or officials. However, a significant number were 'ordinary' villagers who found themselves caught between the guerrillas and government forces. These individuals often had neither the experience of engaging government officials in the courts that nationalist leaders had, nor the military and political training that guerrillas had. Arrest was usually followed by severe torture, and it was not uncommon for people to die in police custody.[61] As Munochiveyi shows, many civilians endured the detention and torture at the hands of security agents and exercised agency in the face of prosecution. However, more often than not, civilians did not take the defiant approach of guerrillas discussed earlier. Instead, they sought legal representation and made efforts to defend themselves in the courts. Some of the common strategies they used in court included denying involvement, alleging coercion, feigning ignorance and colluding in order to give conflicting evidence that would jeopardise the state's case.[62]

Notwithstanding these forms of legal agency, by the 1970s it was becoming increasingly difficult to use the law as a shield against persecution by the government. In Buhera, for example, Austin Mhizha and Sebbedia Masomera were called as state witnesses in the trial of another

---

[60] NAZ MS591/2/4, Legal Sheridan, Winterton, Holmes and Hill to Bernard Sheridan and Company, 6 May 1976.
[61] For detailed accounts of the harrowing experiences of African arrested for political offences by Rhodesian authorities, see Munochiveyi, *Prisoners of Rhodesia*, 98–120.
[62] For examples of this, see NAZ MS589/7/3, Kurehwandada Muzheri vs The State; and Munochiveyi, *Prisoners of Rhodesia*, 67.

Figure 4.4 A political gathering in Salisbury in 1972

African charged under the Law and Order (Maintenance) Act.[63] Much
to the disappointment of the prosecutor, the two recanted their sworn
statements resulting in the collapse of the state's case. However, after
the trial, the prosecutor decided to bring charges against them for
making conflicting statements under oath.

The state faced a similar problem in the 1976 trial of Reverend
Kadenge, a United Methodist Church minister who was charged with
encouraging youth to go to Mozambique to train as guerrillas during church services and meetings. The trial of Kadenge was scheduled to go on for three days, and the prosecution had indicated that
it would call twelve witnesses, all of whom were young members of
Kadenge's congregation. However, the witnesses all recanted their
statements and the prosecution was forced to withdraw its charges
against Kadenge.[64] Nevertheless, the collapse of the state's case did not
guarantee the defendant's freedom. Often they were immediately re-
arrested and detained under the Emergency Powers (Maintenance of

---

[63] NAZ MS591/2/4, Legal Sheridan, Scanlen and Holderness to Bernard Sheridan
and Company, 19 January 1976.
[64] Ibid., B. Elliot to Bernard Sheridan and Company, 3 March 1976.

Law and Order) Regulations. Section 23 of these regulations allowed the police to detain a person without warrant for thirty days, and then for a further thirty days if they felt there were grounds for continued detention. In Kadenge's case, he was taken back to the Rusape police who subsequently informed his lawyer, Bryant Elliot of Scanlen and Holderness, that they were applying for a Ministerial Order for his detention.

In 1975 a similar fate befell Jeremiah Masiyane who was due to stand trial at the Bulawayo Regional Magistrate's court charged with 'recruiting for the terrorist cause'.[65] Upon discovering that he had been tortured into admitting the offence, his law firm, Lazarus and Sarif, informed the prosecutor of their intentions to challenge the admissibility of Masiyane's statement, and the prosecution decided to withdraw the charges before the case came to trial. However, Masiyane was subsequently detained under the Emergency Powers Act and confined to Whawha Prison. Such trials were evidently not about proving guilt. They served as instruments by which the Rhodesian government sought to persecute its perceived enemies and their supporters. As such, when evidence or legal procedure stood in its way, the government resorted to other means.

Despite their limited success in the courts, 'ordinary' Africans continued to seek legal representation or sought the assistance of organisations like the Catholic Commission for Justice and Peace (CCJP), Christian Aid, and the Interdenominational Legal Information Centre (ILIC) in securing legal representation. This trend continued even during the martial law period in the late 1970s as is clear in Joshua Shumba, the ILIC secretary's March 1979 report to the IDAF team in London. He wrote:

I am sorry that I have not been able to send you the weekly reports from 15th January. The truth is that this has occurred owing to circumstances completely beyond my control. The period from December to now has been one of my busiest occasions since I joined the Legal Information Office. I have been, and I am still getting clients almost every ten minutes. They knock at my door one after another and most of the cases they bring are such that one has to listen and sympathise.[66]

[65] Ibid., Lazarus and Sarif to Bernard Sheridan and Company, 19 September 1975.

[66] NAZ MS587/4, Untitled, J. J. Shumba to Roy, 5 March 1979.

Given this trend, it is worth asking the question, Why did Africans continued to seek legal recourse at a time when the courts had been so blatantly restructured to serve the repressive interests of the state? In addition, did these continued appeals to the courts legitimise the legal system as Stephen Ellman argues in the case of South Africa during the apartheid period?[67]

Part of the explanation lies in pragmatic reasons. Given the harrowing experiences of being in Rhodesian custody alluded to earlier, most civilians would do whatever they could to secure their release. The assistance offered by organisations such as the CCJP, ILIC and IDAF also made legal services more accessible to Africans regardless of class. Once a relation was known or suspected to have been arrested or detained by the government, one of the few options available for civilians was to approach a lawyer or these organisations. The prestige lawyers had come to possess as individuals who were fluent in the language of law and were therefore uniquely equipped to engage the state in the courts also reinforced the decision to approach them. In addition to the pragmatic reasons, seeking legal recourse was also driven by a sense of outrage and injustice over the treatment they were being subjected to by the state. This was in turn rooted in an imaginary of rights-bearing citizenship, and the attendant ideas about the limits of state power. However, such legal action did not necessarily legitimise the Rhodesian legal system – partly because in the course of the 1970s, it became increasingly difficult to succeed in the courts. More importantly, the Rhodesian state was beyond legitimation in the minds of the vast majority of Africans.

A development which compounded the difficulties civilians faced was the increasing involvement of the military in the administration of 'justice'. As the guerrilla war intensified, large portions of the country were placed under martial law, and this was accompanied by the establishment of Special Courts Martial which heard cases involving people charged under the security legislation. The declaration of martial law led to a marked deterioration of procedural standards in the administration of the law, and this was particularly troubling because Special Courts Martial had the authority to hand down the death

---

[67] Ellman, 'Law and Legitimacy'.

sentence.[68] Special Courts Martial operated on the assumption that the accused was guilty until proven innocent and therefore torture was a routine experience for accused individuals. In addition, access to legal representation was left to the discretion of the President of the court, and defendants could be denied the opportunity to call witnesses to speak in their defence. Unlike the Special Courts where the existence of an audience was a central part of their operations, Special Courts Martial hearings were held behind closed doors, and this further undermined the procedural standards observed by these courts. Individuals who were tried by these military courts did not have the right to file an appeal in civilian courts. Instead, their appeals were heard by another body that fell under the military body, a Reviewing Authority which was set up under the Emergency Powers (Special Courts Martial: Martial Law) Regulations of 1978.[69]

Prior to the declaration of martial law, there had been the possibility that High Court judges would be outraged by the excesses of the army. However, as the military took charge of both the security functions and the administration of justice, there was very little to check its actions. Its impunity was reinforced by the fact that the Indemnity and Compensation Act protected state officials from legal action in a wide range of circumstances. Consequently, in some cases, accused people were not only tortured into signing admission statements, but their torturers were called as witnesses for the prosecution. The presidents of Special Courts Martial would then use this flawed evidence as the basis for a conviction and the handing down of death sentences.[70] Shumba thus sombrely observed of the martial law dispensation that: 'My very grave concern is that a situation has been reached where sometimes innocent tribesmen lose their property or are incarcerated in prison without any remedy available in law.'[71]

Owing to such travesties of justice, in August 1979 the CCJP decided to intervene, and it applied to the High Court for a ruling quashing the decision by the Executive Council that petitions made by people

---

[68] For a detailed account of the difficulties experienced by Africans who found themselves detained by the military, see Munochiveyi, *Prisoners of Rhodesia*, 95–6.

[69] NAZ MS587/4, Untitled, *The Acting President of Rhodesia, The Director of Prisons, The Commander Combined Operations v. John Antony Deary.*

[70] For examples of such cases, see NAZ MS587/4 Untitled.

[71] NAZ MS587/4, Untitled, J. J. Shumba to Roy, 3 May 1979.

sentenced to death 'be forwarded to the Commander, Combined Operations, for consideration by the Review Authority established pursuant to the proclamation of martial law whose decision will be final.'[72] The High Court found in its favour and ruled that according to Section 60 of the 1969 Constitution, which provided for the exercise of the prerogative of mercy, the President had to have the opportunity to 'address his mind' to the petitions.[73] However, the CCJP's victory was short lived as the government appealed the ruling, arguing that the President had the powers to delegate the prerogative of mercy to the Review Authority. The ruling, which was written by Chief Justice Macdonald, read in part:

> ... in my view there can be no doubt that the Acting president, acting on the advice of the Executive Council, was entitled to exercise his prerogative of mercy in the manner set out in the letter of the 15th March, 1979 in the same way as the monarch in Britain delegates the exercise of that power to the Home Secretary. Just as the Home Secretary is not obliged to refer the refusal of the petition to the monarchy for even formal ratification, so too the review authority is not obliged to do so.[74]

At least two things are significant about this ruling. The first was that the judges, who had formerly been scrupulous about legal procedure, had effectively endorsed the rough justice of the army. Second, the decision removed the legal obstacle to continued executions, and within days of the ruling the CCJP was unpleasantly surprised to hear that the government was moving ahead with executions.[75]

The CCJP resorted to appealing directly to Bishop Abel Muzorewa, who was the Prime Minister under the Internal Settlement. It requested that civilians arrested in martial law areas be allowed legal representation and that they be tried in civilian courts, given the severity of the sentences being handed down by the Special Courts Martial.[76]

---

[72] Ibid., *The Acting President of Rhodesia, The Director of Prisons, The Commander-Combined Operations v. John Antony Deary.*
[73] Interview with Bryant Elliot, Harare, 4 April 2011.
[74] NAZ MS587/4, Untitled, The Acting President of Rhodesia, The Director of Prisons, *The Commander-Combined Operations v. John Antony Deary.*
[75] Ibid., Telegram from CCJP to the Prime Minister, Abel Muzorewa 24 June 1979.
[76] NAZ MS590/15, Political Trials, Scanlen and Holderness to Prime Minister, 3 August 1979.

As an alternative, they requested that all who were convicted by Special Courts Martial be at least allowed to present their petitions of mercy to the President. However, the response from George Smith, the Secretary to the Cabinet, was uncompromising. Regarding the first request, he replied, 'The position regarding legal representation cannot be changed. The question of legal representation was considered very carefully at the time when the present policy was agreed.'[77] On the question of the petitions of mercy, his answer was, 'At this point cabinet is not prepared to consider allowing all persons convicted by special courts martial to present their petitions for mercy to the president.'

Conclusion

Although there had been some debate in the 1950s and early 60s about how to strike a balance between the coercive and the legitimating functions of the law in dealing with African nationalism, the RF hardliners had no ambivalence about the course of action they needed to take. They operated on the reasoning that the more repressive the laws were, the greater their effectiveness as a deterrent. Consequently, detention without trial, large-scale arrests of civilians, extensive use of mandatory death sentences and the application of martial law became key features of the administration of the law. In addition, the uneasy combination of the state of exception and legalism that prevailed produced a situation where the application repressive laws operated hand in hand with numerous instances of covert illegality committed by government officials. However, the repressive measures did not achieve the desired effect and were actively contested. Executions were re-interpreted in nationalist newsletters and cast as acts of martyrdom, and accused guerrillas challenged the efforts to use their trials to frame their actions within a discourse of crime and terrorism. Instead, they used the dock as a platform to stage a moral defence which, in effect, placed the government on trial. Nationalist newsletters regularly carried articles that drew on alternative ideas about the law and justice and unmasked the repression beneath the legalism of the Rhodesian government. However, legal agency was not limited to nationalist politicians and guerrillas. Despite the fact that over time it became difficult to use the courts as a shield against persecution by the government, the

[77] Ibid., G. Smith to Scanlen and Holderness, 30 August 1979.

many civilians who were hauled before the courts also exercised legal agency in diverse ways. This was partly based on pragmatic considerations. However, their decision to seek legal recourse was driven by a sense of outrage and injustice that was in turn rooted in their self-identification as rights-bearing citizens.

5 | Intermediaries, Intellectuals and Translators: African Lawyers and the Struggles in the Legal Arena, 1950–1980

Introduction

In examining legal struggles between Africans and the state officials, the previous chapters have highlighted the argument that these legal encounters gave expression to emergent political imaginaries, shifting ideas of personhood and alternative visions of the colonial social order. I have argued that these were connected to long-term social, economic and political changes that African communities experienced during the colonial period. This chapter develops this argument by focusing on the role played by African lawyers as intermediaries and 'translators' in the legal struggles between Africans and the colonial authorities and their contribution to the reshaping of African subjectivities. Examining the experiences and roles played by African lawyers also casts a light on another dimension of the legal struggles in the colony: that over the distribution of the symbolic capital of the legal profession. In addition, lawyers acted as intellectuals who formulated and articulated critiques of the law and also provided legal advice to nationalist movement, most crucially during the constitutional negotiations on the eve of independence. In examining the contributions of lawyers, the focus of this chapter is specifically on the ways they applied their legal training in the struggles between Africans and the colonial state, both inside and outside the courtroom.[1]

With the exception of a few studies on South Africa, research on the history of African lawyers in countries following the common-law

---

[1] I am less interested in their roles as politicians as this is an aspect that has already been accorded some attention in the literature. Studies about Chitepo's political career include L. White, *The Assassination of Herbert Chitepo: Texts and Politics in Zimbabwe* (Bloomington, 2003); W. Z. Sadomba, *War Veterans in Zimbabwe's Revolution: Challenging Neo-colonialism and Settler International Capital* (Suffolk, 2011), 9–19; and D. Martin and Phyllis Johnson, *The Chitepo Assassination* (Harare 1985).

tradition has largely focused on West Africa.[2] Omoniyi Adewoye's work on Nigeria, for example, looks at the origins and growth of the legal profession between 1865 and 1962. He maintains that African lawyers formed a 'fearless bar' which 'constituted a threat to the prestige of the colonial rulers'.[3] Chidi Oguamanam and Wesley Pue have similarly argued that lawyers in Nigeria played an important role in challenging colonial rule as they 'challenged arbitrary power, asserted local values, played to, but also promoted Nigeria's incipient "public"'.[4] In his work on African lawyers in Ghanaian politics between 1900 and 1945, Bjorn Edsman is, however, less inclined to see their challenges to colonial authority as stemming from an alternative vision of the Ghanaian social and political order. He argues that their 'opposition to the British did not signify opposition to the social order represented by alien rule, but signified resentment at being denied full recognition within it'.[5] Richard Rathbone has broadened the focus to the cultural agency of lawyers, and he highlights the role of lawyers in the Gold Coast in contributing to the acceptance of English law amongst the coastal trading elite.[6] Similarly, Mitra Sharafi argues that the early Ghanaian lawyers were 'cultural translators and ethnographic intermediaries', who produced ethnographic studies of the legal systems of local communities and aided the imposition of colonial rule.[7]

These studies provide useful insights into the experiences and contributions of African lawyers. However, the story they tell differs in several important respects to the experiences of their counterparts in British colonies outside West Africa, especially those in settler colonies such as Southern Rhodesia. In the first instance, the development of a legal profession composed largely of Africans who used their legal training to acquire wealth, power and influence, and who at times

---

[2] For studies of black lawyers in South Africa, see K. Broun, *Black Lawyers, White Courts: The Soul of South African Law* (Athens, 2000); and A. Sachs, *Justice in South Africa.*

[3] O. Adewoye, *The Legal Profession in Nigeria, 1865–1962* (Nigeria, 1977).

[4] C. Oguamanam, and W. Wesley Pue, 'Lawyers, Colonialism, State Formation and National Life in Nigeria, 1900–1960: "the fighting brigade of the people"', *Social Identities: Journal for the Study of Race, Nation and Culture*, 13 (2006).

[5] B. Edsman, '*Lawyers in Gold Coasts Politics, c. 1900–1945*' (Ph.D. Dissertation, University of Uppsala, 1979), 250.

[6] R. Rathbone, 'Law, Lawyers and Politics in Ghana'.

[7] M. Sharafi 'A New History of Colonial Lawyering: Likhovsky and Legal Identities in the British Empire', *Law and Social Inquiry*, 32 (2007).

engaged in 'bargains of collaboration' with colonial authorities, does not resemble the experience of British colonies in East and Southern Africa. In Southern Rhodesia, for example, Africans were actively excluded from the profession and only began to enter it from 1953, in the context of rising nationalism and demands for majority rule. Their self-image as lawyers, and the roles they played, were substantially shaped by this political context. Up to the attainment of independence, these lawyers remained on the margins of a profession dominated by European lawyers. In addition, Sharafi's view of indigenous lawyers as 'cultural translators' and 'ethnographic intermediaries' largely applies to colonies in which indigenous lawyers emerged before or around the time of colonial occupation. What is more, because of the specific historical experiences of Gold Coast and Nigeria, the aspect of race is not significant. By contrast, race was a central factor which shaped the experiences of African lawyers in East and Southern Africa.

This chapter shifts the scholarly focus onto African lawyers in a settler colony in which the profession was dominated by European lawyers, and in which Africans had to struggle to enter and survive. Secondly, it takes the notion of indigenous lawyers as translators in a different direction to that of Sharafi and views them as cross-cultural brokers who were constantly involved in a two-way translation. This entailed translating the concepts of Western law to their African clients, as well as translating their clients' grievances into the language of the law. This process of translation in turn acted as a catalyst in the reshaping of subjectivities and enabled their expression in the legal arena.[8] Last, it explores their role as intellectuals who articulated critiques of the law and the political situation in Rhodesia.

Becoming a Lawyer

Administrative officials in Southern Rhodesia had long been opposed to Africans having access to lawyers as it was felt that this would lead to unacceptable interference with their efforts to administer their areas. It was not surprising, therefore, that they were opposed to Africans actually becoming lawyers because they feared that African lawyers would not only undermine the authority of state officials, but

---

[8] See S. Engle Merry, 'Transnational Human Rights and Local Activism: Mapping the Middle', *American Anthropologist*, 108 (2006), 38–51.

would also gravitate towards politics. This opposition to African lawyers was shared by the vast majority of European lawyers in Rhodesia, and their hostility arose out of racial prejudice and a desire to control the supply of legal services in the colony. The government and European-owned law firms thus joined forces to restrict African entry into the profession, a move that was made feasible by the existence of a large settler population. As in East Africa, the fear of African lawyers found expression in the area of scholarship provision.[9] Although the government provided some scholarships for Africans to pursue university studies related to the teaching or the medical profession, there was no such provision for the study of law.[10] The few Africans who managed to overcome the challenges of acquiring the necessary financial resources and educational qualifications to pursue a legal career, were soon confronted with the reality that law firms were generally unwilling to take them on as articled clerks.

As a result, while colonies like Ghana and Nigeria already had indigenous lawyers by the late nineteenth century, it was only in 1953 – over half a century later – that the first African, Herbert Chitepo, joined the Southern Rhodesian legal profession.[11] By 1960 there were only three African lawyers in Southern Rhodesia, compared to approximately 540 in Nigeria.[12] The situation in Rhodesia had not improved much by 1978. Of the 175 attorneys and 40 articled clerks in Rhodesia, five attorneys and seven clerks were Africans, and only seven of the 56 advocates were Africans.[13]

The circumstances which led the members of the first generation of African lawyers into a legal career were diverse. However, a common factor underlying their motives was an understanding of the instrumental and symbolic power of the law, and a desire to gain possession of the symbolic capital that came with being a lawyer. Many hoped that legal expertise would provide an avenue for personal advancement, as

---

[9] S. D. Ross, 'Rule of Law and Lawyers in Kenya', *Journal of Modern African Studies*, 30 (1992), 422.

[10] Interview with S. Mubako, Harare, 26 April 2011.

[11] Mlambo, *Rhodesia*, 305.

[12] Despite the higher number of lawyers in Nigeria, their activities were tightly circumscribed up until the reforms of the 1930s. See Adewoye, *The Legal Profession*, 179.

[13] NAZ RG4, Committee of Enquiry into the Legal Profession, Provisional Report, April 1978. This figure excludes those African lawyers who were practising outside the country.

well as a means of aiding other Africans in their everyday struggles under settler rule. Godfrey Chidyausiku, for example, was inspired by Herbert Chitepo's use of the law to defend the interests of Africans:

He had such a reputation as a good lawyer and when I was in primary school I always admired what he did and especially that he used his legal knowledge in order to advance the interests of his fellow blacks. That was one thing that really inspired me.[14]

Honour Mkushi's motivations were linked to defending the rights of Africans living under settler rule, as well as more personal concerns around masculinity. He explained:

… my father had schooled me into believing the law profession was the right profession for a man, and it was the sort of profession he thought would equip me to go into the world and fight for myself … I know very well that he pounded that into my mind and I never really let go and thank God up to now I don't think I could have done any other profession.[15]

As Jocelyn Alexander's work on political prisoners' memoirs shows, this concern with defending a threatened masculinity was something which Mkushi and his father shared with a host of nationalists who were held in Rhodesian detention camps.[16] That the idea of pursuing a career in law could be encouraged at an early age reflected the social class of his family. His father was a trained teacher who had taught for a few years before going into business in Gutu district. Consequently, Honour Mkushi had received a good education and could realistically aspire to a career as a lawyer from an early age. Significantly, he spoke of his legal career almost as a vocation and much of his narrative revealed how being a lawyer was an important aspect of his identity.

Chitepo's path into the Southern Rhodesian legal profession, like that of the African lawyers who came after him, was a difficult one. He completed a Bachelor of Arts degree at Fort Hare University in South Africa specialising in History and English in 1949, after which he left for London where he took up a job as a teaching assistant at the

---

[14] Interview with Godfrey Chidyausiku, Harare, 14 March 2011.
[15] Interview with Honour Mkushi, Harare, 23 March 2011.
[16] J. Alexander, 'Political Prisoner's Memoirs in Zimbabwe: Narratives of Self and Nation', *Cultural and Social History*, 5 (2008), 398–403.

School of Oriental and African Studies.[17] During his time in London, Chitepo studied law and was called to the Bar in Middle Temple in 1953. Having completed his studies, Chitepo made plans to return to Southern Rhodesia to pursue a career in law. However, he anticipated problems joining the legal profession and therefore wrote to the Chairman of the Bar Association of England, Sir Hartley Shawcross, requesting his assistance.[18]

A central question for officials in London and Salisbury was whether Chitepo should join the profession as an advocate or an attorney, and the consensus that emerged was that he be discouraged from trying to practice as an advocate. The reasons cited for this position by V. L. Robinson, the Southern Rhodesian Attorney General, all had to do with Chitepo's race.[19] The first was that he was unlikely to take up offices in the Salisbury Advocates' Chambers as the lessor would most probably be unwilling to lease an office to an African. The problem of where Chitepo would conduct business was further complicated by the stipulations of Section 41 of the Land Apportionment Act which restricted Africans from owning or leasing land in areas designated as European areas. Last, Robinson pointed out that the 'great majority of the cases where counsel are [sic] briefed are cases in which the client is a European, and however willing attorneys might be to brief Chitepo, they might find themselves in difficulties with their clients because I doubt whether public opinion has advanced sufficiently in the colony for Europeans engaged in litigation to accept an African as their counsel.'[20]

Although Chitepo had been willing to follow this advice, he found law firms in Southern Rhodesia unwilling to take him on as an articled clerk.[21] Chitepo eventually joined the Bar as an advocate and the Land Apportionment Act was amended to enable him to take up chambers in Salisbury where he began to provide legal services to a predominantly African clientele.[22] However, in 1962 Chitepo voted with his feet

---

[17] Mlambo, *Rhodesia*, 305.
[18] BNA DO35/7726, Sir Hartley Shawcross to Sir Kenneth Roberts-Wray, Colonial Office, 26 June 1953.
[19] Ibid., V. L. Robinson to Sir Hartley, 31 July 1953.
[20] Ibid.
[21] Cited in BNA DO35/7726, Laurens Van der Post to Under Secretary of State, John Foster, 1 June 1954.
[22] BNA DO35/7726, E. Lucas to Mr Aspin, 24 August 1954.

and left for newly independent Tanzania to take up an appointment as the Director of Public Prosecutions.[23] Two other Africans, Walter Kamba and John Shonhiwa, joined the legal profession in the 1950s but also left the country after a few years. Shonhiwa had trained as a barrister in London and joined Gill, Godlonton and Gerrans in 1959, but left the firm before completing his articles and took up a seat on the bench in newly independent Zambia.[24] Kamba had studied law at the University of Cape Town before being articled by Scanlen and Holderness, but by the mid-1960s he too had left the country.[25] This was to be the path of the few Africans who tried to enter the legal profession in the 1960s. Consequently, by the late 1960s there was not one African lawyer practising in the country.[26]

With the launching of a law degree at the University College of Rhodesia and Nyasaland in 1965, a new wave of African lawyers began to seek entry into the profession and, like Chitepo, they found the doors closed. The challenges for this new wave of lawyers began in university where they were faced with hostile lecturers and the reality that their employment prospects after graduating were bleak. Chidyausiku recalled that 'the first day I went to the university I was told ... "you are on a wrong course, law is not advisable for blacks because when you finish you will not get a job." And indeed that very first year when I went to university the first two black graduates from law school were roaming the streets without a job and eventually they had to leave the country to get a job in Malawi.'[27] Mkushi was more fortunate than most of his colleagues. Although he struggled for several months to get a job in a law firm, he ultimately got the first opening that arose for an African articled clerk in the 1970s with the law firm Winterton, Holmes and Hill.[28] A few others would follow

[23] Mlambo, *Rhodesia*, 305.
[24] Interview with K. Reagan, Harare, 13 April 2011. M. E. Currie, *The History of Gill, Godlonton and Gerrans, 1912–1980* (Harare, 1982), 39.
[25] Interview with S. Chihambakwe, Harare, 16 March 2011.
[26] For an account of the experiences of black lawyers in South Africa during this period, see Sachs, *Justice in South Africa*, pp. 209–229; Mandela, *Long Walk to Freedom*, 140; Broun, *Black Lawyers, White Courts;* and Chanock, 'The Lawyer's Self.
[27] Interview with Chidyausiku, and Interview with S. Chihambakwe, Harare, 15 March 2009.
[28] Interview with Mkushi. The firm appears to have required an African clerk in order to take advantage of the demand for legal services amongst Africans.

Mkushi's path of entering the legal profession as an articled clerk. These included Simplisius Chihambakwe who joined Gill, Godlonton and Gerrans, Sidney Mafara who was articled by Gallop and Blank, as well as Patrick Chinamasa who was employed by Honey and Blanckenberg.[29]

The experience for most of Mkushi's colleagues was one of constant rejection by law firms, and the only path that was open to them was to join the Rhodesian bar as advocates. After completing his law studies at the University of Natal, S. K. M. Sibanda returned to Rhodesia in 1970 to pursue his career. Like many other African law graduates, he was unable to find a placement in a law firm, and had to take up a pupillage with the advocates in Bulawayo. After passing his Advocates exam in 1971, Sibanda was soon confronted with the reality that the majority of law firms were reluctant to brief him.[30] The few firms that were prepared to brief him generally offered him 'marked briefs' which carried a set fee regardless of the amount of work the advocate did.[31] The situation was equally difficult for the African advocates in Salisbury who had to depend on the poorly paid *pro deo* cases in which the state paid for legal representation to be provided to indigent defendants who were facing the possibility of the death sentence.[32] The irony in this was that, in the 1970s such cases were almost always related to the Law and Order (Maintenance) Act. Therefore, after all its efforts to prevent Africans from entering the legal profession for fear they would engage in politics, the government ended up paying these lawyers to represent other Africans on trial for political 'crimes' directly related to the anti-colonial struggle.

Translating the Law

Having gotten into the profession, African lawyers went on to play an important role as legal intermediaries who 'translated' the law for their African clients. The political ideas of the post-World War II period, rural to urban migration and education, among other things, were important in reshaping the way Africans perceived themselves in relation to the state. To this list we must add the role of translation

[29] Interview with Chihambakwe, 15 March 2009.
[30] Interview with Kennedy Sibanda, Bulawayo, 28 November 2010.
[31] Ibid.
[32] Interview with Chidyausiku.

played by lawyers. A number of studies in legal anthropology have drawn attention to the role of translation in the legal arena and its influence on legal consciousness and legal struggles. Sally Engle Merry, for example, demonstrates that human rights 'become a part of local social movements and local legal consciousness' through the efforts of intermediaries who 'translate global ideas into local situations and retranslate local ideas into global frameworks'.[33] However, Harri Englund's work on the linguistic dimension of translating human rights discourse in Malawi and Zambia shows how human rights discourse 'can be deprived of its democratising potential' by the decisions made regarding what is translated as well as the lexical choices made during the process of translation.[34]

These insights about the possibilities and constraints of 'translation', both in terms of concepts and language, are useful in reflecting on the roles played by African lawyers and their impact on the legal consciousness and subjectivities of their clients.[35] Virtually all of their clients were Africans, and their work invariably involved a significant amount of translation of both kinds. On the one hand, they interpreted the concepts and stipulations of Rhodesian law for their clients. On the other, they translated their clients' grievances into the language of law. In the process, they reframed disputes into questions of rights and informed their clients of the legal limits of the state's power over them. This interaction with lawyers helped to reshape how Africans viewed their relationship with the state and enabled them to assert themselves as rights-bearing citizens. As Oguamanam and Pue observe, '... the nature of the forensic contests pits rights against power, employs the language of justice, and, where state power is involved, begins down the road of constituting the subjects of state power as rights-bounded citizens.'[36]

Touching on both his desire to defend his African clients' rights and the translation he engaged in during his day-to-day work, Mkushi

---

[33] Merry, 'Transnational Human Rights', 38.
[34] H. Englund, *Prisoners of Freedom: Human Rights and the African Poor* (Berkley, 2005), 47–69.
[35] Diana Jeater's study, *Law, Language and Science*, has examined translation in the legal sphere in Southern Rhodesia, and focuses on the short-lived efforts of colonial officials to translate African legal concepts during the early colonial period. My focus here is on the opposite process, i.e., Africans' efforts to come to terms with colonial legal concepts.
[36] Oguamanam and Pue, 'Lawyers' Professionalism', 774.

observed that 'the legal profession from a black man's point of view was a very unattractive profession, and it was a profession where you went in to try and help a lot of people who were ignorant about their rights. They had ideas about what is right and what is wrong but being able to champion what they felt was right is difficult unless you follow certain routes.'[37] Law, for him, was the 'route' through which this could be done. As it became widely known that there was an African lawyer in Salisbury, Mkushi began to attract a large African clientele.[38] Regarding the reasons that many Africans preferred to consult him Mkushi explained:

It was language and culture and the fear of being misinterpreted in an oppressive system. Going to somebody who you don't actually have confidence in, okay he may be a professional, but the whites were at that time looked at generally as people who belonged to an oppressive system. So they would obviously feel much better sitting down and speaking in their vernacular language telling you everything, the relevant and the irrelevant stuff and you then have the time to sift through whatever is coming on your desk.[39]

Mkushi's reference to sifting 'the relevant and irrelevant stuff' indicates the ways in which the translation at play here reduced the complex nature of the disputes to matters deemed relevant by the courts. Notwithstanding the fact that much was lost in translation during the course of legal action, something important was also gained. In addition to the legal issue at hand, what was at stake in the clashes between Africans and the state in the 1970s was the question of the status of Africans in the Rhodesian polity and the extent of the state's power over them. In this context, legal representation was important in both reshaping Africans conceptions of themselves and their relationship with the state, and enabling them to assert themselves as rights-bearing citizens.

This trade-off between the broader and complex set of grievances, and the narrow 'cause of action' that could be taken up in a court of law was evident in a case which Mkushi took on involving a clash

---

[37] Interview with Mkushi.
[38] Ibid. This point was also made in my interview with Kennedy Sibanda, 28 November 2010.
[39] Interview with Mkushi.

between the residents of the Chamburukira area in Zaka District and the local District Commissioner.[40] The case arose out of the government's realignment of the border between Zaka and Bikita Districts, which resulted in the area under Headman Chamburukira being moved from the Nhema chieftaincy in Zaka to the Mabika chieftaincy in Bikita. The action was driven by the government's efforts at administrative rationalisation, as was backed by the findings of the delineation exercise which indicated that, Headman Chamburukira had historically owed 'traditional allegiance' to Chief Mabika and not Nhema. However, this was only one of the many versions of the area's contested history. The VaZuruvi people, for example, maintained that the current Headman Chamburukira was illegitimate and argued that they were the rightful holders of the headmanship.[41] For their part, the VaHove people claimed that the VaZuruvi had only received the title after conspiring with Chief Mabika to depose their ancestor, Nerongwe, who was the original ruler of the area.[42] Based on these alternative accounts, the VaHove and the VaZuruvi people opposed the boundary realignment and the DC's attempt to enforce it by ordering them to exchange their Zaka registration certificates for new ones that recorded Mabika as their chief and Bikita as their district of origin.

Owing to their resistance, the forty-eight village heads of the VaHove and VaZuruvi people were charged under Section 43 (2) of the African Affairs Act for defying an order by the DC. The magistrate convicted them and sentenced them to fifty days in prison or a fine of R$50, of which thirty days or R$30 were conditionally suspended. Instead of paying the fine, the VaZuruvi village heads decided to seek legal counsel from Mkushi, while the VaHove people consulted the Fort Victoria office of the law firm Winterton, Holmes and Hill. The lawyers lodged an appeal in the High Court which challenged the legality of the DC's order, and further argued that the magistrate had erred procedurally by trying the forty-eight as a group and not individually. Justice Macdonald who heard the case found in their favour, and his ruling was particularly critical of the DCs arbitrary use of his power. It read in part:

---

[40] For a detailed account of this clash, see Karekwaivanane, 'It Shall Be the Duty', 343–8.

[41] Interview with P. Dzoro, Chiredzi, 30 March 2009.

[42] Interview with C. M. Kunodziya, Zaka, 31 March 2009.

... an order is not a lawful order because it is so described in a summons or other document. It assumes its lawful character not from the simple fact that it is given but from the legality of the reason for which it is given. An order for which no reason is apparent is, on the face of it, an unlawful order since until it is clothed in reason, it would appear in its nakedness to be capricious only.[43]

Justice Macdonald went on to underscore the limits of DC's authority over Africans by asserting: 'It cannot be said of tribesmen as it can of soldiers – "theirs not to reason why... "'.[44] The lawyers had not dealt with the deeper and contentious questions about traditional allegiances and the conflicting claims to the Chamburukira title, from which their clients' outrage flowed. However, the ruling which explicitly indicated the limits of state officials' power over Africans, was significant.

Sibanda's work with the Bulawayo Young Women's Christian Association (YWCA) in the mid-1970s illustrates the way translation could act as a catalyst in the reshaping of African subjectivities. Owing to the numerous difficulties faced by their members on the grounds of their gender, the YWCA leadership asked Sibanda and Washington Sansole, another Bulawayo-based advocate, to advise them on the issue of legal status of African women in Rhodesia. Constance Mabusela, the regional Secretary for the YWCA at the time, explained: 'One of the sorest points was you went to the post office to take some money from the post office. If somebody sent you a parcel from somewhere you had to bring an ID [identity document] and those days women had no IDs. So they would say bring your husband and if you're not married bring any man.'[45] She went on:

... we saw many other areas where women were really ill-treated. Then we said "what is our status in this country?" And that's when we organised a conference which we invited Advocate Sibanda. He had newly come from South Africa. He came and somebody else I can't remember, and addressed the women about the status of the women, the fact that you have no status at all. You are minors from birth until death. When you are born you are a child of your father, you are a minor under your father. When you get

---

[43] Cited in NAZ S3700/16, *Kwangware & 47 Others v. State*, 10 October 1974.
[44] Ibid.
[45] Interview with C. M. Mabusela, Bulawayo, 29 November 2010.

Figure 5.1 YWCA leaders Agnes Dhlula (left) and Constance Mabusela in 2010

married you are a minor under your husband. And if your husband dies you are still a minor under your sons! That, we thought, that, we can't take that!

The YWCA decided to take action and organised a rally in Bulawayo on 15 November 1975, during which the two lawyers addressed the crowd alongside the YWCA leaders. Part of Mabusela's speech at the rally read: 'We feel we are being discriminated against and hope with the aid of legal advisors, to make representations to Government to have legislation affecting women changed.'[46] Their plans to hold similar rallies in different towns and cities in the country were frustrated by the escalating guerrilla war and opposition from ZANU supporters who associated the YWCA with ZAPU. However, what is clear is that African lawyers helped to trigger the shift in the way the YWCA women understood their situation, and enabled them to make claims for a different legal status.

---

[46] Cited in *The Sunday Mail*, 16 November 1975.

Defending Political 'Offenders'

Legal scholars writing on the Rhodesian legal profession have identified a commitment to formalism as a central feature of the self-image of lawyers.[47] Feltoe suggests that this formalist identity partly explains their failure to object to the repressive legal measures that were being implemented by the Rhodesian Front during the 1960s and the 1970s.[48] These observations about the centrality of formalism to the Rhodesian legal fraternity were confirmed by my own interviews with white lawyers who practised during this period.[49] However, a number of qualifications are necessary. First, there were a handful of white lawyers who objected to the actions of the Rhodesian authorities and fought tirelessly on the behalf of their clients. These included Bryant Elliot, Antony Eastwood, Ken Reagan and Leo Baron. Second, the public espousal of formalism did not necessarily mean that these lawyers were apolitical. Formalism could often be used to cloak sympathies for the Rhodesian Front. Third, interviews with black lawyers revealed that their views of law and justice often went beyond a commitment to rules and procedures, and encompassed a concern for the substantive outcomes of those rules. In addition, their self-conception as lawyers was tied to the endeavour to use the law to bring about more just outcomes.

A number of formative experiences shaped the way African lawyers conceived of their role as lawyers, and important amongst these was the experience of being part of the colonised population. Studies of African lawyers in Nigeria and South Africa show that it was not unheard of for them to buy into the 'civilising mission' and take on conservative views.[50] However, many of the first generation of African lawyers in Southern Rhodesia identified with the broader African population. This was clear in Mkushi's description of his early years as a lawyer as being 'a fighting phase where you are fighting what you

---

[47] See Feltoe, 'Law, Ideology and Coercion' and W. Ncube, 'Legal History in Law: A Zimbabwean Perspective', *Zimbabwe Law Review (ZLR)*, 12 (1995).

[48] Feltoe, 'Law, Ideology and Coercion', 82.

[49] Interview with A. Masterson, Harare, 28 April 2011; Interview with H. Simpson, Harare, 16 April 2009; Interview with Reagan, 13 April 2011; and Interview with G. Smith, Harare, 16 April, 2009.

[50] Sachs, *Justice in South Africa*, 210 and Adewoye, *The Legal Profession in Nigeria*, 180.

felt was unjust generally around you. Unjust in the sense that you felt that you were part of the society which was being victimised.'[51]

Another factor which had a significant influence on them was the hostility of the broader legal fraternity towards them. Describing the experiences of his generation of lawyers, Chidyausiku put it thus: '... we really had to push our way through the narrow gate from the beginning right up to the end.'[52] This experience of hostility in the profession echoed the experience of discrimination of the wider African population in the country, and made African lawyers more likely to identify with other Africans than with the legal profession. In addition, African exclusion meant that they were not subjected to the same degree of professional socialisation which fostered a formalist self-image in European lawyers. This allowed them to imagine their role as lawyers in ways that contrasted to the legal profession at large. The nationalist politics of the 1960s and 1970s, and the attendant ideological currents, also shaped their self-image as lawyers.[53] As such, many African lawyers put their legal skills to use in the service of the anti-colonial struggle and provided legal representation to Africans who were charged with political 'offences' in the Rhodesian courts.

Chitepo, the most famous lawyer of this generation, began his political involvement in the 1950s as a member of the 'inter-racial' organisations that had been popular with members of the African middle class at the time. However, as the disillusionment with 'racial-partnership' set in, he embraced nationalist politics and soon began providing legal representation to nationalist politicians and supporters who were arrested or detained by the state. The legal representation provided by Chitepo was significant, because his successful cases punctured the colonial state's aura of invincibility. In addition, he was able to use the courtroom to invert the racial hierarchies that were central to Southern Rhodesian society. In the end, Chitepo, like his counterparts Nelson Mandela and Oliver Tambo, decided to shift his struggle against settler repression from the court of law to the battlefield.[54] Following the Unilateral Declaration of Independence and the decision by ZANU to wage an armed struggle, Chitepo left his job in

---

[51] Interview with Mkushi.
[52] Interview with Chidyausiku.
[53] Ibid.
[54] Sadomba, *War Veterans in Zimbabwe's Revolution*, 9–19.

Figure 5.2 Herbert Chitepo (right) conferring with Ndabaningi Sithole in 1974

Tanzania and moved to Lusaka where he led ZANU's military efforts up until he was assassinated in March 1975.

The lawyers who practiced in Rhodesia during the 1970s did so in a markedly different environment. By the 1970s the basic principles of due process had been significantly undermined by security legislation, and practices such as torture and the denial of legal representation were the order of the day. Chidyausiku described the challenges of defending political prisoners in the 1970s as follows:

... I do recall one day going to Mbare Police Station to visit a client and being told to my face 'you will not be able to see your client until he has confessed to the police that he did what he did' and you literally had no recourse to anybody because that was the way blacks were treated at that time. And this was coming from the Member in Charge and you couldn't complain to anybody above him because he would have the same attitude. So you had just to wait until your client has been beaten and … made to confess. After that you would go into court and hope that the court would overrule the statement for having been obtained through undue influence.[55]

African lawyers were able to have some impact in their work due to the government's desire to present the appearance of adhering to the law. However, the situation progressively deteriorated as the government repeatedly amended the laws and undermined the procedural safeguards in the legal system. Ultimately, the declaration of martial law in large parts of the country in the late 1970s made it very difficult for lawyers to locate, let alone defend, their clients.

Despite these difficult conditions, many African lawyers threw themselves into the task of providing legal defence for their clients. In the course of the 1970s, Sibanda travelled the length and breadth of Rhodesia tracing and defending hundreds of Africans who had been detained or brought before the Rhodesian courts as well as representing those who sought to make claims against the state for damages to their property.[56] Although he benefitted financially from this work, Sibanda's motives were also tied to his nationalist political convictions. Reflecting on his difficulties in getting a position as an articled clerk, Sibanda observed:

The question is why? Why did they refuse to take me, to give me articles over them … when they were actually giving people articles? In Harare, when Chihambakwe completed he was given articles. I can't remember the other chap who was also given articles in Harare but not me. Why? Well I discovered later that the reason they wouldn't give me articles is because I had a role to play in the armed struggle defending 'terrorists' and I defended them. Yes I defended them![57]

Sibanda is correct in noting the irony that, had he been able to secure employment in a law firm, he would not have been able to devote as much time and effort as he did to defending Africans accused of political offences. His statement also reveals an alternative imagining of

---

[55] Interview with Chidyausiku.
[56] This figure is based on statistics from the Interdenominational Legal Information Centre's Bulawayo office and my own assessment of the files in Sibanda's private archive.
[57] Interview with Kennedy Sibanda, 28 November 2010.

his role as a lawyer, one that was tied to making a contribution to the armed struggle.

Among the many cases Sibanda dealt with were those involving Africans who were being convicted on the basis of confessions acquired by means of torture. Due to the fact that many Africans were not aware of the procedures of the court, they did not challenge their admissions of guilt in court. Instead, their statements were confirmed by the magistrate and incorporated into the state's evidence. The problem was compounded by the fact that even when the tortured individuals were able to secure legal representation through the ILIC, many of the European lawyers who dealt with their cases often failed to challenge the statements.[58] Consequently, Sibanda and a fellow lawyer, Dennis Mapani, secured an office from the African National Council (ANC) where they processed all the cases coming to the ILIC. By doing so, they ensured that all the cases involving the possibility of a death sentence came to Sibanda, who challenged the admissibility of confessions acquired by means of torture.

Another important part of Sibanda's work was searching for missing persons who had often been detained by the government. This involved travelling to remote police stations around the country, often at considerable personal risk, and communicating with army and police officials who were often hostile and uncooperative. In order to deny Sibanda and others lawyers access to their clients, the police often imposed impossible conditions. Such was the case with the police in Wankie, who were annoyed at having to deal with Sibanda's enquiries about the whereabouts of his clients, and his request for access to their sworn statements. In reply to Sibanda's enquiries they wrote:

With reference to your letter dated the 2nd instant under your reference DM/PWM concerning the above named persons, I wish to advise that as a result of considerable research performed by this office, your 'clients' may appear to be similar to a certain Moffat Nkomo R.C. X24116 Lupane and Ndabezinhle Nkomo R.C. X24111 Lupane District.

In the event of these persons being your 'clients' I wish to advise that both were arrested on the 18th January 1979, both persons were dealt with in accordance with the Martial Law Regulations. Any further enquiries in this

---

[58] Interview with Kennedy Sibanda, Bulawayo, 30 November 2010.

regard should be directed to Assistant Commissioner Jones, C/O Combined Operations Headquarters in Salisbury.[59]

The letter went on:

I take this opportunity of advising you that difficulty is often experienced when insufficient particulars of your clients is provided. If you have been instructed to represent persons, you should at least be aware of their full particulars. It would be of considerable assistance to this department.

Secondly, I am bound by instructions from the Commissioner of Police, in that, statements will only be submitted upon the written consent being made available from your client. The possibility of you being unable to obtain such written consent is not acceptable.

This condition, that a lawyer obtain written consent from his client in order to get police co-operation, when the lawyer was in the process of trying to locate the said client, was clearly devised to prevent arrested individuals from getting legal representation.

Like Sibanda, Mkushi was also involved in defending Africans accused of political offences, and his memories about the political cases of the 1970s were centrally about fighting injustice. What emerges clearly from his narrative is a belief in upholding 'Law' and 'Justice':

... you remember there used to be those politically charged cases where people were being arrested for assisting terrorists – freedom fighters. Where people were hung. Where people lost their lives through the legal system. We had the High Court set up what were called the Special Courts to quickly look at politically motivated cases and they really fired you into having to fight and they fired you into sometimes having to be very political because sometimes you came face to face with injustice.[60]

He went on: 'I remember one case which made me very very angry, of a headman down in Nyazura who obviously was forced to supply certain things to the freedom fighters and he had a son who was a medical doctor here in Harare and we fought! He was sentenced to death, and three days before the execution I managed to get that sentenced

[59] Sibanda Private Archives (hereafter SPA) File, Bulawayo Law and Order Cases, Sibanda to ILIC, 17 July 1979.
[60] Interview with Mkushi.

reduced to life imprisonment …'[61] However, once martial law had been declared in the late 1970s, lawyers were often powerless in the face of the rough justice of the military, and narrow escapes such as the one recounted by Mkushi became increasingly rare.

Beyond the Courtroom

Sibanda and his colleagues' contribution to the anti-colonial struggle were not limited to the courtroom. Many became closely involved with the nationalist political parties and put their legal skills at their disposal, and an important role they played was providing legal counsel during the 1976 and 1979 constitutional conferences in Geneva and London, respectively. Sibanda, who was then an active member of ZAPU, was incorporated into its legal team along with Reg Austin, Leo Baron and Cyril Ndebele.[62] In conjunction with the ZANU legal team, which consisted of Eddison Zvobgo, Mubako, Kamba, Chihambakwe and Mkushi, they advised the Patriotic Front and translated its demands into legal language, and devised ways out of deadlocks during the negotiations.[63] As Fay Chung notes, '… many of the details that were to form the final independence constitution were hammered out in Geneva.'[64]

African lawyers also voiced their own critiques of the legal system in Rhodesia in different forums. Zvobgo, who had a doctorate in law from Harvard University, published a booklet that drew on Karl Marx's theory of history to develop a general theory about 'the role of law as an instrument of oppression'. His musings formed part of the broader efforts by nationalists to critique Rhodesian law. Zvobgo posited that: 'There is a dialectic of law which is evident in all countries. In Rhodesia, as we have seen, each stage had its own marked characteristics.'[65] The five stages he identified, which developed as a result of clashes between Africans and the colonial state, were 'the law of conquest', 'the law of dispossession', 'the law of suppression',

---

[61] Ibid.
[62] Interview with Kennedy Sibanda, 28 November 2010.
[63] Interview with Mkushi, and Interview with Mubako.
[64] F. Chung, *Reliving the Second Chimurenga: Memories from the Liberation Struggle in Zimbabwe* (Harare, 2006), 166.
[65] E. Zvobgo, *The Role of Law as an Instrument of Oppression* (Melbourne, 1973), 57.

'the law of oppression' and finally 'the law of terror'. He predicted that the majority would ultimately emerge victorious, and ended his analysis by observing that: 'I am led to the conclusion that Rhodesia has become a full blown Police-state. The notion of law as arbiter in the orderly resolution of conflict has vanished. Law has achieved the opposite effect in man. It has become his enemy, as visible and as cruel as the racial clique that has enacted it in the quest of a dream – the perpetual rule of a black majority by an alien white minority clique.'[66]

For his part, Chidyausiku made use of the Rhodesian Parliament as an arena in which to challenge the government's actions. 'When I left university', he explained to me, 'I practised for about two years then there was an election and some of my colleagues including Dr Sithole said "well let's use this platform" because when you are in Parliament you enjoyed a certain degree of privilege or latitude. In other words you could say things that you couldn't say outside.'[67] He stood as an independent candidate and won the Harari[68] Parliamentary seat with the support of the ANC. During his time in Parliament, Chidyausiku was forthright in his criticism of the Smith regime and firmly supported the nationalist cause. In addition, many of his contributions to Parliamentary debates indicated how a sense of being part of the larger subjugated African population was at the base of his political convictions.[69]

Chidyausiku's contributions to Parliamentary debates were also coloured by his training as a lawyer. He frequently challenged the Smith administration on the grounds that it was failing to live up to the ideals of the rule of law, and pointed out the counterproductive nature of the repressive laws being passed by the Parliament. During the debate on the Law and Order (Maintenance) Act Amendment Bill of 1974, which sought to deter Africans from recruiting or encouraging others to go for training as guerrillas by making it a capital offence, Chidyausiku pointed out that:

[66] Ibid., 56.
[67] Interview with Chidyausiku.
[68] Harari constituency covered the African township of the same name that lay to the south of the Salisbury central business district, and was renamed Mbare after independence.
[69] See, for example, *Rhodesia Parliamentary Debates*, 18 August 1976, 972.

... the Law and Order (Maintenance) Act may be unwittingly in fact recruiting terrorists. In fact the law is becoming so severe that it is driving people into frustration. In fact if this law is meant to deter people from committing such crimes I consider it will not fulfil its object. The tribesman who is mainly affected by the law will only become aware of this law when he has been arrested and is liable to be sentenced to death. The knowledgeable African or the urban African who has the opportunity to read these Acts, when he sees such Acts and the penalties they are providing for, he is not frightened but he sees the need to overhaul the whole system.[70]

During the debate on the 1974 Constitutional Amendment Bill that contained the provisions relating to the appointment of judges, Chidyausiku underscored the importance of the principle of the independence of the judiciary and insisted on a system whereby judges were appointed by a college of retired judges and senior lawyers, as opposed to the Minister of Justice.[71] Chidyausiku ultimately left the Rhodesian Parliament in frustration. 'At the end of the day', he explained, 'you said to yourself "what have I achieved, it's still the same we are not getting anywhere." So in the end I just decided it's not worth the effort.'[72]

Sottayi Katsere, an advocate and the ZAPU Director for Planning, articulated his critique of the Rhodesian legal system in a higher forum: the United Nations Human Rights Commission which met in Lusaka in July 1978. His submissions to the commission echoed the critiques of the legal system that had been made by guerrillas and nationalists since the late 1960s. However, whereas the guerrillas had challenged the legitimacy of the state and framed their arguments in a nationalist language of self-determination, Katsere's critique was couched in the language of human rights. Among other things, he pointed out the widespread use of torture on Africans suspected of political offences, the violation of the rights of captured guerrillas and the biased nature of the Rhodesian courts. He also extended the human rights critique to the issue of settler rule in Rhodesia in arguing thus: 'We contend, in the Patriotic Front, that the very existence of a minority colonial regime itself is an infringement of human rights because legislative power resides in the hands of a few people.'[73]

---

[70] *Rhodesia Parliamentary Debates*, 14 November 1974, 914.
[71] *Rhodesia Parliamentary Debates*, 13 November 1974, 794–5.
[72] Interview with Chidyausiku.
[73] NAZ MS589/7/4, Katsere, Statement to the United Nations Commission on Human Rights.

Conclusion

The first generation of African lawyers in Rhodesia participated in the struggles in the legal arena in several ways. Their struggles to enter the legal profession constituted one dimension of the legal struggles in Southern Rhodesia – namely, over who could possess the symbolic capital that came with being an 'authorised interpreter' of the law. African lawyers also played an important role of 'translating' the law. On the one hand, they translated the concepts of state law for their African clients. On the other, they translated their clients' grievances into the language of the law. Over and above its practical purpose, this translation acted as a catalyst in the reshaping of African ideas of personhood. The legal representation these lawyers provided also enabled their clients to assert themselves rights-bearing citizens. Furthermore, they acted as legal intermediaries in the cases of Africans who were charged with political offences.

In doing so, African lawyers were not acting out of a formalist commitment to rules and procedures. Their experience of marginalisation in the profession had contributed to their development of a more politically-engaged conception of their roles as lawyers. Breaking away from a rigid formalism, some like Mkushi defined their roles as lawyers as being more than just a commitment to rules and procedures but to fighting for justice in its substantive sense. Others like Sibanda drew on the law pragmatically, and understood their roles as connected to a broader nationalist political project. Yet others like Chitepo decided to shift their focus from taking on the Rhodesian government in the courts to engaging it in the battlefield. Significantly, these lawyers would go on to play an important role in transforming the legal system after independence, and their experiences during the 1970s played an important part in shaping the policy decisions they made. The next chapter turns to these efforts to transform the legal system after independence.

6 Law and Transformation: Remaking the Legal System in Post-colonial Zimbabwe, 1980–1990

'Law is necessary in another but equally vital sense even though it may be less obvious even to lawyers. In order for a country to develop it needs good laws that will induce development. You need law in order to protect and promote the interests of the workers and peasants. Our minimum wages regulations have greatly improved the lot of the poor, and the coming Labour Bill is designed to do even more. Similarly, our policies to create equal opportunities for all, tax reform, new parastatal control of multinational investment, – all these can only be effective in the context of law. In order to transform Zimbabwe into a socialist society we can only do that through the instrumentality of laws.'[1] Minister of Justice, Simbi Mubako, 1984

Introduction

The Lancaster House conference that took place between September and December 1979 yielded a new constitution and paved the way for elections in February 1980, which were won by ZANU (PF). The new government inherited an established set of legal institutions that were staffed by experienced and well-trained professionals.[2] However, these institutions were founded on racial difference, and had long been used in its authorisation and reproduction. This was reinforced by the fact that senior personnel in the legal system, such as prosecutors, magistrates and judges, were almost exclusively white. The structure of 'traditional' courts had also been used to implement a system of differentiated citizenship. Finally, during the long decades of political unrest since the 1950s, successive settler governments had built up an

---

[1] S. Mubako, 'The Law and the Judiciary in Zimbabwe', Department of Information Press Statement, 20 August 1984.
[2] For a broader discussion of the colonial legacy that the new government was confronted with, see Colin Stoneman (ed), *Zimbabwe's Inheritance* (New York, 1982).

elaborate armoury of repressive legislation that was used to clamp down on dissent, and had cemented the 'state of exception' as a feature of Rhodesian statecraft. The new government was therefore faced with the challenge of transforming this system in which the law, violence and racial domination had become intricately connected. In this chapter, I examine the new government's effort to transform this inherited legal system, and its attempts to draw on the law in order to constitute state power and legitimacy.

In grappling with these questions, this chapter contributes to the debates on state-making and nation-building in post-colonial Zimbabwe. One strand in this literature has highlighted the importance of land and agrarian policies and shows how questions of authority over land and its use were important to the projection of state authority across space.[3] Another strand has drawn attention to the memorialisation of the anti-colonial war and the use of the memory of the armed struggle for the purposes of nation building, as well as legitimating the state and the ruling elite.[4] Building on this literature, I examine the role played by law in the new government's state-making project. I argue that although a central legitimating claim for the new government was the promise to bring about development and modernisation, it was 'through the instrumentality of laws', as Simbi Mubako put it, that these promises were to be fulfilled. In addition, the new courts introduced by the government were to serve as sites whose procedures, rituals and symbols instantiated the state.[5]

The chapter focuses on three of the main areas of legal reform in the 1980s: the government's 'Africanisation' policy which was aimed at

[3] M. Drinkwater, *The State and Agrarian Change in Zimbabwe's Communal Areas* (New York, 1991); W. Munro, *The Moral Economy of the State: Conservation, Community Development and State Making in Zimbabwe* (Athens, 1998); and Alexander, *The Unsettled Land*.

[4] N. Kriger, 'The Politics of Creating National Heroes: The Search for Political Legitimacy and National Identity' in N. Bhebe and T. Ranger (eds), *Soldiers in Zimbabwe's Liberation War* (Oxford, 1995); R. Werbner, 'Smoke from the Barrel of a Gun: Postwars of the Dead, Memory and Reinscription in Zimbabwe', in R. Werbner (ed), *Memory and the Postcolony: African Anthropology and the Critique of Power* (London, 1998); Alexander et al., *Violence and Memory*, chapter 11.

[5] Hansen and Stepputat, 'Introduction: States of Imagination', 7–8 and A. Gupta and A Sharma, 'Rethinking Theories about the State in an Age of Globalisation', in A Gupta and A Sharma (eds), *The Anthropology of the State: A Reader* (Oxford, 2006), 13.

democratising the legal system and doing away with its racist under-
pinnings; the reorganisation of chiefs' and headmen's courts in order
to 'modernise' them and undo their complicity in the system of differentiated citizenship; and lastly the reforms to the laws regarding
women's rights which sought to remove the legal impediments to full
citizenship for black women that had been in place during the colonial period. The changes in these three areas were amongst the most
important areas of legal reform soon after independence and, therefore, provide a useful lens into the importance of the law as a means
of enacting the modernising ambitions of the new government. At the
same time, these changes were important because they created new
avenues for the exercise of legal agency, and this was particularly the
case in the way they enabled the renegotiation of gender relations. This
chapter also adopts a wider analytical lens than most studies of the
1980s which have tended to limit their focus to specific spheres such
as gender relations, politics or labour.[6] Although these studies have
offered valuable insights, the reforms in these areas need to be located
within the context of long-term legal changes prior to independence,
as well as the broader designs of the new government.

'Africanising' the Legal System

The task of transforming the legal system fell to Simbi Mubako, who
was appointed the country's first Minister of Justice. In the course
of the 1960s and 1970s, Mubako had accumulated five law degrees,
three of which were at Masters level from University College-Dublin,
the London School of Economics and Harvard University.[7] Mubako
had also taught Constitutional Law at the University of Zambia in
Lusaka during the 1970s. It was during this time that he became an
active member of ZANU and worked together with Herbert Chitepo
in drawing up legal positions for the party on issues such as the 1972

---

[6] E. Batezat, M. Mwalo and K. Truscott, 'Women and Independence: The
Heritage and the Struggle', in C. Stoneman (ed), *Zimbabwe's Prospects: Issues
of Race, Class, State and Capital in Southern Africa* (London, 1988), 153–73;
J. L. Kazembe, 'The Women Issue', in I. Mandaza (ed), *Zimbabwe: The Political
Economy of Transition 1980–1986* (Harare, 1986); B. Raftopoulos and L.
Sachikonye (eds), *Striking Back: The Labour Movement and the Post-Colonial
State in Zimbabwe, 1980–2000* (Harare, 2001).

[7] Interview with S. Mubako, Harare, 26 April 2011.

Figure 6.1 President Canaan Banana swearing in the first Cabinet in 1980

Pearce Commission. Mubako became more closely involved in the legal affairs of the party after it was thrown into disarray by the assassination of Chitepo in 1975, and the subsequent arrest of most of the senior leadership in Lusaka. He arranged legal representation for the leaders who were accused of the assassination by the Zambian government. His next important task for the party was to lead its legal team at the constitutional conferences in Geneva and London.

At the end of the Lancaster House Conference, Mubako left for Roma University in Lesotho and took up an appointment as the Dean of the Law School. However, soon after doing so he was selected to be the first Minister of Justice.[8] Upon taking up office, Mubako proceeded to push for a series of significant changes in the legal system, and sought to balance transformation with maintaining the 'confidence, efficiency and professionalism of the legal system.' High on his list of reforms was the Africanisation of the legal system:

… the first challenge was to make sure that the legal system became African rather than what it was. It was dominated by whites and it was very difficult

[8] Ibid.

to find lawyers, to find judges, to find anything. There was not even a single black judge at the time. There was not even a single magistrate at lower levels. No no no, there were two who were very junior magistrates ... The question is how do you then Africanise the system without the African lawyers?[9]

For Mubako, transforming the racial composition of the personnel in the legal system was about democratising it, as well as altering the status of the courts as symbols of settler rule. He explained, '... if I didn't do that we would only have white judges still continuing and the impression would have been that there is no change and I was determined that at least there must be some change ...' It should be added that, although Mubako's efforts to Africanise the system were politically driven, his hand was also forced by the exodus of large numbers of white prosecutors and magistrates, which left a huge gap in the legal system.

Apart from the low number of African legal professionals, Mubako's efforts at Africanisation were hindered by the structure of the profession, and the legislation that governed it. The existing system of a 'divided profession' placed control over entry into the legal profession in the hands of the white-owned law firms. In addition, the constitutional stipulations regarding the qualifications of judges restricted Mubako's ability to appoint African lawyers to the judiciary. One such stipulation stated that candidates for appointment to the judiciary had to have been practising *advocates* for at least seven years, which effectively ruled out all of the African lawyers who had qualified as attorneys in the 1970s. In order to deal with these impediments, Mubako had the Legal Practitioners Act passed by Parliament in 1981.[10] The Act fused the legal profession and removed the privileges that had been reserved for advocates, such as their exclusive audience in the High Court and eligibility for appointment as judges. In addition, the period of articled clerkship was shortened from three years to one, thereby allowing newly trained lawyers to set up their own practices much earlier than before. At the University of Zimbabwe, efforts were made to enrol more black law students, while the Legal Resources Foundation set up a library for new lawyers to conduct their research.[11] The Ministry of

---

[9] Ibid.
[10] Ibid.
[11] Interview with R. Austin, Harare, 29 April 2011.

Justice also initiated fast-track training programmes for prosecutors and magistrates at the government training centre in Domboshawa.

There were also concerted efforts to get members of the first generation of African lawyers to serve in the new administration. Eddison Zvobgo was appointed to the post of Minister of Local Government, while Godfrey Chidyausiku was initially appointed Deputy Minister of Justice, then Attorney General, and ultimately a High Court Judge. Simplisius Chihambakwe was appointed as the government's representative on the Law Society Council and later became the President of the Council. He was also appointed to chair the Detainees Review Tribunal and the 1983 Special Commission of Enquiry into the disturbances in Matabeleland. George Chinengundu was appointed Deputy Minister of Local Government and Town Planning, and Honour Mkushi continued in private practice but was called upon to prosecute in high-profile political cases during the 1980s.[12] S.K.M. Sibanda was appointed as the government's second representative on the Law Society Council and later became the Vice President of the council. During the early 1980s he also sat on the ZANU (PF) Central Committee and was appointed to the board of the government-owned financial institution Zimbank.[13]

Despite the changes to the Legal Practitioners Act, Mubako continued to face difficulties in his effort to Africanise the judiciary because many experienced African lawyers preferred to stay in private practice which had much better remuneration.[14] He therefore had to look further afield and was able to get two judges from Ghana, which was experiencing political unrest due to a military coup. He also managed to negotiate with the Tanzanian government to have two judges seconded to Zimbabwe. In addition, Mubako persuaded Telford Georges, a West Indian jurist who had served as the Chief Justice in Tanzania after independence, to serve on the Zimbabwean bench.

The goal of Africanising the bench was always weighed against other considerations, however. One such consideration was ensuring that the legal system continued to operate in an efficient and professional manner, so as to retain its legitimacy in the eyes of citizens. The appointment of judges was also an inherently political task, as the new

[12] Interview with H. Mkushi, Harare, 23 March 2011.
[13] Interview with S. K. M. Sibanda, Bulawayo, 28 November 2010.
[14] Interview with Mubako.

government generally sought, as far as possible, to appoint judges who would be 'sympathetic' to it. The uneasy interaction between these different considerations was evident in the efforts to replace Chief Justice Hector Macdonald, who had openly supported the Smith regime and declared his unwillingness to serve under a nationalist government. In this instance, the goal of Africanisation took a back seat to concerns about maintaining the credibility of the justice system and political considerations. Rather than appoint Enoch Dumbutshena, who had limited experience as a judge, he appointed John Fieldsend, one of the two judges who had resigned in protest after the courts endorsed UDI in 1968.[15]

During Fieldsend's leave pending retirement in 1983, Justice Leo Baron was appointed acting Chief Justice. However, his appointment was not made substantive. Despite the fact that Baron was the most senior judge on the bench, ZANU (PF) officials were reluctant to make his appointment permanent, because he had been a close advisor of Joshua Nkomo and a member of the ZAPU.[16] The government thus announced its intention to appoint a black Chief Justice, and appointed Dumbutshena instead. By 1984, the vast majority of the judges were appointees of the new government, and Mubako expressed optimism that the relations between the executive and the judiciary would henceforth be less strained.[17] However, as I show in the next chapter, his optimism was soon proven wrong.

Reorganising Chiefs' Courts and the Administration of 'Customary Law'

Another set of important changes in the legal sphere during the 1980s was in the area of chiefs' courts and 'customary law'. As we have seen, during the 1960s the Rhodesian Front had elevated 'customary law' and chiefs' courts in its attempts to counter nationalist agitation, and re-legitimise the state. By contrast, the new government sought to modernise the 'manner of administration and substantive content' of 'customary law', and bring it into step with social and economic changes in the country. As part of its 'modernisation' efforts, the new

[15] Ibid.
[16] NAZ ORAL/239 Leo Baron.
[17] Mubako, 'The Law and the Judiciary in Zimbabwe'.

government sought to introduce the symbols, procedures and concepts of state law into 'customary law' courts. However, these efforts came up against resistance from 'traditional' leaders. This was not because chiefs were inherently opposed to the incorporation of 'modern' features in their courts. After all, they had lobbied for precisely that from the 1950s. The problem in the 1980s was that the new government's plans to reorganise the local courts side-lined 'traditional' leaders.

Two key factors help to explain this reorganisation of courts and the resultant marginalisation of chiefs. The first was the fact that, unlike the Smith regime, the new government no longer depended on chiefs as a major source of legitimacy. This was not an outright rejection of chiefs, as had been the case in Mozambique after independence. However, what was clear was that chiefs were no longer seen as being at the centre of the new government's designs. Instead, it promised to implement development programmes, to create a modern society, and to adopt a more democratic approach to governing.[18] Although the government's rhetoric emphasised democratising local government, in practice it retained the top-down approach employed by the Rhodesian Front.[19] The second factor that shaped the changes in the primary courts system was the shift of decision-making authority on the question of 'customary law' courts away from the Ministry of Home Affairs (formerly called the Ministry of Internal Affairs) to the Ministry of Justice.

In presenting the Customary Law and Primary Courts Act in Parliament, Mubako made it clear that the government intended to reorganise the administration of justice in line with its broader modernising project. In this regard, he explained that 'The Bill before this House seeks to introduce a system of customary law and courts which will be seen by the people as being part of the new society.'[20] He further argued that 'Any system of law which does not develop with the times in the manner of its administration and its substantive content will be discredited and decay ... No system of law which wants to survive, can escape that process of modernization.'[21] The legislation was also aimed at re-establishing state authority over the administration

---

[18] See *Zimbabwe Parliamentary Debates*, 10 February 1982, 1610–1611.
[19] For a broader discussion of the fate of chiefs and the shortcomings of the participatory approach in the 1980s, see Alexander, *The Unsettled Land*, chapters 5, 6 and 7.
[20] *Zimbabwe Parliamentary Debates*, 3 February 1981, 1498.
[21] Ibid.

of justice in the face of political party committees which continued to arbitrate local disputes in the rural areas during the early 1980s.[22] As Mubako later conceded 'these could have led to a breakdown in the administration of justice had the government not intervened quickly'.[23] Another important goal in the reforming of the local courts system was to break away from the practice under settler rule where chief's courts buttressed settler state's efforts to treat Africans as ethnicised, custom-bound citizens.

Under the Act, the old racially segregated courts were abolished and a single court hierarchy was established. The old courts that had been run by District Commissioners, Headmen and Chiefs were replaced by a 'Primary Courts System' made up of two tiers of courts. The first tier consisted of the Village Courts (*matare apamusha*) which were run by elected Presiding Officers (POs), whereas the second tier was made up of Community Courts (*matare makuru*) run by POs who were trained and appointed by the Ministry of Justice.[24] Primary Courts mostly heard civil cases and a limited range of criminal cases that were seen as determinable by 'customary law'. The courts were supervised by an inspectorate headed by Justice Brobbey, one of the judges recruited from Ghana. It is worth pointing out that the legislation on primary courts was more concerned with the administration of customary law, as opposed to its codification. Consequently, more attention was given to procedural aspects, especially in the Community Courts which were to be administered by trained POs.

From 1982, the Primary Courts System was implemented, and new courts were established in large numbers across the country. In carrying out their everyday duties, these newly instituted courts enacted the modernising ambitions of the state, and made it present at the local level. Andrew Ladley notes that by the end of 1982, there were approximately 1500 village Courts and 50 Community Courts in operation. Together the courts heard about 2500 cases each month, and this figure continued to rise in the course of the 1980s.[25] In a

---

[22] Ibid, 1497. See also N. Kriger, *Zimbabwe's Guerrilla War: Peasant Voices* (Cambridge, 1992), chapter 6.
[23] Mubako, 'The Law and the Judiciary in Zimbabwe'.
[24] Next in the hierarchy of courts were the Magistrate's Courts, followed by the High Court and finally the Supreme Court.
[25] Ladley, 'Changing Courts in Zimbabwe', 113.

small number of cases, white Zimbabweans were involved in community courts both as defendants and plaintiffs.[26] In Zaka district (previously Ndanga), the Primary Courts had mixed fortunes. The District Administrator for Zaka, J. P. Chataurwa, made the following comments on the situation in his area:

Some chiefs/headman who are popular/acceptable to the people have been made court presiding officers, assessors, councillors etc. However, certain chiefs/headmen who were against the people's revolution were either killed or fled their homes thereby bringing the institution of chieftainship into doubtful integrity. From my contact with people on the ground, it is generally acceptable to the majority of the people. They (the mass/people) have not advocated for a complete abolition of the institution of chieftainship.[27]

Chief Ndanga, whose chiefdom fell within Zaka district, was amongst those chiefs who were not 'popular/acceptable' enough to be elected as POs. During the early 1980s, party affiliation was an important form of currency in getting elected as a PO in the Ndanga Village Courts.[28] Consequently, it was Simon Musuka, a ZANU (PF) official and a member of one of the rival houses eligible for the Ndanga chieftaincy, who was elected as the PO.[29]

Although the government had hoped that the democratic selection of POs would provide the new judicial officials with legitimacy, in practice things turned out to be much more complicated. 'Traditional' leaders contested the legitimacy of these POs on several grounds. Some argued that they were new comers who could not be expected to exercise authority over the autochthons, while others invoked 'custom' as the true basis for the legitimate exercise of judicial power.[30] In Zaka, the severe drought of 1982–1984 provided a basis for Chief Ndanga to reclaim judicial authority. As in Chimanimani District, the 'traditional' leadership in Ndanga interpreted the drought as a sign

---

[26] Ibid., 113.

[27] NAZ-Masvingo: CHK & HM 14 1975–1982, District Administrator for Zaka, J. P. Chataurwa, to Undersecretary Development, 14 April 1982.

[28] Group interview with four Ndanga village heads – M. Magora, C. Ndume, J. B. Ngwaru and F. Mutape – Ndanga, 2 February 2011.

[29] Interview with R. Ndanga, Ndanga, 18 April 2011.

[30] M. Magura, Group interview with Ndanga village heads. See also Alexander, *The Unsettled Land*, 166.

that the ancestors were angered by the marginalisation of chiefs.[31] Consequently, from the mid-1980s Chief Ndanga was able to re-assume judicial authority.[32]

The Primary Courts System and the modernising impulse behind it were ultimately abandoned in 1990, due to a combination of factors, one of which was the pressure from chiefs for the restoration of their judicial powers. At the same time, the ruling party progressively came to see chiefs as an important source of political support and thus became more amenable to their demands. This shift towards chiefs occurred in the context of growing frustration within grassroots party and local council structures, arising from the government's centralised approach to decision making in important issues such as land distribution. As Jocelyn Alexander points out, 'the weaknesses of vidcos [village development committees] and the apathy within the party created space for the emergence of customary leaders as, at one and the same time, populist critics of state policy and a pivotal means for officials to implement policies and for politicians to build support.'[33] Consequently, during the run up to the 1985 elections, Prime Minister Robert Mugabe promised to restore chiefs' judicial powers, and this promise was fulfilled in 1990 through the Customary Law and Courts Act.[34]

However, the passage of the 1990 law did not amount to a full return of judicial powers to 'traditional' leaders. Many important areas of social dispute such as child custody, wills and inheritance, maintenance and the dissolution of marriages were placed under the jurisdiction of magistrates. In addition, the jurisdiction of headmen and chiefs was limited to cases in which the value of claims did not exceed $500 and $1000, respectively. As Welshman Ncube observed: 'Considering that maintenance, custody and divorce claims probably take up more than 95 percent of the business of the current community courts, it is difficult to envisage what meaningful cases will be left to be heard by headmen and chief's courts.'[35]

---

[31] Group interview with Ndanga village heads; and Interview with R. Ndanga, 18 April 2011.
[32] Interview with R. Ndanga, 18 April 2011.
[33] Alexander, *The Unsettled Land*, 165.
[34] Ibid., 166.
[35] W. Ncube, 'Customary Law Courts Restructured', *ZLR*, 7 (1989–1990), 16.

Law and Gender Relations

Whereas many of the reforms to the 'traditional' courts were reversed by 1990, the legal reforms dealing with the legal status of women proved to be more durable, despite the widespread opposition they provoked. The 1980s witnessed the passage of several important laws such as the Equal Pay Regulations of 1981; the Matrimonial Causes Act of 1985 which, among other things, provided for the equal division of property between husband and wife in the event of a divorce; and the Labour Relations Act of 1984, which explicitly made discrimination on the grounds of gender illegal in the workplace. These Acts reflected the new government's modernising ambitions; but more importantly, they provided new opportunities for women to renegotiate gender relations by means of the law. My focus here will be on the Legal Age of Majority Act of 1982, which had far-reaching implications for women's rights. In addition, I will illustrate the forms of legal agency the reforms enabled by examining the surge in maintenance cases that were heard in Community Courts during the1980s.

From the early colonial period, African women had been defined in colonial law as 'perpetual minors', who were under the legal guardianship of a male relative from birth to death.[36] Calls to improve their legal status had been made during the mid-1970s by organisations such as the Young Women's Christian Association (YWCA), the National Federation of Women's Institutes of Rhodesia and the Anglican Church.[37] However, the focus of these calls was often limited to 'emancipated' women, a category that included widowed or divorced women who had contracted a 'Christian' marriage, and economically self-sufficient women.[38] Despite the narrowly targeted lobbying, the Ministry of Internal Affairs firmly resisted this pressure for fear of antagonising the Council of Chiefs. It chose instead to continue pursuing 'Community Development', with its less controversial emphasis on 'self-help', 'popular participation' and 'decision making'.[39] However, after independence, the new government resolved

---

[36] Schmidt, 'Negotiated Spaces', 630.
[37] See NAZ S3700/15, Legal Status of African Women.
[38] Chidyausiku also raised the question of the legal status of 'emancipated' African women in Parliament in 1974. See *Rhodesia Parliamentary Debates*, 15 November 1974.
[39] Interview with Betty Mutero, Harare, 22 March 2011.

to implement policies that would improve women's legal status and empower them economically. The driving force behind these policies was the Ministry of Community Development and Women's Affairs led by Teurai Ropa Nhongo, supported by groups such as female ex-combatants, feminist legal activists, academics based at the University of Zimbabwe, and members of the YWCA.

One of the key laws that this coalition of activists successfully lobbied for was the Legal Age of Majority Act of 1982 which stipulated that all Zimbabweans, irrespective of race, gender or class would 'assume the full rights and obligations of citizenship' upon reaching the age of 18.[40] An important factor that helped to get the legislation passed through Parliament was the support of senior ZANU (PF) officials who used their political clout, in the face of substantial resistance from within the party, and the country at large.[41] Thanks to this high-level backing, the Legal Age of Majority Bill was tabled on the 16th of June and moved through the first, second and third readings, as well as the committee stage, in just three days and was subsequently passed.[42]

The legislation was legitimated by invoking the liberation war and the country's professed ideology of socialism. In presenting it to Parliament, Mubako highlighted women's contribution in the recent liberation struggle and emphasised the fact that they had earned their right to equal citizenship. 'The law', he argued:

... will remove away any doubt surrounding the legal status of African women and will ensure that all our women will have all the legal rights that citizens of a democratic country should possess. They have fought in the war and thousands of them died just like their male comrades. They may still be called upon to defend their country at age 18, they pay taxes at the same age as men, they vote at that age; it is therefore only just and proper that women like men should become majors at the same age of eighteen.[43]

This position was reinforced by Nhongo at a colloquium on the rights of women organised by the Ministry of Justice. Her speech, which

---

[40] *Zimbabwe Parliamentary Debates*, 17 June 1982, 67.
[41] *Zimbabwe News*, February 1985.
[42] See *Zimbabwe Parliamentary Debates*, 17 June 1982, 65–100; and *Zimbabwe Parliamentary Debates*, 18 June 1982, 117–18.
[43] *Zimbabwe Parliamentary Debates*, 17 June 1982, 68.

appealed to the government's declared ideology of socialism, read in part: 'It should be borne in mind also, that in the context of the national ideology and the principles on which the liberation struggle was fought, a perpetuation of inferior status of women is a real embarrassment for it negates the very principles of socialism...'[44] Countering the argument about preserving culture that was frequently advanced by opponents of the legislation, she maintained that 'Cultures and traditions are not static but change as circumstances and situations change. Customs are made by people and it is people who can change them. They are fashioned to suit the prevailing socio-economic order and it is on this basis that women feel certain aspects of customary law are simply obsolete and out of step with the situation in Zimbabwe today.'

The objections to the legislation expressed in Parliament during the brief debate, echoed those that had been made by male elders in the early decades of colonial rule to laws that enabled women to challenge patriarchal authority.[45] MPs invoked an essentialised notion of 'African culture' which was discursively constructed in opposition to 'western culture' and predicted that social degeneration would follow the Bill's passage.[46] One critic of the Bill was S. D. Malunga, a ZAPU MP from Matabeleland North. He spoke at length about the importance of 'culture' and 'customs' for the nation and the importance of preserving it.[47] Malunga was particularly concerned about the provision that girls over the age of 18 would be able to marry without their parent's consent. This, he argued, went against 'African customs' and he asserted that: 'An African girl will continue to seek permission from the parents, and if there is trouble it is a matter of must – she will go back to her parents, or brothers, or whatever relatives are there to talk about the problem.'[48]

For his part, J. E. G. Ntuta, also a ZAPU MP from Matabeleland North, was worried about the implications of the bill on gender and generational relations. He warned that the Bill might lead to

---

[44] Cited in W. Ncube, 'The Decision in Katekwe and Muchabaiwa: A Critique', *ZLR*, 1 & 2 (1983–4), 218.

[45] See Schmidt, 'Negotiated Spaces'.

[46] Similar arguments were made by opponents of the Matrimonial Causes Act. See Kazembe, 'The Women Issue', 390.

[47] *Zimbabwe Parliamentary Debates*, 17 June 1982, 69–70.

[48] Ibid.

further degeneration in the behaviour of the youth. Like the Minister, he invoked the liberation struggle but used it to make an opposing argument:

We fought for this country because our customs were not recognised. At my age, born in 1924, I am still answerable to my brother. I have a widowed mother to whom I am still answerable. I never steamroll my mother. I have due respect for her, and I let her enjoy her maternal role. That maternal instinct must not be blocked by law. I believe if the Minister's speech is misinterpreted, it will make our children worse than they are.[49]

Part of Ntuta's concerns arose out of the tensions between the notion of personhood on which the Bill was based and that on which customary social relations were founded. For him, the notion of moral personhood that underlay customary social relations was incompatible with the idea of individual rights on which the legislation was based.

However, the patriarchal anxieties exhibited by many of the Bill's opponents were challenged by Naomi Nhiwatiwa, the ZANU (PF) MP from Manicaland, who questioned the focus on girls by some of the Bill's opponents, and their underlying assumption that women were incapable of using the freedom the Bill gave them responsibly. Instead, she highlighted their important roles as mothers of the nation: '... they are the cradle of this country, they are the ones who have nursed this nation, they are the ones who have nursed our leaders today.'[50] For her part, Ruth Chinamano, an MP from Matabeleland North, was much more forthright: 'If I do not support this Bill I would be doing an injustice to womenkind – [HON. MEMBERS: Hear, hear] – It is long overdue to introduce such a Bill for women. The days when eggs were only for men and not for women are gone. – [HON. MEMBERS: Hear, hear] – *Chikanganwe hama* [a chicken gizzard]. The days when part of a chicken was only for men and not for women have gone. This is the year for social changes and the changes must be for everyone.'[51]

After the legislation was passed, there was a huge public outcry. At one level, this outcry was in large part a patriarchal backlash triggered by the realisation that the legislation posed a threat to patriarchal control, and in particular, the practice of *roora* or bride wealth payment.

[49] Ibid., 73.
[50] Ibid., 72.
[51] Ibid., 78.

The way that the legislation was publicised by the government did not help matters. Julie Stewart, who assisted with the drafting of the legislation, noted that the publicity material gave prominence to the fact that the new legislation enabled girls to get married without parental approval.[52] Consequently, even those who had no qualms over the issue of equal rights for women became suspicious of the legislation. At another level, the public outcry was an expression of anxieties about rapid social change and its impact on the behaviour of the youth. These anxieties were in turn blamed on the efforts to accord women equal rights.[53] The debate about the legislation also came to encompass questions about the broader direction of the nation and the place of African culture within it.

The Legal Age of Majority Act led to a number of landmark rulings in the course of the 1980s. One of the significant impacts of the rulings was that they invalidated the claims of particular categories of men over their daughters or wives. The first was handed down in the 1984 test case between Katekwe and Muchabaiwa which was sponsored by the University of Zimbabwe Law Department. The case dealt with the question about whether a father had the right to sue for seduction damages in the case of a daughter who was above the age of eighteen.[54] From the Community Court through to the High Court, the rulings handed down all held that a father no longer had this right. In doing so, the courts indirectly undermined a father's claim to bride wealth with respect to a daughter who was over eighteen years of age. The second important ruling was handed down in the 1987 case between Auxillia Mangwende and her uncle Leonard Chihowa which concerned the former's right to be considered an heir to her father's estate. In this case, the Community, the Magistrate's and the Supreme Courts all ruled that, following the passage of the Legal Age of Majority Act, there was nothing that prevented a daughter from being appointed an heir in the event that her father died intestate.[55]

Despite the existence of progressive legislation and supporting judicial rulings, translating these legal reforms into actual improvements in women's lived realities was a longer struggle. For many women,

---

[52] Interview with J. Stewart, Harare, 12 April 2011.
[53] Kazembe, 'The Women Issue', and Interview with Stewart.
[54] Ncube, 'The Decision in *Katekwe v. Muchabaiwa*'.
[55] J. Stewart, 'Legal Age of Majority Act Strikes Again: *Chihowa v Mangwende* SC 84.87', *ZLR*, 4 (1986).

financial limitations, illiteracy, lack of information and concerns about possible marital disharmony all influenced the extent to which they took advantage of the legal remedies available to them.[56] In addition, the publicity given to the rulings led to intensified public outcry against the Act. As a result, in 1984, Eddison Zvobgo, the new Minister of Justice indicated that the government was looking into passing an amendment that would allow fathers to claim damages for seduction, regardless of whether the daughter in question had attained the legal age of majority.[57] Similarly, Nhongo, the Minister of Community Development and Women's affairs, felt the need to promise a gathering of parents in Mount Darwin that 'We want to retain our cultural values and we shall invite parents, elders, and traditional leaders to advice [sic] us on the necessary amendments needed to retain those social values we cherish.'[58] However, in the end, the Act was not amended.[59]

Notwithstanding the many challenges in implementing the legislation, the reforms of the 1980s did open up new spaces in which gender relations could be renegotiated. One such space was the Community Court. This was in part the result of an amendment to the Customary Law and Primary Courts Act in October 1982, which empowered Community Courts to adjudicated over maintenance cases.[60] For much of the colonial period, the practice of paying maintenance had largely been restricted to the European population. In the event of a divorce within African families, the question of child custody was dealt with by family elders. If the wife's family took care of the children, the father would be expected to make a *chiredzwa* payment in recognition of this.[61] With respect to family property, the bulk went to the husband, and there was no obligation for men to make any payments to their estranged partners. As such, the law on maintenance introduced a new social norm and allowed for the renegotiation of

---

[56] Tsanga, 'Reconceptualizing the Role of Legal Information Dissemination in the Context of Legal Pluralism in African Settings', in A. Hekkum et al. (eds.), *Human Rights, Plural Legalities and Gendered Realities: Paths Are Made by Walking* (Harare, 2007), 440–5.

[57] Cited in Ncube, 'The Decision in Katekwe v Muchabaiwa'.

[58] Ibid.

[59] See Kazembe, 'The Women Issue'; and Batezat et al., 'Women and Independence'.

[60] Kazembe, 'The Women Issue', 387. See also *Zimbabwe Parliamentary Debates*, 24 June 1982.

[61] Interview with M. Mufuka, Jerera, 4 February 2011.

gender power relations. The use of the courts by women in these cases should also be understood within a much longer history of African women's engagement with the law.[62]

The number of maintenance cases heard in Community Courts around the country rose sharply between 1983 and 1990. This rise was partly influenced by the fact that the Legal Age of Majority Act enabled women to sue without the assistance of a legal guardian. Significantly, maintenance suits were not limited to urban areas or to upper class women. The rise in maintenance litigation was also spurred by the publicity campaigns about the new legal provisions that were carried out by the government, women's rights groups and the Legal Resources Foundation.[63] The fact that these suits were generally successful also contributed to the increase in cases. In cases in which men did not attend the hearings, a default ruling was handed down against them and an order for deductions to their salaries was made. However, these rulings were not always successfully implemented. By the mid-1980s, several districts were convening separate maintenance courts in order to deal with the sheer volume of cases. Such was the case in Zaka and Bikita districts where maintenance cases came to constitute a significant proportion of the civil cases heard by Community Courts. As shown in Tables 6.1 and 6.2,[64] the total number of maintenance cases in some years equalled or exceeded the number of all other types of civil cases put together.[65]

An examination of the court records for maintenance litigation in Zaka and Bikita reveals that there were two main categories of women who made filed these suits. The first were young women whose erstwhile lovers had deserted them and refused to take responsibility for their child together.[66] For these women, the courts helped to ensure

---

[62] See Schmidt, 'Negotiated Spaces', and Zimudzi, 'African Women'.

[63] W. T. Manase 'Grassroots Education in Zimbabwe: Successes and Problems Encountered in Implementation by the Legal Resources Foundation of Zimbabwe', *Journal of African Law*, 36 (1992).

[64] The statistics in the two tables were compiled using records from the Magistrate's and Community Courts in the two districts.

[65] A study carried out by a University of Zimbabwe research team in the mid-1980s showed that, on average, around a quarter of all cases heard in the 19 Community Courts surveyed were maintenance suits. See Kazembe, 'The Women Issue', 388.

[66] For an example, see the case between Shylet Gondo and Philip Tapfuma discussed later in this chapter.

Table 6.1 *Bikita District Civil Court Statistics*

Year	No. of Maintenance Cases	No. of Civil cases
1980	No Records (NR)	2
1981	NR	70
1982	NR	218
1983	NR	187
1984	NR	276
1985	300	191 plus
1986	360	394
1987	179	215
1988	127	160
1989	91 plus	182
1990	122	147

that such men provided for their welfare and that of their children. This was particularly important in instances in which the parents of the young mother refused to support their daughter. The second category consisted of women who had been married for a number of years and had children but were faced with husbands who were not providing for the family. These husbands were often migrant workers that had taken up with a new partner in the towns or cities where they worked. The first step often taken by wives was to seek arbitration within the family, and if this failed, they turned to the courts. The institution of court action in such instances was often an attempt to rebalance the marital relationship and renegotiate the distribution of household resources. This was evident in the case of Sylvia Mujaya who sued her husband, Wellington Madzimure, for maintenance in the Zaka Community Court in 1985. During the pre-trial conference she informed the court that, 'I made these maintenance summons to respondent because I was not aware of his whereabouts so I am asking the court to withdraw the claim so that we go and discuss the whole issue at home. If he declines to maintain his child I will come back and cause maintenance summons against him.'[67]

---

[67] NAZ Masvingo, Zaka Community Court Maintenance Cases, Loc 7-1-8F, Box 3563, *S. Mujaya v W. Madzimure.*

Table 6.2 *Zaka District Statistics for Civil Cases*

Year	No. of Maintenance Cases	No. of Civil cases
1980	No Records (NR)	Records Missing (RM)
1981	NR	RM
1982	NR	RM
1983	33	RM
1984	100	RM
1985	148	411
1986	266	264
1987	306	229
1988	219	293
1989	RM	203
1990	194	167

As in other districts, the courts in Bikita and Zaka tended to be sympathetic towards the women who filed maintenance suits.[68] The ruling handed down in the maintenance case brought by Shylet Gondo against her erstwhile lover Philip Tapfuma provides an example of the tone taken by presiding officers and is worth quoting at some length. In giving his reasons for ruling against Tapfuma, the Presiding Officer, T. Kwenda, made the following observations:

Assuming that the respondent never fell in love with the applicant let alone to have sexual intercourse with her then why would the applicant had [sic] the audacity to falsely implicate him. The applicant gave her evidence well to the satisfaction of the court neither did she contradict herself under cross examination. The respondent did not adduce any evidence that the applicant was having affairs with other men besides him. It is highly improbable for a woman to falsely implicate a man she never had an opportunity to have sex with for having impregnated her. The child is similar to the respondent in every respect particularly the facial structures and the complexion. Although the court cannot rely on this phenomenon in paternity dispute but the probative value of this evidence combined with other factual issues relevant to a particular case cannot be completely ignored. In actual

---

[68] Kazembe makes a similar observation about Community Court rulings in custody cases in 'The Women Issue', 389.

words the respondent is being falsely implicated for fathering a child whom by coincidence bears a striking resemblance to him despite the fact that he never had any sexual intercourse with the applicant.[69]

In some cases, just filing a maintenance suit was sufficient to persuade the errant husband to agree to support his child(ren). In such instances, the husband signed a consent order which was ratified by the court. The wording of these consent orders clearly captures the role played by the Community Courts in enforcing this new social norm. In the case of *Loveness Mbetu v. Servias Gwenhure*, the consent order read: 'I Gwenhure Servias have freely and voluntarily without influence entered a consent agreement with applicant (LOVENESS MBETU) whereby I will pay to her $60-00 per month as maintenance for three children namely Callisto, Elizabeth and Memory. That I shall purchase clothing for the children every month the amount of which is not included in the aforesaid maintenance fees. This agreement shall be effective as from the 30th of December 1985 and thereafter payments shall be made on the 31st of each succeeding month.'[70]

Conclusion

The 1980s witnessed a substantial degree of transformation in the legal system in Zimbabwe. Under the banner of building a modern socialist society, the new government took several steps to change the racial composition of the personnel in the legal system, and the legal provisions governing the status and rights of women. There were also efforts to replace the system of chiefs and headmen's courts with the Primary Courts system. These reforms were progressive in as far as they democratised the legal system and removed the racial and gender barriers to full citizenship. However, the reforms were also connected to the new government's state-making project. Africanisation allowed for the new government to staff legal institutions with its

---

[69] NAZ Masvingo, Bikita Magistrates Court Maintenance cases 1990, *Shylet Gondo v Philip Tapfuma* M108/09.

[70] NAZ Masvingo, Zaka Community Court, 1985, Loc 10-6-6R, Box 3567, *Loveness Mbetu v. Servias Gwenhure*, case M139/85. The following cases in the same file have similarly worded consent orders: *Emmaculate Chirombedze v. Francis Chirombedze*, case M36/85; *Tendai Makovera v. Marron Kujere*, case M35/85; *Franscisca Tapudzayi v. Jabson Tapudzayi*, case M125/85.

own appointees, and the creation of the Primary Courts System was in part about ensuring the state's monopoly over the exercise of judicial authority. In addition, the moves by the state to 'modernise' the administration of 'customary law' led to an increased degree of inter-penetration between state law and 'customary law'. This was evident in the curriculum for trainee Community Court POs, and the increasing incorporation of the symbols, concepts and procedures of state law into primary courts. This process was to some extent reversed by the Customary Law and Courts Act of 1990 and the attendant resurgence of 'traditional' leaders. However, the fact that social disputes were placed outside chiefs' jurisdiction ensured that the gains, with respect to women's rights, were not reversed.

7 | Continuity and Consolidation: Law and Politics in Zimbabwe, 1980–1990

Introduction

In a much celebrated speech made on the eve of independence, the Prime Minister, Robert Mugabe, announced a policy of national reconciliation declaring: 'If yesterday I fought you as an enemy, today you have become a friend and ally with the same national interest, loyalty, rights and duties as myself. If yesterday you hated me, today you cannot avoid the love that binds you to me and me to you. The wrongs of the past must now stand forgiven and forgotten.'[1] Mugabe followed up this language of reconciliation with the laudable gesture of appointing to his cabinet five ZAPU officials and three from the Rhodesian Front.[2] These developments signalled the possibility that the country could make a break with its long history of political turmoil and state repression of political dissent. However, these positive steps were outweighed by a number of historical and contingent factors that ultimately pulled the country back into the violence and intolerance that had characterised its politics for the last three decades. Between 1980 and 1990, the government repeatedly renewed the nationwide state of emergency that had been in place since 1965. During this period, thousands of citizens were abducted, tortured, maimed and killed by government forces. Like its predecessors, the new government reverted to using law and legal discourse in order to justify and facilitate its repression of political dissent.

[1] R. Mugabe, 'Long Live our Freedom', 17 April 1980, http://www.kubatana.net/ html/archive/demgg/070221rm.asp?sector=OPIN&year=2007&range_start=31, retrieved, 14 December 2012.
[2] ZANU (PF) won 57 of the 80 common roll seats in 1980, whereas ZAPU won 20 seats. The remaining three seats went to the Muzorewa-led United African National Council. The Rhodesian Front won all 20 parliamentary seats that were reserved for white Zimbabweans. As a result, Ian Smith and some of his close associates from the 1970s continued to be involved in politics during the 1980s.

Whereas the previous chapter examined the progressive, if contested, efforts to transform the legal system in Zimbabwe during the first decade of independence, this one shifts the focus onto an area in which the working of the law was characterised by continuity and consolidation. It makes three main arguments. First, it argues that in the area of politics, the government followed in the footsteps of its predecessors and mobilised a discourse of law and order to criminalize political opposition. In doing so, it drew on the same institutions and practices, and invoked the same justifications in order to silence political dissent. However, these continuities were not solely about the legacies of settler rule. They were partly a product of the authoritarian tendencies that had begun to emerge within the nationalist movement from the mid-1970s, especially within the military camps.[3] Second, it maintains that, although the legal system had become one of the few available avenues of challenging political persecution in the 1980s, the circumstances were such that citizen's legal agency proved to be largely ineffective against a vindictive state. Last, it shows that after independence the content and administration of the law continued to be a source of tension within the state. However, in the 1980s the most significant tensions were between senior members of the executive and the judiciary. In analysing these tensions, the chapter challenges the argument advanced by legal scholars that the actions of the judiciary in the early 1980s were shaped solely by its commitment to the rule of law.[4] Instead, it factors politics into our understanding of the decisions made by the judiciary.

The Slide Back to Political Repression

One of the factors that explain the continued legal repression in the political sphere is the institutional legacy of the settler state. In 1980,

---

[3] See J. Alexander, 'View from the Liberation Movement Camps in Zambia', paper presented at the Britain Zimbabwe Research Day, June 2012; and G. C. Mazarire, 'Discipline and Punishment in ZANLA: 1964–1979', *Journal of Southern African Studies*, 37 (2011). See also Chung, *Reliving the Second Chimurenga*.

[4] See J. Hatchard, *Individual Liberties and State Security in the African Context: The Case of Zimbabwe* (Harare, 1993); and T. Biti, 'The Judiciary, the Executive and the Rule of Law in Zimbabwe', in S. Kayizzi-Mugerwa, A. O. Olukoshi, L. Wohlgemuth (eds), *Towards a New Partnership with Africa: Challenges and Opportunities* (Uppsala, 1998).

the new government inherited a security apparatus that had increasingly been oriented towards crushing political dissent. The new Constitution agreed to at Lancaster House had a number of provisions that could, in theory, be used to check state repression. The Bill of Rights, for example, provided for a range of justiciable individual rights and freedoms which were applicable to all Zimbabweans regardless of race or gender. These included the freedoms of speech, association and movement, as well as the freedom from arbitrary search and discrimination.[5] The Supreme Court Act also stipulated that anyone who believed that the Bill of Rights had been violated could apply directly to the Supreme Court for a hearing.

However, these progressive legal provisions were weakened by the stipulation that, for the first five years of independence, none of the inherited laws could be struck down on the grounds that they contravened the Bill of Rights. In addition, the legal protections could easily be invalidated by the constitutional provision which empowered the President to declare a state of emergency for a maximum of six months. Under emergency powers, the executive could effectively make law without reference to Parliament, and it could take actions that violated the provisions of the Bill of Rights such as effecting detention without trial. Admittedly, the declaration of a state of emergency was subject to approval by a simple majority of Parliament within fourteen days, and could only be renewed by means of a vote in Parliament. However, ZANU (PF) could easily overcome these checks and balances using its overwhelming majority in Parliament.

The second important factor was the authoritarian tradition of maintaining law and order that had emerged within ZANU (PF) during the 1970s particularly in the military camps. As Gerald Mazarire's study of ZANLA camps shows, internal dissent was met with severe corporeal punishment, and this became part of the military command's standard approach to maintaining discipline.[6] There was, of course, another legal tradition in ZANU (PF), one which was reflected in the critiques of the Rhodesian legal system articulated by nationalists, lawyers and guerrillas. This tradition held justice, rule of law and the respect for human rights as important ideals. Nevertheless, it

---

[5] Constitution of Zimbabwe (Lancaster House), chapter three – Declaration of Rights.
[6] Mazarire, 'Discipline and Punishment', 579–82.

was the more authoritarian tradition that asserted itself in the political sphere during the 1980s.

A third factor was the reality that beneath the euphoria of independence and the rhetoric of reconciliation were simmering tensions that rendered the country's peace and unity precarious. Soon after independence, the new government was faced with the complex task of integrating the three armies – ZIPRA, ZANLA and the Rhodesian Security Forces – that had recently been enemies on the battlefield. The two guerrilla armies had a history of tense relations and had clashed on a number of occasions during the 1970s, and the antipathy between them was worsened by the negative propaganda that was spread in their respective camps during the 1970s. The transition from war to peace was also impeded by indiscipline amongst ex-combatants, the provocative actions of the Rhodesian Security Forces, as well as armed criminals that were terrorising the countryside.

The law and order problems in the country were initially not viewed in partisan terms, but were instead seen as being part of the aftermath of a long and bitter war. When Herbert Ushewokunze, the Minister of Home Affairs, approached Parliament to request the renewal of the state of emergency in July 1980, he presented the security problems as being due, among other things, to interparty rivalry, frustration and boredom within the assembly points, as well as the 'possession of firearms and grenades by unauthorised persons'.[7] Regarding the problem of dissidents, he explained: 'I am not talking here of persons who have temporarily left assembly places. I am talking about people who have no loyalty to any political party or to Government. They use their weapons to force innocent civilians to hand over food and money. They commit robbery, rape and generally harass the population in rural areas.'[8]

Ushewokunze was also anxious to see key institutions of the state, such as the police, regain legitimacy in the eyes of the political leaders and the public to help in restoring law and order. He thus observed:

Another source of security problem [sic] is the hostility shown to Government agencies, particularly the Police as a body. The Police can only operate effectively if they have the backing and the confidence of the majority of

[7] *Zimbabwe Parliamentary Debates*, 23 July 1980, 1097.
[8] Ibid., 1096.

the population ... Disparaging statements by some party officials and others about the Police and other lawful authorities can only erode the public confidence in these authorities. The power of the Police and of the courts and of other Government agencies, must be protected so that they are not usurped.[9]

He also tried to allay any concerns about his request for the renewal of the state of emergency by assuring the House that many aspects of the security legislation which had been passed in the 1970s would be repealed. These included the power of the police to seize, destroy or confiscate property, and to impose curfews. In addition, the legislation providing for the censorship of all information relating to security forces and the imposition of collective fines and the establishment of special courts would also be repealed.

The second reason he gave for the renewal of the state of emergency was that, without it, many important regulations which had not yet been transferred to the statute books would fall away, thus creating a regulatory vacuum.[10] Although this argument seemed plausible in 1980, it continued to be used throughout the 1980s and became one of the standard pretexts for perpetuating the state of emergency.[11] The government increasingly made use of emergency powers in matters that had little to do with the security situation. Of the seventy-three Statutory Instruments introduced under emergency powers during the 1980s, fewer than fifteen were related to security, and the rest dealt with routine administrative matters such as changing the names of towns and cities, and revising liquor prices, taxes and minimum wages.[12]

The Minister's request was met with discomfort by many MPs who felt that the measure bore too strong a resemblance with the practices of the Smith Regime. The sentiments expressed by Swithun Mombeshora, a ZANU (PF) MP and the Deputy Minister of Agriculture, were shared by several legislators. He observed: 'I would like to say that I support the State of Emergency as proposed but also sincerely hope it will be the last time we sit in this House asking for the renewal of the State of Emergency.'[13] Notwithstanding these reservations, the renewal of the State of Emergency was supported by all ZANU (PF) and ZAPU MPs.

---

[9] Ibid., 1097–8.
[10] Ibid., 1100.
[11] Hatchard, *Individual Liberties and State Security*, 23.
[12] Ibid., 187–8.
[13] *Zimbabwe Parliamentary Debates*, 23 July 1980, 1120.

However, the unanimity around the state of emergency was short lived. This was in large part due to the armed clashes between ZANLA and ZIPRA ex-combatants in the Bulawayo township of Entumbane in November 1980. The clashes were triggered by inflammatory comments made by Enos Nkala, the ZANU (PF) Minister of Finance, to party supporters at the White City Stadium in Bulawayo. In his speech, he had threatened ZAPU members with violence and declared 'I will crush Joshua Nkomo'.[14] ZANU (PF) members later claimed that they had been provoked by ZAPU supporters who were throwing stones at them during the rally.[15] However, what is clear is that it was Nkala's inflammatory language and his public call for retaliation that led to the clashes between supporters of the two parties. The ex-combatants of both parties, who had by then been moved from the assembly points and settled in Entumbane Township, joined the clashes in support of their respective party members, and the result was two days of armed battles in the city.

The government's biased response to these clashes played a key role in escalating the conflict. To begin with, the clashes were followed by selective arrests and prosecutions which targeted ZIPRA ex-combatants. In addition, ruling party politicians largely blamed the law and order problems on ZAPU, and its officials and supporters began to be discursively constructed as being outside of the nation and posing a threat to it.[16] Through this process, they were rendered legitimate targets of government-directed violence and, by extension, the rights of citizenship enshrined in the country's new Constitution were seen as not being applicable to them.

When Herbert Ushewokunze came before Parliament in January 1981 to request a further renewal of the state of emergency, it was clear that ZANU (PF) now viewed ZAPU as the problem. Although the ZANU (PF) MPs were convinced that the state of emergency was necessary to deal with the threat to law and order, they were at pains to distinguish their actions from those of the Rhodesian Front. Senator George Chinengundu, a lawyer and the Deputy Minister of Local Government, for example argued that 'The State of emergency in the past was primarily directed at muzzling all political opposition,

---

[14] Lawyers Committee for Human Rights, *Zimbabwe: Wages of War, A Report on Human Rights*, (New York, 1986) 51.
[15] *Zimbabwe Parliamentary Debates*, 21 January 1981, 1316.
[16] Werbner, 'Smoke from the Barrel of a Gun', 92–3.

imprisoning all politicians, and such like things. The State of Emergency at the moment is directed at violent sections [sic] by dissidents, and it is not directed at any particular party.'[17] Chinengundu defended the actions of the government on the grounds that such exceptional powers were necessary to protect the rights of citizens:

Indeed we need to protect the rights of the individuals and the state of emergency should not unnecessarily derogate from those rights of individuals. But if the State of Emergency is not strong enough to protect the rights of individuals, those rights will become useless because the State itself cannot protect them. The state needs to strengthen itself in order to be able to protect the rights of the individual and this is what the Minister is seeking to do.[18]

Contrary to Chinengundu's claims, the government was in fact 'muzzling all political opposition' as the RF had done. In addition, his justifications were reminiscent of the arguments advanced by the hardliners in the Southern Rhodesian Parliament from the 1950s in order to justify the repressive legal measures that were being passed in order to quell nationalist agitation. Above all, they contradicted the critiques of the law that had been forcefully articulated during the 1960s and 1970s by black lawyers like himself as well as nationalists and guerrillas.

By contrast, ZAPU MPs were no longer convinced that the state of emergency was an appropriate solution to the country's problems. Their arguments were summed up by Edward Ndlovu, the MP for Matabeleland South, who pointed out that 'Peace and unity cannot be achieved by State of Emergency.'[19] Amidst heckling from ZANU members, including the Minister of Home Affairs, Ndlovu voiced his misgivings about ZANU PF's intentions:

I tend to agree with some people who may claim that too much power can be dangerous, and by the way there is a danger of misusing the State of Emergency. – [AN HON MEMBER: Anybody who is not subversive, has nothing to fear.] – [HON MEMBERS: Hear, hear.] This interrupting has let the cat out of the bag because we demand peace and unity, and

[17] *Zimbabwe Parliamentary Debates*, 21 January 1981, 1308.
[18] Ibid., 1307.
[19] Ibid,. 1305–6.

certain people fail on how to approach this particularly important problem of peace and unity. Then when they are criticised they say some people are subversive.[20]

The ZAPU leader, Joshua Nkomo, called for dialogue pointing out that it was unnecessary to resort to such extreme measures. Instead, he proposed that the party caucuses be tasked with devising more effective solutions; however, his suggestions went unheeded. The misgivings of ZAPU legislators about the state of emergency were shared by members of the Rhodesian Front. Mr Goddard, the MP for Lundi, for example, was not far from the truth in arguing that 'the government is seeking to renew a State of Emergency not because there is a threat to national security but rather that the Government wants to continue to abuse the powers that it is afforded under a State of Emergency for its own party.'[21]

In February 1981, directly following the renewal of the state of emergency, serious armed clashes between ZANLA and ZIPRA ex-combatants erupted again in Entumbane and some areas in the Midlands Province, resulting in the deaths of over 300 people.[22] Soon after these clashes, thousands of ZIPRA ex-combatants in the army began to desert out of fear for their safety. Some of the deserters took to the bush as 'dissidents' and perpetrated numerous robberies, murders, rapes, and acts of sabotage in Matabeleland, Midlands, and Masvingo provinces.[23] The strained relationship between ZANU (PF) and ZAPU was worsened by a number of incidents that occurred in 1981 and 1982. A key incident was the discovery of arms caches, in February 1982, on properties owned by the ZAPU company Nitram and in areas close to ZAPU assembly points. The properties in question were confiscated, all the ZAPU cabinet ministers were dismissed and former ZIPRA commanders were charged with treason.[24] Although the arms caches were treated as irrefutable evidence of a treasonous plot, in reality both ZANLA and ZIPRA ex-combatants had stashed arms during

---

[20] Ibid., 1306.
[21] Ibid., 1332.
[22] Catholic Commission for Justice and Peace (CCJP) and Legal Resources Foundation (LRF), *Breaking the Silence, Building True Peace: A Report on the Disturbances in Matabeleland and the Midlands, 1980–1988* (Harare, 1999), 5.
[23] Ibid., 32–3.
[24] Alexander et al., *Violence and Memory*, 188.

the 1970s, and in the aftermath of the Entumbane clashes.[25] In addition, some of these caches had been planted by Central Intelligence Organisation (CIO) double agents who were being paid by the South African government to foment tension between ZANU (PF) and ZAPU. The attack on the Prime Minister's residence in June 1982, and the killing of six tourists in Matabeleland North by ZIPRA ex-combatants, worsened relations further and strengthened the government's resolve to crack down on ZAPU.

The security situation was also compounded by the efforts of the apartheid government in South Africa to destabilise Zimbabwe, actions which increased the sense of siege on the part of the Zimbabwean government.[26] As alluded to earlier, South African authorities recruited CIO officers as double agents who sabotaged several key sites in Zimbabwe and disseminated false allegations that ZAPU was planning to overthrow the government. In August 1981, South African agents attacked a munitions store at Inkomo Barracks on the outskirts of Harare, destroying Z$50 million worth of ammunition. In December that year, they bombed the ZANU (PF) headquarters in Harare and almost killed many senior leaders including Mugabe. This was followed by the bombing of the Thornhill Airbase in July 1982, which destroyed thirteen military planes, and a month later three white South African soldiers were killed during armed clashes in Zimbabw.[27] Another aspect of the apartheid government's destabilisation efforts was Operation Drama which was launched in late 1982. The operation involved the training of approximately 100 armed dissidents who came to be known as 'Super ZAPU' and operated in Zimbabwe in 1983 and 1984.

It cannot be denied that the new government was faced with a complicated security situation in the 1980s. Nevertheless, as ZAPU politicians like Nkomo pointed out, the problems did not necessitate a nationwide state of emergency. The attacks by South African agents could have been treated as criminal offences under existing legislation, and the disturbances in areas such as Manicaland and Matabeleland could have been dealt with by means of a localised state of emergency.[28]

---

[25] Ibid.
[26] *Breaking the Silence, Building True Peace: A Report on the Disturbances in Matabeleland and the Midlands 1980–1988*, Catholic Commission for Justice aand Peace and Legal Resources Foundation (Harare 1999), 29–30.
[27] Alexander et al., *Violence and Memory*, 89.
[28] Hatchard, *Individual Freedoms and State Security*, 24.

What is more, the 'dissident problem' was at its core a political problem which required solutions of the sort that ZAPU MPs were suggesting. By choosing to see the problem as one of law and order which required the extraordinary powers provided for under the emergency powers legislation, the government not only foreclosed more appropriate solutions, it also worsened the situation. The brutal crackdown on citizens in Matabeleland by state agencies pushed ex-combatants and youth into the ranks of the dissidents and led to increased attacks by dissidents. It also engendered an enduring sense of political alienation for many residents of the region.

Like the Rhodesian Front, ZANU (PF) had embraced the state of exception as a feature of its statecraft. The national state of emergency was declared largely because it enabled the executive to bypass the Parliament in making legislation, allowed for the deployment of the security forces, and provided for indefinite detention of ZANU (PF)'s political opponents. However, the most serious abuses that were perpetrated in the 1980s, such as the abductions, rapes, brutal assaults and mass murders, were not sanctioned by the state of emergency. In these instances, the state of emergency did not suspend the juridical order, so much as it enabled the government to create zones that were relatively closed to scrutiny where security forces were given free reign. As a consequence, one of the first moves taken by the President after the massacres in Matabeleland was to grant blanket amnesty to all the government forces and 'dissidents' who had been involved in it.

The most notorious of the state bodies which were actively involved in terrorising ZAPU supporters was the Fifth Brigade. The Brigade consisted of ex-ZANLA combatants selected from the Tongogara Assembly Point, and, unlike other Brigades in the army, it reported directly to Mugabe. Whereas the rest of the army had been trained by British Instructors, the Fifth Brigade was trained by North Korean instructors. In the areas in which the Brigade was deployed, it was a law unto itself and it wantonly killed, wounded, raped and destroyed the property of residents.[29] The enactment of the violence often took on an ethnic character, with predominantly Shona-speaking soldiers brutalising Ndebele and Kalanga-speaking villagers and forcing them

---

[29] *Breaking the Silence*, 45–60. See also Alexander et al., *Violence and Memory*, chapter 9; and R. Werbner, *Tears of the Dead: The Social Biography of an African Family* (Edinburgh, 1991).

to sing Shona songs. Moreover, the killings were systematic, and the dead were ferried by government vehicles and disposed of in mass graves and abandoned mines. In addition to the violence, the Brigade imposed a curfew in Matabeleland South in 1984 which included a restriction on food movements, and this had a devastating effect on the region which was already suffering from a severe drought.[30]

Although the military operation in Matabeleland was premised on the grounds that the populace was in support of the dissidents, in reality the dissidents enjoyed little popular support. As Alexander, McGregor and Ranger note, the residents of Matabeleland did not identify with this new war in the way they had done with the anti-colonial struggle.[31] The demands made by dissidents placed a burden on their food supplies during the extended drought of the early 1980s. Moreover, the violence and robberies perpetrated by the dissidents, and the fact that their presence exposed civilians to attacks by government forces, made the residents of Matabeleland less inclined to support the dissidents. The government's attacks on the residents of Matabeleland by state forces had more to do with crushing ZAPU than with dealing with the 'dissident problem'. At the root of the government-directed violence was an intolerance of political dissent, which was also evident in its aspirations of creating a one-party state.[32]

In the run up to the 1985 general elections, the government adopted a new strategy in its efforts to crush ZAPU.[33] More emphasis began to be placed on targeting all levels of the ZAPU leadership. As a result, in the first four months of 1985, dozens of local ZAPU officials were abducted from their homes at night by armed men. The ZAPU victory in all fifteen Parliamentary seats in Matabeleland proved that the party was still strong, and resulted in an intensified crackdown on its officials, directed by the new Minister of Home Affairs, Enos Nkala. Although Nkala was originally from Matabeleland, he took to the task of cracking down on ZAPU with fervour, and announced to the Senate in September 1985 that 'the policy of reconciliation toward ZAPU has been withdrawn.' In his characteristically inflammatory language, he declared: 'We want to wipe out the Zapu leadership. You've only seen

---

[30] *Breaking the Silence*, 56.
[31] Alexander et al., *Violence and Memory*, 210–17.
[32] A motion proposing a one party state was debated in Parliament in September 1984. See *Zimbabwe Parliamentary Debates*, 5 September 1984, 1568–95.
[33] *Zimbabwe: Wages of War*, 30.

the warning lights. We haven't yet reached full blast. I don't want to hear pleas for mercy. I only want encouragement to deal with this dissident organisation ... the murderous organisation and its murderous leadership must be hit so hard that it doesn't feel obliged to do the things that it has been doing.'[34]

Consequently, from 1985 there was a significant rise in the number of abductions by the CIO and the Police Internal Security Intelligence (PISI) Unit, two institutions with roots in the period of settler rule. Following the elections, all the black councillors on the Bulawayo City Council were detained, as were five ZAPU MPs, Sidney Malunga, Kembo Mohadi, Stephen Nkomo, Edward Ndlovu and Welshman Mabhena. In addition, eight senior members of the army who were ZIPRA ex-combatants were also detained in 1985. Malunga, who was the ZAPU Chief Whip and a vocal critic of the massacres in Matabeleland, was later tried for treason in 1986.[35]

Alongside this crackdown on ZAPU, negotiations were initiated between ZANU (PF) and ZAPU in 1985.[36] Throughout 1986, the parties failed to reach an agreement, and the talks broke down in April 1987. Nkala responded by banning ZAPU public meetings and rallies, closing all ZAPU offices around the country, and dissolving six ZAPU-dominated local authorities in Matabeleland North. This increased pressure forced ZAPU back to the negotiating table and culminated in the December 1987 Unity Accord, which brought about an end to the violence of the 1980s and led to ZAPU's absorption by ZANU (PF).

In sum, during the period immediately following independence, there were some reasons to hope that law and order could be restored, that politics would be conducted in a more tolerant way and that the new Bill of Rights would protect all citizens against political persecution. However, these hopes were soon dashed. The combination of ZANU (PF)'s authoritarian traits, the legacy of state repression and the animus between ZAPU and ZANU (PF) ultimately led the new government to revert to the practices of its predecessors. The state of emergency, which had initially been renewed in order to give the government time to transfer important regulations onto the statute books, ultimately came to be used as a means of targeting and

[34] *The Herald*, 19 September 1985.
[35] *Breaking the Silence*, 70.
[36] Alexander et al., *Violence and Memory*, 229.

persecuting political opponents and their supporters. The new government embraced the institutions and the laws established by the Smith regime, and in some cases, even the personnel that had served that regime. Political dissent came to be viewed as 'subversive', and 'security' was placed above the rights of citizens. In the face of this continued state repression, it is worth asking: To what extent could, and did, citizens employ the law as a shield against state repression? It is to this question that the chapter now turns.

Engaging the Government in the Courts

During the 1970s, the legal system had been one of many sites of engaging the settler state and was certainly secondary to the armed struggle. By contrast, in the 1980s it was one of the few potential sources of protection for individuals facing political persecution, as the vast majority of these individuals were neither engaged in, nor supportive of an armed struggle. Nevertheless, the extent to which the law could be used as a shield during this period was limited. This was largely because in the area of politics, the new government had deliberately chosen not to adhere to the legalism of the settler state. This unwillingness to be bound by the law was evident in the fact that new institutions such as the Ombudsman's Office, that were created to ensure the accountability of state officials were not granted oversight over the security forces.[37] It is not a coincidence that all of the state bodies which were central to the brutal repression of political opposition in the 1980s, such as the army, the police, the prison service and the CIO, were exempt from the Ombudsman's oversight.

Statements by senior government officials also attested to the new government's unwillingness to be hindered by the law from taking any actions it deemed to be necessary in dealing with its political opponents. In an address to Parliament in 1982, Mugabe made it clear that his government was willing to take what he described as 'extra-legal' measures to deal with the security problems in the country.[38] The Deputy Prime Minister, Simon Muzenda, also invoked the 'state of exception' argument in a way that was eerily reminiscent of the RF. In

---

[37] G. Feltoe, 'A Survey of Major Legislation in the Period 1980–1984', *ZLR*, 1 & 2 (1983–1984), 278.

[38] *Zimbabwe Parliamentary Debates*, 29 July 1982.

a response to the Report of the Lawyers Committee for Human Rights on the gross abuses in Matabeleland, he argued,

Human rights are not *per se* legal questions but also inextricably part and parcel of the POLITICAL fabric and stability of any Nation state. While you have observed the near complete disappearance of human rights in Matabeleland (1st paragraph page 33 of your draft report), you do not seem to have drawn the correspondingly necessary conclusion, namely that there comes a time when a government has to assert its authority in the name of, and for the sake of the majority when a recalcitrant tiny minority is persistently violating the human rights of the majority. It takes such action in ORDER TO RESTORE AND UPHOLD HUMAN RIGHTS. This is precisely what is taking place in Western Zimbabwe.[39]

The capacity of the law to protect citizens was also undermined by the weak capacity of institutions such as the Zimbabwe Republic Police and the Attorney General's office. The repeated renewal of the state of emergency since the 1960s had undermined the respect for and ability to follow due process in these institutions.[40] This was reinforced by the fact that new personnel employed after 1980 were being trained in an environment where proper legal procedure was routinely subordinated to the goal of quelling political dissent.

The effectiveness of the law as a shield for citizens was also undermined by the fact that the dock had limited value as a platform from which to articulate critiques of the state. This was partly because the local and international audience for courtroom oratory in the 1980s was small and often lacked influence. In addition, while earlier critiques from the dock had drawn their power from being wedded to the broader nationalist struggle, in the 1980s there was no broader political movement for the victims of government-directed violence to tap into. Another key challenge facing the victims of political persecution in the 1980s was their limited access to legal representation. Whereas in the 1970s organisations such as the International Defence and Aid Fund, Christian Care, Amnesty International and the CCJP had provided funding for the legal representation of political prisoners, during

---

[39] Letter from Deputy Prime Minister S. V. Muzenda to Michael Posner, 30 April 1986. Cited in *Zimbabwe: Wages of War*, 164. (Emphasis in original).
[40] Interview with Bryant Elliot, Harare, 4 April 2011. See also *Zimbabwe: Wages of War*.

the 1980s there were limited funds for this purpose. This limited access to legal representation was confirmed by Simplisius Chihambakwe, the chairperson of the Detainees Review Tribunal, who noted that only a third of those who appeared before it were legally represented.[41] Due to the costs involved in instituting legal action, many of the prominent cases involving citizens who sued the state for violation of their rights were filed by white Zimbabweans.[42] In a number of cases, these individuals were successful in their suits, and the Supreme Court awarded damages for abuses by government agents. However, the practical implications of these rulings in these cases were limited as the judgements were not publicised; therefore, there was limited knowledge of the protection that the law provided in such instances. In addition, the government often refused to pay the damages, and there were no legal means of enforcing payment because the State Liabilities Act prohibited plaintiffs from attaching government property.

One of the early cases against the state was filed by Wally Stuttaford, a Rhodesian Front MP who was charged in December 1981 with plotting to overthrow the government. He was held in custody for a month during which he was tortured and denied access to a lawyer.[43] After he was acquitted of the criminal charges against him, Stuttaford instituted legal action against the government. In order to avoid negative publicity, the Minister of Justice, Simbi Mubako, resorted to a tactic used by his predecessors in the 1970s and ordered the trial to be conducted *in camera*.[44]

Following the ruling in the Stuttaford case, the government introduced the Emergency Powers (Security Forces Indemnity) Regulations in 1983, which were meant to protect state officials from civil or criminal action if they were acting 'in good faith' for the protection of state

---

[41] *Zimbabwe: Wages of War*, 154.
[42] See the following High Court cases: *J. S. V. Hickman and P. T. McDonald v. Minister of Home Affairs and the Chairman of the Detainee Review Tribunal; A. F. York and N. E. York v. Minister of Home Affairs and the Director of Prisons; R. H. Wood v. Minister of Home Affairs; C. J. van der Walt v. The State; C. D. Evans and P. E. Hartlebury v. The Chairman of the Review Tribunal and the Minister of Home Affairs; J. V. Austin and K. N. Harper v. The Minister of State (Security) and the Commissioner of the Zimbabwe Republic Police.*
[43] *Zimbabwe: Wages of War*, 99–100.
[44] It later emerged that Stuttaford had been awarded the equivalent of US$ 4,500 in damages by the High Court. See *Breaking the Silence*, 69.

security. However, the regulations came under judicial scrutiny in a Supreme Court case brought by Dennis Granger, a lawyer who had been detained and tortured by the CIO on suspicion that he was a foreign spy. The CIO's suspicions had been aroused by the fact that he had been seen taking photographs on a road in Harare. Granger was in fact photographing the scene of an accident for a case he was handling. He won his case and the Supreme Court awarded him Z$1,200.00 in damages. An important outcome of the trial was the Supreme Court decision that the 'good faith' provision of the Emergency Powers (Security Forces Indemnity) Regulations was declared 'void by reasons of inconsistency with the Constitution'.[45]

Amongst the most prominent political cases of the period were the series of lawsuits brought on behalf of the ex-ZIPRA commanders, Dumiso Dabengwa and Lookout Masuku. In one case, the wives of the two men sought a court order to enable them to have access to lawyers.[46] Another lawsuit challenged the legality of Dabengwa's continued detention, on the grounds that he was not being brought before the Detainees Review Tribunal every six months as stipulated in the law. In yet another lawsuit, Dabengwa applied to the High Court for permission to attend the funeral of Lookout Masuku whose health had deteriorated severely during his time in custody.[47] In most of these cases, Dabengwa was unsuccessful, and while the court found in his favour during the treason trial of 1982, he was immediately served with a detention order and was released only in 1986.

Notwithstanding their gruelling experiences, in some respects senior ZAPU officials such as Dabengwa and Masuku were more fortunate than local party officials and supporters and rank-and-file ex-combatants. For the most part, they were not subjected to torture and had access to lawyers and the courts. By contrast, many lower level ZAPU officials and ZIPRA ex-combatants were simply abducted in the night and were never heard from again, and others were detained under emergency powers. These detentions were effected by means of Section 21,

---

[45] SPA File, *Sledge Muradzikwa and 8 other v. The Honourable Emmerson Mnangagwa.*

[46] See the following High Court Cases: *Z. Dabengwa and G. Masuku v. Minister of Home Affairs, The Protecting Authority Harare North Province and The Commissioner of the Zimbabwe Republic Police,* as well as *D. Dabengwa v. Minister of Home Affairs and the Director of Prisons.*

[47] See the High Court Case *D. Dabengwa v. Minister of Home Affairs.*

which allowed the police to detain anyone for up to thirty days if they thought there were grounds for their indefinite detention. Alternatively, state officials could employ Section 53 (1), which provided for detention for up to thirty days regardless of whether there were grounds for indefinite detention via Ministerial order. Regarding the experiences of individuals detained under these two clauses, the LCHR observed that

Many individuals initially detained under Section 21 or 53 (1) remain in detention for periods exceeding 30 days, in some cases significantly longer. These individuals receive the fewest possible protections because their detentions are technically illegal. The vast majority of these individuals are not prominent enough to attract public attention. They are likely to have limited financial resources and thus cannot afford legal representation, and so they simply languish in detention until the authorities decide to release them.[48]

It went on to note that: 'The few who do have legal counsel often are advised not to assert the illegality of their continued detention. Attorneys fear that a successful challenge would not lead to the release of the detainee but would instead provoke retaliation against the detainee in the form of a Section 17 Ministerial Order permitting indefinite detention.'[49]

As a lawyer based in Bulawayo, S. K. M. Sibanda dealt with numerous cases involving people accused of political offences by the government. One of the senior ZAPU officials he represented was Swazini Ndlovu, who had been taken into custody in March 1982 on suspicion of being connected to the ZIPRA arms caches. He was initially detained in Khami Prison outside Bulawayo, before being transferred to Chikurubi Prison in Harare. Despite being cleared of any involvement with the arms caches, he was kept in detention as new investigations over his involvement in the murder of Stanislus Marembo, a ZAPU official, were being carried out. Subsequent enquiries by Sibanda revealed that Ndlovu was being investigated for yet another case involving the shooting at the Prime Minister's residence in June 1982.[50] What was troubling about Ndlovu's case was that, not only had he said the shooting happened after he had been detained, but

---

[48] *Zimbabwe: Wages of War*, 151.
[49] Ibid.
[50] SPA File, *State v. Swazini Ndlovu*, Sibanda to Senior Public Prosecutor, 1 December 1982.

when he was brought before the magistrate during the bi-weekly remand hearings at Chikurubi Prison, he was repeatedly told that there was no official record of his detention. After eight months in custody without being formally remanded or issued with a detention order, Ndlovu wrote to Sibanda in desperation. Ndlovu's letter revealed both his persistence in seeking legal recourse and his self-identification as a rights-bearing citizen. The letter read as follows:

Dear Sir

I am certain that if the magistrate fulfilled his promise he will have contacted you by the time you receive this letter. All the same I have decided to write you because this is the only means of contact provided by the authorities of this place. Sincere apologies for writing you c/o Stephen Mbizo. This has been necessitated by the fact that I do not have your address.

Well the first point that has necessitated my writing you is that the magistrate does not seem to have my name under those people he is remanding. If I am right, therefore, technically I have not been appearing before him.

There are a number of issues I had thought to raise with you including a direct appeal to the Chief Justice which I have not done up to now because I anticipated your arrival here. I would therefore want to know what the position is *vis a vis* the development in this case. What is my position as regards the investigating officer? Do I give them any statement in your absence or demand your presence?

I believe some movement is absolutely necessary so that I know if I am merely a political detainee rather than remaining a secret detainee camouflaged under spurious reasons. My rights as a citizen have been curtailed and I am not told why?

I am getting concerned very seriously about my 8 months detention with no reasons given at any time and I think that if it is impossible for any reason, on your side, to make any move, do inform me. I have nothing more to lose than my life

In anticipation
I remain
Swazini Ndlovu[51]

After receiving the letter, Sibanda entered into correspondence with the Attorney General's office in order to secure Ndlovu's release. In a letter to the Senior Public Prosecutor, Sibanda highlighted the plight of

[51] Ibid., Swazini Ndlovu to Sibanda, 3 November 1982.

his client and pointed out that 'the interest of the state should surely be balanced against the rights of the individual'.[52] Ndlovu was ultimately released in February 1983 after a year in detention without any charge having been made against him.

In another case, Sibanda defended Elias Mejo Sakana and Timothy Dube who had been arrested in 1982 under the Law and Order (Maintenance) Act for distributing subversive material. In this case, it was not the vindictiveness of the government that worked against Sakana and Dube, but the repressive provisions of the legislation which criminalised legitimate political activity. This in turn made it difficult for the two to offer an effective defence in court. The charges against the two men were based on a political pamphlet that Dube had picked up on the roadside in the Plumtree area. After reading it, he decided to pass it on to his friend Sakana, who was a ZAPU member and the Vice Chairman of the District Council. The pamphlet in question was addressed to 'All Patriots in Zimbabwe' and made a comprehensive critique of the new government's policies and challenged its Socialist claims.[53] The pamphlet proceeded to highlight the government's betrayal of the goals of the liberation struggle, and its divisive politics then concluded with a call for unity. Sakana distributed some copies amongst his friends in Plumtree, and a few days later he was informed that the police were looking for him. He reported to the police station where he was promptly arrested and charged with printing and circulating subversive material. The two men secured the services of Sibanda, but were ultimately convicted of printing and circulating 'subversive' material. Dube was sentenced to eighteen months in prison, twelve of which were suspended, while Sakana was sentenced to two years in prison with fourteen months suspended.

It was not only ZAPU and ZIPRA members that Sibanda defended in the 1980s. He also represented nine ZANU (PF) provincial officials who sued the Minister of State in the Prime Minister's Office responsible for Security, Emmerson Mnangagwa, for their torture at the hands of state agents in 1983. This case illustrates the fact that ZANU (PF) members were not exempt from state-directed violence, and underscores the new government's intolerance of political dissent, regardless

---

[52] Ibid., Sibanda to Senior Public Prosecutor, 28 January 1983.
[53] SPA File, *State v. Timothy Dube and Elias Sakana*, Statement by Sakana to Sibanda, (undated but likely to have been recorded around 23 June 1982).

Figure 7.1 Minister of State in the Prime Minister's office, Emmerson Mnangagwa

of its source. Sledge Muradzikwa, an ex-combatant, and eight other local ZANU (PF) officials in Gweru had fallen foul of the party's national leadership for resisting the efforts by the Central Committee to dismiss Patrick Kombayi from his post as the mayor of Gweru. In March 1983, Benson Ndemera, the party's Deputy Chairperson for Midlands Province, had called an emergency meeting in order to communicate this directive. However, the meeting descended into chaos when Ndemera failed to give a satisfactory reason for Kombayi's dismissal.[54]

The following day, local members of the ZANU (PF) Women's League staged a protest against the attempts by the Central Committee to impose its wishes on them. The protest was violently broken up by

[54] SPA File, *Sledge Muradzikwa and 8 others v. The Honourable Emmerson Mnangagwa*, Statement by Adrian Chinyama.

the police, and several local party leaders were arrested. Although the charges against them were later dropped, nine party officials who were considered to be at the forefront of this 'revolt' were later picked up in the middle of the night by the CIO. They were taken to Inyathi Police Station where they were accused of planning to overthrow the government and subjected to severe torture. Adrian Chinyama, the Deputy Chairperson of the Midlands Women's League, was amongst the nine. Despite the fact that she was pregnant, Chinyama was severely assaulted, subjected to water boarding, and kept in a cage. She ultimately had to be taken to hospital as a result of her torture.[55]

After their release a few weeks later, the nine filed a law suit claiming damages for their torture at the hands of state agents, but, their efforts to pursue the matter were repeatedly frustrated. Medical reports documenting the torture went missing under suspicious circumstances, and the Prime Minister issued a certificate under Section 4 (2) of the Emergency Powers (Security Forces Indemnity) Regulations of 1983, which provided blanket indemnity for the security agents involved. The certificate read:

I, ROBERT GABRIEL MUGABE in my capacity as the Minister of defence do hereby certify that any matter or thing referred to in this case as done by either the officers or members of the Central Intelligence Organisation or the Minister of State was done in good faith for the purpose of or in connexion with the preservation of the security of Zimbabwe.[56]

The case was scheduled to be heard on 24–27 February in 1987 and, given the Supreme Court's ruling in the Granger case, the nine stood a good chance of winning their case.[57] However, the case does not appear in the records for High Court judgments and is likely to have been withdrawn before trial.

Although some victims of government persecution sought legal recourse, there were others who no longer believed that the law held any remedial value. All too often their faith in the legal system

---

[55] Ibid.

[56] Ibid., Prime Minister's Certificate 8 February 1984. (Emphasis in original)

[57] The four-year delay in the case coming to court was due to a number of reasons. These included the state's efforts to undermine the case, the fact that litigants had to change lawyers midway, as well as the decision by Sibanda, their new lawyer, to wait until the Granger case had been decided as it had a bearing on their law suit.

had been shattered by the brutalisation they had experienced at the hands of state agents. Such was the case in Silobela where nine local ZAPU members were abducted from their homes in the night by suspected state agents in January 1985 and were never heard from again. However, the families involved did not report the matter to the police. Their lack of faith that the police would do anything to assist them is likely to have been influenced by the fact that the police had turned a blind eye to the increasing violence perpetrated by the ZANU (PF) Youth Brigade and Youth Wing before and after the 1985 elections.[58] In addition, the appointment of Shona-speaking officers to senior positions in police stations within Ndebele-speaking communities altered the relationship between police and villagers. Whereas in the past villagers had relied on the police to warn them about the Fifth Brigade, they could no longer do so. Consequently, it was over a year later that the CCJP found out about the abduction and initiated legal action against the government.[59] The decision to sue the government was based on the fact that it was well known that abduction was one of its strategies of dealing with political opponents. In a previous case, the CCJP had located twenty-five abductees in a Kwekwe jail in 1985.[60] However, when the Silobela case came to trial, the government's attorney adopted a cynical defence that challenged the allegations by arguing that the kidnappings could also have been carried out by ZANU (PF). In the end, it could not be proven beyond reasonable doubt that the government was behind the abductions, and the suit was unsuccessful.[61]

Accounts by lawyers about the operation of the legal system in the 1980s tend to emphasise the view that the experiences of those accused of political offences became considerably worse than they had been in earlier decades. Bryant Elliot, who defended political prisoners during the 1970s and 1980s, noted the deterioration in the adherence to due process on the part of the new government. Requirements such as the presentation of detainees before the Detainee Review Tribunal were followed less and less.[62] Elliot's observations were echoed by a lawyer interviewed by the Lawyers Committee for Human Rights

---

[58] *Zimbabwe: Wages of War*, 129–34.
[59] Interview with Elliot. See also *Breaking the Silence*, 16.
[60] *Zimbabwe: Wages of War*, 45.
[61] Interview with Elliot.
[62] Ibid.

(LCHR). The lawyer, who had defended nationalists from the 1950s, observed that,

For the lawyers it is more difficult now than it was before. When it was whites arresting blacks, it wasn't all that easy. But when a woman called the office, and said the Special Branch had picked up her husband at 4 a.m., you would say "do you know their names?" and she would say, "No." But through the sort of networks that existed then, it wasn't easy, but within a fairly short time, at least within a matter of hours, it was possible, on the phone, to find out where the bloke was. Now, it is simply impossible.

And when the Special Branch knew that the relatives had contacted a lawyer, we believed that whatever else they might have done to him, they might at least think twice about doing it to him [again]. Our belief was that the sooner we could get to the individual responsible, the more we could do for the protection of the person irrespective of whatever legal proceedings might follow.[63]

Other lawyers interviewed by the LCHR spoke of the 'pattern of lies' told by authorities to mislead lawyers who were searching for their clients.

Notwithstanding the aforementioned points, it is important not to overemphasise the differences, especially when one considers the extent of government abuses during the late 1970s. As demonstrated in earlier chapters, the experience of arrest under the Rhodesian Front was extremely brutal, and re-detention after acquittal was a common practice. Furthermore, the right to legal representation was significantly undermined as Special Courts Martial began to operate around the country. In addition, black lawyers like Sibanda and Chidyausiku were regularly frustrated by police. Part of what the statements by the lawyers interviewed by the LCHR reflected was the reconfiguration of personal networks in the legal system that occurred with the coming of independence and the Africanisation of the legal system. In the 1980s, black lawyers like Sibanda had fewer problems defending political prisoners, given their close relationships with senior politicians and civil servants. These networks proved to be important to securing the release of Joshua Nkomo's lawyer, Bruce Longhurst, who had been detained at the Plumtree border post on his way back from consulting

---

[63] *Zimbabwe: Wages of War*, 71.

with his client in Botswana.[64] Sibanda met with the Minister of Home Affairs to explain that Longhurst 'had only been acting in the interests of his client and was not party to any illegal act'.[65] In addition, Chihambakwe contacted several Ministers, as well as the army official in charge of military and security operations in Matabeleland, and was ultimately able to secure Longhurst's release.[66]

The Executive and the Judiciary at Loggerheads

The content and administration of law, as we have seen, had long been a source of division within the state, and the coming of independence did not change this. What did change, however, was the level at which the conflict occurred. The friction prior to independence had been between low and middle level officials in the Native Affairs Department and those in the Ministry of Justice. However, after 1980 it was senior officials in the executive and senior members of the judiciary who were at loggerheads. Whereas Rhodesian judges had by and large supported the Rhodesian Front government during UDI, after 1980 the High Court and the Supreme Court – which were largely composed of judges appointed by the Smith administration – repeatedly ruled against the government in important political cases. This friction was in part a reflection of the political changes in the country; however, it gradually came to reflect a divergence in the thinking of the officials in the two branches of the state about the relationship between law and the legitimate exercise of state power.

One of the early cases that brought these tensions to the fore was the trial of the Alan and Noel York. The two brothers were arrested in January 1982 after the discovery of a substantial amount of arms on one of their farms. However, during their trial the state's case was substantially weakened by the fact that the judge disallowed the defendants' statements of admission on the grounds that they had been acquired through torture. In addition to this, the government's key witness absconded to South Africa before giving his testimony. As a result, the two brothers were acquitted. Having lost the case, the Minister of Home Affairs, Herbert Ushewokunze, resorted to issuing a detention

---

[64] Joshua Nkomo had fled the country to Botswana in fear of being arrested on the basis of politically motivated charges.

[65] SPA File Law Society 1983, Law Society Minutes, 15 March 1983.

[66] Ibid.

order against the two brothers on the sixth of May. The order was successfully challenged in the High Court. However, Ushewokunze responded by issuing another detention order on the first of July. This order was again set aside by the High Court on the eighth of July, and the brothers were released only to be re-detained on the same day, on a third detention order which the court finally accepted as legal.

These repeated clashes between the High Court and the Ministry of Home Affairs resulted in a withering attack on the judiciary by Ushewokunze in Parliament. 'The manner in which our law courts dispense justice', he railed, 'is gravely frustrating and undermining the work of law enforcement agencies like the police. The security of the state is sacrificed at the altar of individual liberties.'[67] He went on:

But even after this, recalcitrant and reactionary members of the so-called Benches still remain masquerading under our hard-won independence as dispensers of justice or, shall I say, injustice by handing down pieces of judgement which smack of subverting the people's government. We inherited *in toto* the Rhodesian statutes which these self-same magistrates and judges used to avidly and viciously interpret against the guerrillas. What is so different now apart from it being majority rule? Our posture during constitutional negotiations with the British... that the judiciary must be disbanded, can now be understood with a lot of hindsight.[68]

Two points are worth making about Ushewokunze's statement. The first is that he, like other members of the executive invoked the 'state of exception' argument. The second is that the unfortunate reasoning behind Ushewokunze's indignation was that, since the judges had supported the Smith regime in repressing its political opponents under the same legal framework, they should do the same for the new government. During his tenure as Minister of Home Affairs, he repeatedly attacked judges who ruled against the state, and issued detention orders that, in effect, disregarded the rulings. For example, after the acquittal of Dabengwa and Masuku in the treason trial, Ushewokunze dismissed Justice Squires' ruling as 'stranger than fiction', and issued a detention order against the two.[69] Ushewokunze also condemned Justice Dumbutshena's decision to acquit the six Air

---

[67] Cited in Hatchard, *Individual Freedoms and State Security*, 133.
[68] Ibid.
[69] *Zimbabwe: Wages of War*, 158–9.

Force officers accused of assisting South African agents to bomb the Thornhill Airbase in 1982 as showing evidence of 'class bias'. It is not surprising that Ushewokunze's conduct was one of the key concerns raised by the Law Society Council during their meeting with the Minister of Justice in December 1983.[70]

In writing about the conflicts between the bench and the executive in the 1980s, Tendai Biti has explained these clashes in terms of the judiciary's commitment to the rule of law and protecting individual rights.[71] However, such an explanation leaves unaccounted for the fact that many of these judges had supported the Rhodesian Front in applying the same repressive laws. In trying to understand what shaped the decisions of the judiciary in the early 1980s, it is necessary to locate them within the political context of the period, and the tensions between the new regime and the remnants of the old. Chanock's observations about the friction between the South African judiciary and the government following the National Party's victory in 1948 are instructive. This friction, he argues, was in large part because the judges 'were not part of the same political elite as the regime'.[72] The same argument can be made for Zimbabwe in the early 1980s.

That being said, the argument about the judiciary's commitment to rights becomes much more relevant after 1984 when the bench consisted largely of judges appointed by the ZANU (PF) government. In an address to the army in August 1984, Simbi Mubako offered his own reflections on the early tensions between the executive and the judiciary and expressed optimism that with the recent new appointments such clashes would become less likely. 'In the first two years of our independence', he observed:

… the class and ideological unity between the judiciary and the executive had disappeared. A new revolutionary Government had won the war and the elections, but was forced to inherit both the laws and the judiciary from the old regime. Many people expected clashes between units of the different armies which were merged together.

However, by judicians [*sic*] management and following correct policies no major crisis eventuated. We now have a situation in which all the present judges of the Supreme Court and High Court, ninety per cent of

---

[70] SPA File Law Society 1983, Law Society Minutes, 12 December 1983.
[71] Biti, 'The Judiciary, the Executive', 69.
[72] Chanock, 'Writing South African Legal History', 272.

the magistrates and all the presiding officers have been appointed by this Government. In that sense a revolution has occurred in the composition of the judiciary which is more complete than that of the civil service or of the Parliament itself. Clashes may still occur but they are much less likely.[73]

However, despite this 'revolution' in the composition of the judiciary, the clashes between the executive and the judiciary persisted and indeed escalated. While the executive insisted on using the law to pursue its political opponents, an important shift was discernible in the rulings handed down by senior members of the judiciary. Many judges were increasingly moving away from a rigid commitment to formalism and orienting themselves towards human rights. In an article written for the popular magazine *Parade* Chief Justice Dumbutshena argued that 'the High Court and the Supreme Court of Zimbabwe have developed a human rights jurisprudence that is the envy of other countries. In the interpretation of human rights provisions in our constitution, we have applied to good effect international human rights norms.'[74] These divergent paths being charted by the bench and the executive were at the root of the growing dissonance between the two arms of the state in the late 1980s.

This growing tension between the two branches of the state was fuelled by a series of Supreme Court rulings that drew attention to the incompatibility between certain punishments prescribed by law and the country's Bill of Rights. In 1989 the Supreme Court found in favour of a suit challenging the constitutionality of judicial whipping for adults. It ruled that the punishment breached Section 15 (1) of the Declaration of Rights which stipulated that 'No person shall be subjected to torture or to inhuman or degrading punishment or other such treatment.'[75] The ruling read, in part:

By its very nature [corporal punishment] treats members of the human race as non-humans. Irrespective of the offence he has committed, the vilest criminal remains a human being possessed of common human dignity. Whipping does not accord him human status. No matter the extent of regulatory safeguards, it is a procedure easily subject to abuse in the hands of a sadistic and

---

[73] Mubako, 'The Law and the Judiciary in Zimbabwe'.
[74] E. Dumbutshena, 'Justice – the People's Right', *Legal Forum*, 2 (1990), 6.
[75] Constitution of Zimbabwe, (Lancaster House) chapter 3, Section 15 (1).

unscrupulous prison officer who is called upon to administer it. It is degrading to both the punished and the punisher alike.[76]

In another case, the Supreme Court ruled that judicial whipping for juveniles was also unconstitutional.[77] As a result of these rulings, the government repealed sections 329 to 333 of the Criminal Evidence and Procedure Act which provided for corporal punishment. In October 1990 Justice Korsah presided over the case of Wilson Masitere, and ruled that the sentence of solitary confinement and spare diet handed down in the Magistrate's Court was unconstitutional, on the grounds that it too violated Section 15 (1) of the Bill of Rights.[78]

The case that brought matters to a head however, had to do with the constitutionality of hanging as a form of execution and was supposed to be heard by the Supreme Court. The new Chief Justice, Antony Gubbay, instructed the lawyers on both sides to prepare their arguments. However, the government pre-empted the hearing by passing Constitutional Amendment 11. Among other things, it amended Section 15 of the Constitution in order to ensure that male corporal punishment for juveniles and execution by hanging were not construed as inhuman and degrading punishments. In presenting the Bill to Parliament, then Minister of Justice, Emmerson Mnangagwa, argued that: 'Government will not and cannot countenance a situation where the death penalty is *de facto* abolished through the back door by a declaration by the courts that the manner of executing the death sentence by hanging constitutes inhuman and degrading punishment.'[79] With respect to the reintroduction of juvenile corporal punishment, Mnangagwa explained that it was meant to deal with the risng number of juvenile offenders in the prison system. He further argued that the government felt that it was 'undesirable that young offenders should be brought into contact with adult offenders.'

On the one hand, the amendment reflected the government's views on punishment. On the other, it conveyed an underlying message that the executive was not willing to see the judiciary expand its influence through judicial activism and in the process curb the executive branch's powers. This was also clear in the section of the amendment

---

[76] Cited in Dumbutshena, 'Justice – the People's Right', 7.
[77] Ibid.
[78] *The Herald*, 9 October 1990.
[79] *The Herald*, 7 December 1990.

which dealt with land reform. In addition to giving the government powers to compulsorily acquire land, it withdrew the authority previously granted to the courts to determine how much compensation should be paid for expropriated land, and when such compensation should be paid. Chief Justice Gubbay used the occasion of the opening of the High Court in 1991 to publicly criticise the amendment and assert the role of judges:

Judges are the custodians of the Constitution of Zimbabwe. This means that at this moment in time the courts have the power and the duty to ensure that all the provisions of the Constitution – which is the supreme and overriding law of the land – are observed by all instrumentalities of the Government, and to declare invalid any excess of power or Act of Parliament or Presidential or Ministerial Regulation, which contravenes any of the prohibitions contained in the Constitution.[80]

However, Mugabe countered this interpretation of the role of the judiciary by asserting that: 'The work of judges is to interpret the law and not to make it.' He went on to extend an indirect invitation to the Chief Justice to resign pointing out that: 'If certain laws are revulsive [sic] to the conscience of a judge, then that judge and conscience should not sit as a judge. Pure and simple.'[81]

Conclusion

In July 1990 the new Minister of Home Affairs, Moven Mahachi, announced to Parliament that he would not be seeking the renewal of the state of emergency. However, this was no cause for optimism as it was clear from Mahachi's speech that the government was willing to use emergency powers in the future should they be deemed necessary. He expressed no regret at the gross abuses that were committed by the state under the pretext of carrying out anti-dissident operations: 'Yes,

[80] Justice A. R. Gubbay, 'Speech delivered by the Chief Justice, The Honourable Mr Justice A. R. Gubbay at the Opening of the 1991 Legal year, Harare on 14 January 1991, *Legal Forum*, 3 (1991), p. 7. Justice Gubbay had been appointed by the Rhodesian Front in 1977 and continued to serve as a judge after independence. He was appointed as Chief Justice after the retirement of Enoch Dumbutshena. During the 1980s and 1990s, he gained an international reputation of being a human rights judge.

[81] *The Herald*, 18 January 1991.

some fellow Zimbabweans were bruised in the process because of the State of Emergency during the period. Such fellow Zimbabweans are to blame, because in the majority of cases, they were willing to be used by counter-revolutionary elements for monetary gains, and/or were trying to de-stabilise a properly elected democratic government.'[82] The sense of impunity was reinforced by the general amnesty which was declared on the tenth anniversary of the country's independence by Mugabe, who was by then the executive president.[83] Couched in the language of reconciliation, the President extended amnesty to 'dissidents and their collaborators', as well as 'former PF ZAPU fugitives from justice'. However, the real beneficiaries of the amnesty were the members of the security forces who had brutalised and killed thousands of innocent citizens. The amnesty also provided legal cover for those who had committed politically motivated crimes during the elections of 1990.

The LCHR aptly noted of the 1980s that: 'While the balance of power had shifted, the rules of the game remained the same.'[84] The ZANU (PF) government had embraced the repressive laws, institutions and practices that had been used by the settler governments to quell political opposition. This continuity was the product of both, the institutional legacies of settler rule and the authoritarian tendencies within the ruling party itself. In the 1980s, the relative importance of the legal arena as a site in which to challenge government repression was greater, given that there were few other effective sites for members of opposition parties to confront the state. However, citizens' legal agency often proved to be ineffective in shielding them from government persecution. Although many of the government's political opponents turned to the courts to assert their rights as citizens, they found little succour in them owing to the vindictiveness of the state, and the repressive nature of laws like the Law and Order (Maintenance) Act. In addition, whereas in the 1960s and 1970s it had been possible to at least use the dock as a platform, in the 1980s this strategy was largely ineffective as the local and international audience for courtroom performances was small and lacked influence. Moreover, those accused

---

[82] 'State of Emergency to go-Mahachi', Department of Information Press Statement, 23 July 1990.
[83] 'President Announces General Amnesty,' Department of Information Press Statements, 1 August 1990.
[84] *Zimbabwe: Wages of War*, 4.

of political offences lacked a broader political struggle from which to draw strength. An important development during this period was the increasing tension between the upper echelons of the executive and the judiciary. These tensions were initially a reflection of the mutual antipathy between the remnants of the old regime and the officials of the new one. However, they soon came to reflect the divergent thinking between the two arms of the state about the relationship between law and the legitimate exercise of state power. As I show in the next chapter, these tensions continued to be present in the 1990s and early 2000s and led to drastic steps to reconfigure the judiciary in the early 2000s.

8 'The Past as Prologue': Law and the Zimbabwean Political Crisis, 1997–2008

Introduction

In the week leading up to the general elections on 29 March 2008, Masimba Kuchera, Michael Muza and Tafadzwa Rugoho filed an urgent High Court chamber application citing the Minister of Justice, Legal and Parliamentary Affairs as the main respondent.[1] The immediate impetus behind the application was the gazetting of Statutory Instrument 43 of 2008 by President Mugabe on 17 March. The Statutory Instrument authorised police officers to be present in polling stations, and to assist illiterate or disabled voters in the forthcoming elections. In so doing, the legislation reversed the amendments to the Electoral Act, which had only been in operation for two months. Kuchera and Muza, who were both visually impaired, along with Rugoho, who was physically handicapped, argued that the new regulations violated their legal right to vote in secret. They therefore sought a High Court ruling that stopped the statutory instrument from being applied during the forthcoming elections, and allowed illiterate or disabled voters to be assisted by a person of their own choice.

Justice Antonia Guvava, who heard the application, was unsympathetic to their case. She ruled that the litigants' concern about the police's role in elections was unjustified, and that their application could not be treated as urgent. She therefore dismissed the application with costs. The core elements of this case – from the (ab)use of law by the President in order to tilt the electoral landscape in his favour, to the efforts by citizens to take to the courts in order to defend their rights, as well as the tendency of the judiciary to find in favour of the government in sensitive political matters – were all typical of legal struggles dealing with overtly political matters during the post-2000 period. Significantly, these aspects of the legal encounters were reminiscent

---

[1] M. Kuchera, M. Muza and T. Rugoho v. The Minister of Justice Legal and Parliamentary Affairs, Case No. HC 1727/08.

of the longer history of law and its use in constituting and contesting state power in the country.

Recent studies of legal struggles in post-colonial Africa have, however, sought to understand them in terms of a 'judicialisation of politics' in the post-Cold War period.[2] Jean Comaroff and John Comaroff, for example, have argued that political questions in post-colonial Africa (and elsewhere) are increasingly being brought to the courts for resolution to such an extent that 'Politics itself is migrating to the courts – or to their popular, even criminal, replicas.' They further argue that authoritarian governments are increasingly resorting to the law in order to achieve their designs. In illustrating their argument, one of the examples they cite is that of the Zimbabwean government's frequent use of the law in order to repress its political opponents during the post-2000 period.[3]

Although there are certainly new dimensions to recent legal struggles which can be traced to the post-Cold War moment, this chapter maintains that they are best understood in the light of the much longer history of legal struggles in the country stretching back to the last decades of settler rule. As the preceding chapters have shown, the questions vexing the body politic had long been debated within the legal arena. In addition, citizens and successive governments had frequently enlisted the law in the pursuit of their respective goals. The legal strategies adopted by the ZANU (PF) government in dealing with political opposition in the post-2000 period bore many similarities to those it used in the 1980s, and more importantly, to those adopted by settler governments since the 1950s. These similarities are not coincidental, they indicate key continuities in the nature of the state, and the place of law as an element of statecraft during the colonial and post-colonial period.

The explanations for the legal responses of citizens must therefore be sought much further back in history. As we have seen, citizens' appeals

---

[2] See J. Comaroff and J. Comaroff, 'Law and Disorder in the Postcolony: An Introduction', in J. Comaroff and J. Comaroff (eds), *Law and Disorder in the Post-colony* (Chicago, 2006). For variations on this idea see F. E. Kanyongolo, 'The Rhetoric of Human Rights in Malawi: Individualization and Judicialization', in H. Englund and F. Nyamnjoh (eds), *Rights and the Politics of Recognition in Africa* (London, 2004); and J. Gould, 'Strong Bar, Weak State? Lawyers, Liberalism and State Formation in Zambia', *Development and Change*, 37 (2006).

[3] Comaroff and Comaroff, 'Law and Disorder', 24.

to the law were part of long established repertoires of engaging with an overbearing state. However, the role that law played for citizens as a resource in political struggles and its effectiveness varied across time. This depended on, among other things, whether there were alternative avenues of engaging the state, citizens' ability to access legal services, and the strategies adopted by the state itself. The existence of a broader political struggle from which they could draw strength, as well as local and international audiences were also critical factors. It should, however, be underscored that the law has never been the only means by which citizens prosecuted their political struggles.

Although global intellectual currents certainly inflected the legal suits instituted by citizens, the reasons that explain why they sought to use the law must be sought much closer to home. In her study of the rise of opposition parties in hybrid regimes like Zimbabwe, Adrienne LeBas argues that the decisions made by the government in trying to stabilise its rule in the early years of independence shaped the character of opposition parties and their ability to mobilise broader national constituencies.[4] She is referring in particular here to the ZANU (PF) government's corporatist strategy which involved entering into an alliance with organised labour. Consequently, when labour had a falling out with the ruling party, there was an institutional framework which transcended region and ethnicity which could be used as a basis for the formation of an opposition party, and one that could withstand the pressures of ethnic fragmentation. A similar argument can be made about the role of law as a resource for citizens. The choice of the ZANU (PF) government to rely heavily on the law as a tool of oppression also influenced the responses of ordinary citizens, as well as opposition and civil society activists.

The Emergence of an 'Authoritarian Rule of Law'

The cessation of the brutal repression of ZANU (PF)'s political opponents in 1987 and the decision not to renew the state of emergency in 1990 were not necessarily an indication of the government's movement towards greater respect for citizen's rights. Rather, it reflected the ruling party's confidence that it had vanquished its political

---

[4] A. LeBas, *From Protest to Parties: Party-building and Democratization in Africa* (Oxford, 2011).

opponents. Consequently, the early to mid-1990s were characterised by relative political calm. Notwithstanding this, the period witnessed fundamental changes in the political landscape. In the first instance, the political alliance between the state and labour that had stabilised ZANU (PF)'s rule began to come apart. Second, new political alliances between labour unions, the urban poor and civil society organisations began to coalesce. These processes culminated in the formation of the Movement for Democratic Change (MDC), an opposition party that posed the most serious threat to ZANU (PF) rule since independence. The rise of the MDC in turn led to concerted efforts by the government to implement what Jothie Rajah has called an 'authoritarian rule of law'.[5]

The key trigger behind the unravelling of the alliance between the state and organised labour was the adoption of the IMF-backed Economic Structural Adjustment Programme (ESAP) in 1991, in order to deal with the challenges of poor economic growth, growing budget deficits and increasing foreign debt.[6] Among the neo-liberal reforms prescribed under ESAP included the requirement that the government reduce its expenditure on health and education. In addition, it was supposed to allow market forces to determine the value of the local currency and the prices of goods and services. The impact of these policies on households was immediate and devastating. The new policy of cost recovery resulted in a significant increase in fees in the health and education sector, and the removal of price controls led to a sharp rise in the prices of goods and services. The resultant inflation led to a substantial erosion of real wages. These challenges were further compounded by the large-scale retrenchments in the public and the private sectors. In 1992, 25,000 jobs were lost in the public and private sectors, and a further 23,000 jobs were lost in the private sector alone in 1994.[7]

The economic hardship that accompanied ESAP drove civil society organisations to become more forthright in their criticism of the government and to press for inclusion in policy making. An important organisation in this regard was the National Constitutional Assembly (NCA), a broad civil society coalition formed in 1997 in order to foster debate on the existing Lancaster House Constitution and press for a new

[5] J. Rajah, *Authoritarian Rule of Law: Legislation, Discourse and Legitimacy in Singapore* (Cambridge University Press, 2012).
[6] LeBas, *From Protest to Parties*, 116.
[7] Ibid., 118.

'people-driven constitution'. The emergence of the NCA represented the success of alliance building across a number of civil society organisations which had joined forces in order to lobby the government. These alliances proved to be important in launching the MDC and in mobilising against the government's draft constitution during the February 2000 referendum. The NCA's activities also provided a forum for the public discussion of politics. As part of its activities it published several pamphlets which dealt with a range of topics such as citizenship, the declaration of rights, the principles of democracy and the functions of the different arms of government.[8] In addition, six hundred facilitators were trained and deployed in all ten provinces in the country in order to promote grassroots discussions about the constitution. As Sarah Rich Dorman points out, the framework of the constitutional debate provided 'a "non-political" way of talking about the exercise of politics.'[9]

A second consequence of the increasing economic hardships in the country was the rise in workers' strikes, student demonstrations and street protests from 1995 onwards. The demands of the Zimbabwe Congress of Trade Unions (ZCTU), which often coordinated these protests, were initially economic in nature, and gradually came to encompass political demands. However, it soon came to a realisation that an alternative political party was necessary to take forward the workers' aspirations. In 1997, the ZCTU began organizing a Working People's Convention which would bring a range of stakeholders to discuss the crisis in the country and devise solutions. The preparations involved wide ranging consultations with civil society organisations across the country. These meetings, LeBas notes, 'served the ZCTU's strategy of alliance-building. By incorporating grassroots activists into the pre-convention process, the ZCTU was building links with civic organizations at the local as well as national level.'[10] The deliberations and the resolutions that emerged out of the Working People's Convention of February 1999 provided the basis for the political platform of the MDC, the labour-backed party that was launched in September 1999.[11]

---

[8] S. Rich Dorman, 'NGOs and the Constitutional Debate in Zimbabwe: From Inclusion to Exclusion', *JSAS* 29, (2003).

[9] Ibid., 849.

[10] LeBas, *From Protest to Parties*, p. 141.

[11] B. Raftopoulos, 'The Labour Movement and the Emergence of Opposition Politics in Zimbabwe', in B. Raftopoulos and L. Sachikonye (eds) Striking Back: The Labour Movement ant the State in Zimbabwe 1980–2000, p. 16.

The MDC's threat to ZANU (PF)'s political dominance was made real by two significant political victories that were scored by the opposition and civil society organisations in the year 2000. The first was the rejection of the government-sponsored draft constitution by a margin of 54.7 percent to 45.3 percent during the February 2000 referendum, largely due to a successful campaign by the MDC and the NCA. The second was the substantial success scored by the MDC in the June 2000 Parliamentary elections. Although ZANU (PF) had seemed unchallengeable throughout the 1990s, in the June 2000 elections the MDC won 57 seats, drastically reducing ZANU (PF) presence in Parliament to 62 seats, and ZANU-Ndonga retained one seat in Chipinge. In addition to wresting these parliamentary seats from ZANU (PF), the losing MDC candidates challenged the results in thirty-nine constituencies on the grounds that the elections had been marred by substantial violence and intimidation. The MDC had therefore not only taken a substantial number of seats and asserted itself as a political force to be reckoned with, it also threatened to overturn ZANU (PF)'s slim majority in Parliament. This triggered a determined bid by ZANU (PF) to hold on to power at all costs.

ZANU (PF)'s efforts to hold on to power drew on a number of strategies. Prominent among these was the use of the coercive apparatus of the state, war veterans and the youth militia to intimidate, assault and, in some cases, kill political opponents.[12] However, the use of law remained a key feature of the government's tactics. Presidential powers were regularly used to impose *ad hoc* regulations when swift action was deemed necessary. One of the most egregious examples of this was the clemency order that Mugabe issued on the 6th of October, which extended amnesty to all individuals who had committed politically motivated crimes between 1 January 2000 and 31 July 2000.[13] In December, he issued an executive order that sought to invalidate

---

[12] See Solidarity Peace Trust, 'Policing the State: An Evaluation of 1981 political Arrests in Zimbabwe – 2000–2005', December 2006; Solidarity Peace Trust, 'Punishing Dissent, Silencing Citizens: The Zimbabwe Elections 2008', May 2008; and Solidarity Peace Trust, 'Destructive Engagement: Violence, Mediation and Politics in Zimbabwe', July 2007. See also Zimbabwe Human Rights NGO Forum's monthly Political Violence reports.

[13] Solidarity Peace Trust, 'Subverting Justice: The role of the Judiciary in denying the will of the Zimbabwean Electorate since 2000', March 2005, 12.

the thirty-nine electoral challenges filed by the MDC, by declaring the election free and fair.

The government also passed several laws whose combined effect was to severely restrict the rights and freedoms of Zimbabwean citizens, while providing state officials with additional powers to control virtually all avenues of expressing political dissent. These laws were meant to work in conjunction with ZANU (PF)'s exclusionary political discourse, which divided the populace into 'patriots' who supported ZANU (PF), and 'sell-outs' in the opposition who were said to be complicit in a regime change agenda being orchestrated by western powers.[14] As had been the case in the 1950s and 1960s, the way political dissenters were discursively constructed fed directly into state responses at the level of legislation. The raft of repressive laws passed by the government from 2001 was therefore meant to equip state officials with sufficient powers to 'protect' the nation and deal decisively with the 'sell-outs'.

In April 2001, Jonathan Moyo, the Minister of State for Information and Publicity tabled a new Broadcasting Services Act that was fast-tracked through Parliament. The legislation was a response to Capital Radio's successful legal challenge in September 2000, to Section 27 of the previous Act which gave the government-controlled Zimbabwe Broadcasting Corporation (ZBC) a monopoly over broadcasting in the country. On the basis of this ruling, Capital Radio began broadcasting but was shut down within days and its equipment seized. As the new legislation was being drawn up temporary Broadcasting Regulations were put in place by means of Presidential Powers. The new Act, which was passed in April 2001, gave the government substantial control over broadcasting within the country. Among other things, the law set short licencing periods for private radio stations and barred community radio stations from broadcasting 'any political matter, including the policy or launch of a political party'. In addition, the number of licences for national broadcasters and signal carriers other than the ZBC was restricted to one, and the Minister of State for Information and Publicity was given the ultimate authority to determine who was granted a licence.[15]

---

[14] See M. Tendi, *Making History in Mugabe's Zimbabwe: Politics, Intellectuals, and the Media*, (Oxford, 2010).

[15] D. Coltart, A critique, www.davidcoltart.com/2001/10/a-critique-of-the-zimbabwean-broadcasting-services-and-political-parties-finances-acts/. Retrieved 7 July 2014.

The Political Parties (Financing) Act, which was also passed in April 2001, was aimed at financially crippling the opposition by means of a provision that prohibited political parties from accepting direct or indirect 'foreign' donations. The definition of 'foreign' donations was conveniently broadened to include donations from Zimbabwean citizens who were resident outside the country. This provision was based on the knowledge that, given the deepening economic recession in the country, new political parties would struggle to finance their operations solely from local sources. It therefore sought to choke off any external funding for the MDC thereby hampering its ability to expand its structures and operate effectively.

The piece of legislation that was especially devastating for the efforts of opposition and civil society activists to mobilise was the Public Order and Security Act (POSA) of 2002. The Act, which was passed during the run-up to the March Presidential elections, replaced the Law and Order (Maintenance) Act. As had been the case in the 1950s, concerns about public order and security were used to disguise efforts to use the law to protect the ruling party's hold on power by drastically limiting the rights and freedoms of citizens, and providing state officials with broad powers to silence dissent. The Act made it mandatory for all organisers of public gatherings to inform the police of their plans at least four days in advance.[16] This was ostensibly to enable the police to make the necessary preparations to avoid any public disorder. However, the police used this provision to gain advance knowledge of the plans of opposition and civil society organisations in order to ban their events. Police were also empowered to disperse 'unlawful gatherings' using 'all reasonably necessary measures including force'. In the event that a police officer killed a citizen who was said to be resisting their efforts to disperse public gatherings, such a killing was deemed legal under POSA. In effect, it became legal for police to use lethal force on citizens who were exercising their freedom of assembly and expression. Following the passage of the law, public meetings and peaceful protests organised by the MDC and civil society organisations such as the NCA and ZCTU were routinely prohibited, and where activists persisted, they were frequently assaulted by the police and arrested. It is little wonder that POSA soon acquired the dubious

---

[16] Public Order and Security Act 2002 [Chapter 11: 17].

distinction of being more repressive than its predecessor LOMA which had been drafted during colonial rule.

Two weeks after the passage of POSA, Parliament passed the Access to Information and Protection of Privacy Act which gave the government substantial powers over public and private media organisations. Although the two Acts were tabled in Parliament by different ministers, the fact that they were passed in quick succession was not coincidental. It was indicative of the concerted efforts being made at the Cabinet level to put in place a series of laws that would enable the government to effectively silence political dissent. The Act undermined the freedom of the press in a number of ways, including by making it mandatory for all journalists and media organisations operating in Zimbabwe to be registered.[17] A new Media and Information Committee was created to oversee this registration process. In addition, it was tasked with monitoring media content and disciplining 'errant' journalists.

The passage of repressive legislation was followed by the prosecution of numerous individuals and organisations that were perceived to be enemies of the state. Between 2000 and 2008, media organisations, journalists, opposition party officials and supporters, civil society activists, as well as lawyers, became targets of political persecution.[18] Within two years of the passage of the Access to Information and Protection of Privacy Act, two newspapers, *The Daily News* and *The Daily News on Sunday*, which had become the main platforms for voicing criticism of the government, were shut down.[19] In addition, there were over 60 instances of journalists being charged under its provisions. Between 2003 and 2006 the MDC Legal Affairs Department handled 668 cases involving the arrest of 3,468 party members and officials. The top leadership of the party was not spared either. In 2003 Morgan Tsvangirai, Welshman Ncube and Renson Gasela were charged with high treason on the basis of manufactured evidence.[20] As we have seen, similar treatment had been meted out to ZAPU leaders

---

[17] Media Institute of Southern Africa (MISA) and Article 19, 'The Access to Information and Protection of Privacy Act: Two Years On', September 2004, 2.

[18] For an account of the persecution of lawyers, see A. Tsunga, 'The Professional Trajectory of a Human Rights Lawyer in Zimbabwe between 2000 and 2008', *JSAS*, 35 (2009), 984–91.

[19] MISA and Article 19, 'The Access to Information and Protection of Privacy Act', appendices.

[20] See the following High Court case, *State v. Morgan Tsvangirai, Welshman Ncube and Renson Gasela*.

such as Dumiso Dabengwa, Lookout Masuku and Sidney Malunga in the 1980s, as well as Ndabaningi Sithole in the 1960s.

The charges brought against political and civil society activists by the state were often trumped up. As such, it was not uncommon for the state to later withdraw the charges, or for accused individuals to defend themselves successfully in court. Of the 668 cases handled by the MDC Legal Affairs Department, charges were withdrawn before plea in 152 cases. However, this was not necessarily a victory, as these charges could be brought against them in the future. Consequently, the threat of re-arrest continued to hang over opposition activists. As Jocelyn Alexander has observed, the objective in such instances was not necessarily long-term imprisonment.[21] Prosecution itself was a form of persecution whose goal was to demoralise the government's political opponents by subjecting them to periods of temporary confinement during which they were tortured, and made to suffer the squalor and deprivation of a prison system that had all but collapsed. At the same time, state officials sought to ensure that trials were drawn out in order to inflict the maximum amount of suffering and inconvenience. As Susanne Verheul points out: 'The "sociology of political interference", supported by a combination of patronage and intimidation, restrained the prosecution from exercising its professional discretion in particular cases.' As part of this strategy, prosecutors were instructed to routinely oppose bail in cases involving opposition or civil society activists. In the event that bail was granted, they invoked the infamous Section 121 of the Criminal Codification Act, which allowed the state to continue holding an accused in custody for a further seven days if the prosecution indicated its intention to appeal against a ruling.[22]

The abuse of the law by the government also extended to interfering with the operation of the courts, and one of the consequences of this was that many important cases simply stalled in the courts, leaving those who had sought legal remedy frustrated. This strategy was frequently used in dealing with electoral challenges as it meant that the declared winner continued to occupy the contested seat for as long as the matter was *sub judice*. There were also several instances

---

[21] Alexander, 'The Political Imaginaries', 485.
[22] Interview with Josphat Tshuma, 11 September 2013.

where key trial records went missing. In extreme cases, lawyers were prevented from filing court papers by armed police officers.[23] Such was the case in the election petition filed by Morgan Tsvangirai challenging the results of the June 2000 Buhera North Parliamentary election. Justice Devittie who heard the petition declared the results of the election null and void and Kenneth Manyonda, the ZANU (PF) candidate, appealed the ruling. However, the tape recording of the trial and the judge's notebooks went missing from the High Court; as a result, the case was never concluded and Manyonda served out a full term in Parliament.[24]

Another example of a case that was never completed due to government interference with the operation of the courts was the electoral petition filed by Morgan Tsvangirai challenging the results of the March 2002 Presidential election.[25] Given that he was the leader of the opposition, every effort was made to frustrate his attempts to oust Mugabe. As such, it is not a coincidence that the wheels of justice always turned at their slowest when it came to dealing with important lawsuits that were filed by Tsvangirai. His 2002 electoral petition was a critical one as its outcome could have led to the invalidation of Mugabe's presidency. To begin with, the Registrar of the High Court failed to set a date for the hearing of the case for over a year, which forced the MDC to file an urgent application in the High Court in May 2003.[26] All told, the MDC had to file 22 supplementary cases in order to get the main case to progress. These included nine applications to have election documents brought to Harare, six applications to compel the Registrar General to produce documents, and two applications to get the government to produce the voters roll.

It was only after the court had issued an order for the trial date to be set that the MDC's lawyers met with Judge President, Godfrey Chidyausiku, to discuss how the trial would be conducted. They agreed on a two-part trial in which the first would focus on the legal and constitutional arguments raised in the petition, and the second would consider the allegations that the elections were characterised by 'violence, intimidation and

---

[23] Tsunga, 'The Professional Trajectory of a Human Rights Lawyer', 989.
[24] Solidarity Peace Trust, 'Subverting Justice', 29.
[25] See the following High Court case, *Morgan Tsvangirai v. Robert Mugabe and Others,*.
[26] Solidarity Peace Trust, 'Subverting Justice', 31.

corrupt and illegal practices'. Contrary to the usual practice, it was only on the very day of the trial that it became known that the case would be heard by Justice Ben Hlatshwayo.[27] The first part of the trial was conducted in November 2003 and Justice Hlatshwayo initially reserved his judgement. His summary ruling dismissing Tsvangirai's petition was handed down seven months later, and three years after the hearing he had still not given a detailed judgement providing the reasons for his decision. As a result, Tsvangirai was not able to file an appeal, and a date for the second part of the trial was never set. The ultimate, and indeed desired, effect of all these delays was that Mugabe served a full term in office before the case had been concluded.

Statutory Instrument 43 of 2008 which provoked the law suit by Kuchera, Muza and Rugoho must be understood within this context of earlier efforts to use the law to influence the outcome of the elections. By gazetting the statutory instrument using the Presidential (Temporary) Powers Act, Mugabe unilaterally nullified the amendments to Sections 59 and 60 of the Electoral Act that had been passed by Parliament in 2007. These amendments had been enacted as part of the political reforms being implemented under the auspices of the Southern African Development Community (SADC) mediation.[28] Among other things, the amendments removed police officers from the list of individuals that were allowed to assist illiterate or disabled people to vote. However, less than two weeks before the elections, the President, who was himself standing for election, nullified them. This blatant abuse of the law to retain power was not only consistent with a longer set of practices that the ruling party had become proficient in since the 1980s, it was also part of a set of institutional practices that had gradually become embedded within the state during the last decades of settler rule.

Undermining Judicial Independence

The government's ability to abuse the law in the post-2000 period rested partly on its success in undermining the independence of the

[27] When Chidyausiku became the Judge President, he changed the system of allocating cases to judges by rota and introduced a new one in which he would personally allocate cases to judges.

[28] In 2007 SADC formally initiated mediation efforts in order to end the political and economic crisis in Zimbabwe. These were spearheaded by President Thabo Mbeki of South Africa.

judiciary to such an extent that it was unlikely to challenge its actions. The 1980s, as we have seen, had been characterised by growing tensions between the judiciary and the executive that arose from contrasting visions about the relationship between law and the legitimate exercise of state power. Despite this, throughout the 1990s the judiciary continued to hand down rulings that sought to check the powers of the executive. However, with the emergence of the MDC as a credible threat to ZANU (PF)'s hold on power, the clashes between the judiciary and the executive took on greater political significance. In the deeply polarized political context of the period, adverse rulings on crucial issues like the land occupations or election petitions had a direct impact on the ruling party's political survival. Consequently, a fearless and independent judiciary came to be seen as a serious political liability for ZANU (PF).

Despite the tense public exchanges between the Chief Justice and the President over the Constitutional Amendment No. 11 of 1990, the judiciary refused to be cowed into submission. On several occasions in the early 1990s, the Supreme Court struck off sections of legislation that violated citizens' rights, and/or gave government officials too much power. In 1991 and 1993, the Court handed down rulings that protected death row inmates from 'inhuman or degrading punishment' in relation to the conditions and the length of their incarceration pending execution.[29] In 1994, it ruled that Section 6 of the infamous Law and Order (Maintenance) Act, which empowered the police to ban public demonstrations, was *ultra vires* of Sections 20 and 21 of the Constitution.[30] The following year, the Supreme Court struck down a section of the National Registration Act which, much like colonial pass laws, gave police officers the authority to demand identity documents from anyone above 18 years of age found in a public place, and to arrest those who were not carrying their identity documents.[31]

However, it was the illegal arrest and torture of two journalists, Mark Chavunduka and Ray Choto, by the army in January 1999 that

---

[29] A. Gubbay, 'The Light of Successive Chief Justices of Zimbabwe in Seeking to Protect Human Rights and the Rule of Law', Miriam Rothschild and John Foster Human Rights Trust Annual Lecture 2001, 9–10.

[30] D. Matyszak, 'Democratic Space and State Security: Zimbabwe's Public Order and Security Act', unpublished paper, 3. See also *In Re* Munhumeso and Ors, *ZLR* (1994), Part I, 49.

[31] Gubbay, 'The Light of Successive Chief Justices', 10.

brought about another public clash between the executive and the judiciary. The saga was set into motion by *The Standard's* publication of an article on the 10th of January which alleged that 27 soldiers had been arrested for inciting a coup. In an effort to find out the source of the story, military officials detained Chavunduka, who was the editor of the newspaper, for several days inside Cranborne Army Barracks in Harare. This detention was patently illegal as the Defence Act did not empower the military police to arrest civilians. The High Court therefore granted Chavunduka's lawyers an order instructing the Minister of Defence, Moven Mahachi, and Major Mhonda of the Zimbabwe National Army to release Chavunduka unconditionally. However, the Ministry of Defence defied this and two further orders from the Court and, ultimately, released Chavunduka to the police after six days. Upon learning that the army was looking for him, Choto, who had written the story, handed himself over to the police on the 19th of January. The police proceeded to pass both journalists on to army officials who tortured and interrogated them for 24 hours. After being handed back to the police, Choto and Chavunduka were subsequently charged under the Law and Order (Maintenance) Act with 'publishing false information likely to cause alarm, fear or despondency to the public' and were ultimately released on bail on 21 January.

Members of the judiciary were alarmed by the blatant violations of the rule of law perpetrated in the whole saga. Not only had the army illegally detained civilians, it repeatedly defied the High Court's orders to release them. It had then proceeded to take the two journalists out of police custody and torture them at length. What is more, the police, whose role it was to enforce law and order, had been complicit in some of the illegal actions of the army. Of particular concern to the judges was the fact that the executive had remained conspicuously silent in the face of all of these egregious acts. As a consequence, three Supreme Court judges, Wilson Sandura, Simbarashe Muchechetere and Nicholas McNally, wrote a petition to the President which was copied to the Ministers of Justice, Defence, Home Affairs, and National Security, as well as the Attorney General. In it, they called on the President to make a public statement affirming the government's commitment to the rule of law. Shortly afterwards, the acting Judge President, Justice Ishmael Adam, submitted a similar petition on behalf of the High Court bench.

In response, the President arranged an emergency national address during which he sharply reprimanded the judges. He described their

actions as 'an act of utter indiscretion … an outrageous and deliberate act of impudence', and proceeded to lecture them on the constitutional provisions on the separation of powers.[32] In an interview
to mark his seventy-fifth birthday Mugabe took things a step further.
Although he acknowledged that he had no legal power to dismiss the
judges, he pointed out that 'any judge who no longer has our confidence, at conscience, must resign.'[33] The Minister of Justice, Emmerson
Mnangagwa, also released a strongly worded press statement which
critiqued the judges' petition paragraph by paragraph, and accused
them of behaving in a way that was beneath the dignity of their office.
He took particular exception to the fact that the judges had called
on the President to reaffirm the government's commitment to the rule
of law. In this regard, he pointed out that 'Extra-judicial statements
castigating those allegedly involved in the arrest and giving extra-judicial directives to the Head of State and Government, particularly in a
manner reminiscent of a teacher/pupil relationship, e.g.: "we ask you
to state unequivocally that the Government of Zimbabwe …," are not
expected from the judiciary.'[34] He further advised them to avoid making statements on matters that are likely to come before them, 'lest
it may be said that they are polluting at the source the very foun-
tain of justice that it is their duty to protect.' Although the President
and the Minister of Justice castigated the judges, they did not deal
with the issue that was at the root of the clash: the outrageous actions
of the military. What is clear from the indignant tone of the responses
of the Minister of Justice and the President is that, as had been evident
in 1990, the executive remained unwilling to have the judiciary serve
as an active check on its actions.

The decision by the judges to confront the executive in such a public
manner was unprecedented in independent Zimbabwe and reflected
the degree to which they were scandalised by the actions of the army.
It also indicated how far they were willing to go in defending the rule
of law. When the case against Chavunduka and Choto came before
the courts, the two chose not to respond to the charges against them.
Instead they filed a human rights application with the Supreme Court,
arguing that Section 50 (2) (a) of the Law and Order (Maintenance)

[32] Cited in J. W. Chikuhwa, *A Crisis of Governance: Zimbabwe* (New York, 2004), 55.
[33] *The Herald*, 21 February 1999.
[34] *The Sunday Mail*, 14 February 1999.

Act, under which they were being charged, violated their right to freedom of expression. In May 2000, the Supreme Court ruled in their favour. The stance of the judiciary on this matter also provides a useful standard against which to compare the actions of the judiciary a few years later after many judges had been forced out and the bench reconfigured.

The tensions between the executive and the judiciary in 1999 were ultimately ironed out partly with the help of the Law Society. However, the year 2000 presented two further emotive political issues that brought matters to a head once more *viz* the land issue and the contested June 2000 election results. The land question was brought to the centre stage of Zimbabwean politics by the farm occupations that began in February 2000. Following the rejection of the government-backed draft constitution, veterans of the liberation war and their supporters began occupying white-owned farms. These occupations were initiated partly in response to the rejection of the draft constitution which contained a provision which stipulated that the British government would be responsible for compensating farmers whose land was compulsorily acquired. Seeing a political opportunity, ZANU (PF) seized on the land issue as a way of mobilising and rewarding its supporters, and it became central to its electoral platform. The land occupations were thus cast as the 'Third Chimurenga', the struggle to complete the unfinished business of the anti-colonial struggle.

Given the importance that the land issue had come to assume in ZANU (PF)'s bid to hold on to power, rulings by the courts which sought to stop the land occupations were bound to be met with hostility. Consequently, the decision by the Commercial Farmers Union (CFU) to seek a High Court in order to stop the occupations set the judiciary and the executive on a collision course. In March 2000, the High Court issued a consent order which instructed all farm occupiers to vacate the farms in twenty-four hours.[35] However, despite having initially consented to the order, the police subsequently refused to enforce it arguing that the land issue was a political matter which had to be resolved in the political sphere. The High Court issued another consent order on 10 November 2000 which declared farm occupations illegal and instructed the responsible government ministers to see to it that all farm occupiers were evicted. This order also went

---

[35] Gubbay, 'The Light of Successive Chief Justices', 14.

unenforced, and the CFU secured yet another order from the Supreme Court instructing all government ministers in agriculture-related ministries and the police to comply with the High Court Orders.[36]

The ruling party responded to these repeated orders by attacking members of the judiciary, especially white judges who it condemned as being reactionary. These attacks were most clearly dramatised by the storming of the Supreme Court building by about 200 war veterans and their followers on 24 November 2000. The group disrupted the hearing of an application by the CFU by shouting political slogans and waving placards, some of which declared that the judges should be killed. As Chief Justice Anthony Gubbay who was presiding over the aborted proceedings later observed, this was 'a show of absolute contempt for the institution of the courts'.[37] This disregard for the courts evidently had the approval of senior ZANU (PF) leaders as a few weeks later, at the party's annual congress, Mugabe publicly declared, 'The courts can do what they want. They are not courts for our people and we shall not be defending ourselves in these courts.'[38]

The Supreme Court's rulings on the contested results of the June 2000 general elections proved to be the last straw in the clashes between the executive and the Gubbay-led judiciary. In January 2001, the Court, led by Chief Justice Gubbay, ruled that the Presidential Proclamation of 8 December 2000, which was intended to thwart the electoral petitions that were before the courts, violated 'the rights of access of the aggrieved parties to the High Court.' Shortly thereafter, the President, the Minister of Justice, and the leadership of the war veterans began making public statements attacking the judiciary. Patrick Chinamasa, the new Minister of Justice, publicly condemned the judiciary as 'semi-colonial' and declared that it needed to be overhauled. As we have seen, such attacks on judges by ministers were not new, neither was the rhetoric they were couched in. What was new, however, was the extent to which the government was willing to go. A week after the Supreme Court ruling, Chinamasa informed Justice Gubbay that the government would not be able to guarantee his security if he stayed in office.[39] Gubbay understood the implicit message

---

[36] Ibid., 15.
[37] Ibid., 16.
[38] Ibid.
[39] This message was conveyed in the context of the recent invasion of the Supreme Court by war veterans carrying placards that read 'Kill the Judges'.

and tendered his resignation. In the following eighteen months, seven more senior judges resigned, largely due to political interference and/or intimidation.[40]

In addition to pressuring judges into resignation, the government vindictively pursued defiant judges, in some cases even after they had retired. Judges who refused to toe-the-line often faced disciplinary action for alleged misconduct; this sent a clear message to other serving judges that there would be a high price to pay for defiance. A long-serving member of the judiciary who suffered this fate was Justice Fergus Blackie. Prior to his retirement in July 2002, Justice Blackie had sentenced Chinamasa to three months in prison for contempt of court after he had repeatedly failed to appear in court to answer for previous contempt charges.[41] In September, Blackie was arrested at his home in the early hours of the morning, and charged with obstructing the course of justice and engaging in corruption. The charges were related to a ruling he had made in May that year, which overturned the conviction of a white Zimbabwean woman who had been accused of stealing from her employer. During his first day in detention, he was kept in a squalid cell at the infamous Matapi Police Station and was denied food, medication and access to legal representation. It is not a coincidence that this humiliating treatment was meted out to a former judge who had dared to convict the Minister of Justice for contempt. Blackie's ordeal served as retribution for his actions and sent a clear message to old and newly appointed judges about the consequences of defiance.

Justice Majuru's decision to conduct his work without fear or favour also led to victimisation. His misfortunes can be traced to a ruling in a case involving *The Daily News*, a privately owned newspaper which had become a thorn in the government's side. In October 2003, Justice Majuru, in his capacity as the President of the Administrative Court, ruled that the Media and Information Commission's refusal to register the newspaper was illegitimate because the Commission was improperly constituted. In so doing, he frustrated the government's efforts to shut the paper down. The following month, the government-controlled newspaper, *The Herald*, reported that Justice Majuru was

---

[40] The seven judges were Fergus Blackie, Nick McNally, Ahmed Ebrahim, Michael Gillespie, Ishmael Chatikobo, James Devittie and Justice Sandra Mugwira.

[41] 'Cuffed Justice', *The Economist*, 19 September 2002.

under investigation for improper conduct. As a result, Majuru recused himself from the case and, out of fear for his safety, he fled the country and tendered his resignation from South Africa in January 2004.

The resignations of senior judges allowed the government to appoint new ones who were deemed to be sympathetic to the government or, at the very least, pliable. The Chief Justice was replaced by Godfrey Chidyausiku, who had been the Deputy Minister of Justice and later the Attorney General in the 1980s, before becoming a judge. His appointment continued a practice that dated as far back as the 1940s in which the government's senior legal advisers were moved from the executive branch to the helm of the judiciary. This undermined the independence of the judiciary and put the principle of separation of powers into serious question. It would be incorrect to suggest that all judges were ZANU (PF) sympathisers, although there were certainly some who were overtly pro-establishment. The new judges came from a diverse range of backgrounds that included academia, the civil service, and private practice. Nevertheless, what was evident was that through a combination of incentives and subtle pressures, within the context of an economic crisis and political polarisation, judges were gradually placed in a position where the costs of defying the executive were very high.

One of the major criticisms made against the reconstituted judiciary was that they had accepted farms that had been compulsorily acquired under the controversial land reform programme at a time when land cases were coming before the courts. As a result, by 2008, lawyers, civil society activists, academics and journalists had come to view the judiciary's independence as being seriously compromised, and they felt that the new judges were unlikely to act as an obstacle to the abuse of power by the executive in the same way that their predecessors had done since the 1980s.

Judges were not unaware of these criticisms, and on occasion they responded to them and maintained that the judiciary was impartial. However, their statements often did not ring true, in large part because they often bore an uncanny similarity to those being made by Zanu (PF) officials. In addition, they often implicitly admitted that their political sympathies lay with ZANU (PF). A case in point was Chief Justice Chidyausiku's remarks at the pass-out parade of police officers in Harare in October 2005. His speech provided an alternative narrative about the political events in the country and how they had

affected the judiciary. He maintained that the reason for the resignation of many of the white judges from the bench was that 'they were
unable to come to terms with the redistribution of the land on a more
equitable basis.'[42] Positioning the reconstituted judiciary in solidarity with black Zimbabweans, Chidyausiku argued that because many
of the judges who replaced them were black this had had 'the effect
of synchronising the perceptions of the judiciary with those of the
majority of the population of this country', who, he claimed, were
in support of the government's land reform programme. He rejected
the concerns about judges accepting acquired farms and asserted that
'Judicial officers and police officers, like all other Zimbabweans, are
legitimate beneficiaries of the land reform programme.'

What was particularly revealing was the fact that Chidyausiku echoed the ruling party's position on land reform in arguing thus:

As for the allegation that the receipt of land under the land reform programme has compromised the judiciary, I would comment as follows. The
issue of whether or not land should be redistributed is a political issue. It is
not a legal issue. It is a matter of social justice that fairly and squarely is in
the domain of politics and not law. Whether the land has been distributed in
accordance with the law of the land is the legal issue.'[43]

The argument that the land question was a political one, as opposed to
a legal one, had been the basis for the government's rejection of judicial rulings on the land reform. It therefore chose to draft new laws
that reflected its political position and expected the courts to enforce
these new laws. Rather than challenge this reasoning and articulate
an alternative way of approaching the relationship between land, law
and politics, Chidyausiku chose to endorse the ZANU (PF) position.
Significantly, as the head of the judiciary his public statement sent
a clear message to other members of the judiciary as to what was
expected of them.

Although judges' impartiality had become questionable, especially
when dealing with overtly political cases, pointing this out in the courtroom was regarded as unacceptable impertinence. Lawyers who did so
in their court submissions often elicited a stern response and threats of

[42] *The Herald*, 22 October 2005.
[43] Ibid. See also the address by Justice C. E. Bhunu on the opening of the 2006
legal year in Masvingo, published in *The Herald*, 15 February 2006.

censure for 'cast[ing] aspersions on the bench'. Such was the case with
R. C. Shaw's application to the Administrative Court in 2005 which
contested the acquisition of his farm by the government. In requesting the matter to be referred to the Supreme Court, Shaw's lawyer
argued that the judiciary had been 'subjected to improper pressures',
and cited the circumstances surrounding Justice Majuru's departure
from the Administrative Court as an example. Justice Selo Nare who
heard the application, took a very dim view of these comments and
made this clear in his ruling which read in part: 'What counsel did was
merely to cast aspersions on the Bench. His actions border on naked
contempt of the Bench.'⁴⁴ However, Nare's written censure did not go
far enough for Chidyausiku, who felt that lawyers who questioned
the impartiality of the judiciary should be punished more severely. He
therefore pointed out that 'Where legal practitioners who are officers
of the court, and as such, are expected to know better, make totally
irresponsible submissions scandalising the court mere admonition is
inadequate and more appropriate action should be taken to punish
such legal practitioners for contempt of court.'⁴⁵

A consequence of the reconfiguring of the judiciary was that it
became unlikely to rule against the government in politically sensitive
matters. The ruling by Justice Guvava in the case brought by Kuchera
and his colleagues is an example of this tendency within the judiciary.
In dismissing the application, Justice Guvava focused on a number of
technical weaknesses in the papers filed by the Kuchera and his colleagues. However, in doing so, her ruling failed to deal with important
issues that were at the heart of the applicants' case. To begin with, it
did not deal with the question about whether it was proper for an
incumbent, who was participating in the forthcoming elections, to use
Presidential Powers to make amendments to the Electoral Act two
weeks before the polls. In addition, the significance of adding police
officers to the list of officials who would assist voters at the polling
station, when three were already provided for, was not examined sufficiently. On this point Guvava observed that 'The circumstances under
which all four persons, acting together, would interfere with the applicants rights to freely cast their vote is in my view difficult to imagine
nor has it been explained.'⁴⁶ She thus concluded that 'the application

---

⁴⁴ *The Standard*, 25 September 2005.
⁴⁵ Ibid.
⁴⁶ See the High Court Case *Kuchera et al. v. Minister of Justice*, 3.

cannot suddenly have become urgent merely because a fourth person has been included in the number of persons assisting illiterate and disabled voters.'

On the face of it, the judge's reasoning appeared to be sound; however, when viewed in the political context of the period, it evinced a studied effort to ignore the political realities confronting ordinary citizens in Zimbabwe. The misgivings about the police's impartiality raised by Kuchera and his colleagues had become fairly commonplace by 2008. Numerous reports by the media and non-governmental organisations documented growing evidence that the Zimbabwe Republic Police (ZRP), and indeed other arms of the state, were being used to support ZANU (PF)'s efforts to hold on to power at any cost. As early as 2001, the Human Rights NGO Forum observed that 'The ZRP has acquired a poor reputation, both for assaulting citizens exercising their constitutional rights of expression and assembly, and for being thoroughly partisan, allegedly under the direction and control of the State President and the ruling party.'[47] In addition, numerous civil society activists and opposition supporters reported that they had been abducted and/or subjected to intimidation, assault and torture by the police.[48] In the run-up to elections, the media reported numerous instances of the police refusing to take any action against ZANU (PF) members who were accused of political violence, and instead arrested opposition party members who were victims of political violence when they came to file charges.[49]

It is these concerns about the partisanship of the police that had brought about the reforms to the Electoral Act towards the end of 2007. In restoring the police's involvement in the voting process, the President was acting on the basis of an understanding of the political utility of a partisan police force. Kuchera and his co-litigants were therefore justifiably concerned about having members of the police force assist them to vote, especially as the names and addresses of everyone who was assisted to vote were recorded. As such, visually impaired individuals who wanted to vote for the opposition could not be sure that their choices had been accurately recorded, or that they would not suffer political retribution. However, the judge's ruling did

---

[47] Zimbabwe Human Rights NGO forum, 'Enforcing the Rule of Law in Zimbabwe', Special Report 3, 22.
[48] See Verheul, 'Performing the Law', 39–45.
[49] MDC Legal Affairs Department Report 2000–2005, 23.

not appear to be aware of the reality of a partisan police force and its implications for the electoral process.

Citizens versus the State

The introduction of repressive laws, the erosion of judicial independence and the interference with the operation of the courts, meant that the cases brought forward by citizens were less likely to succeed. Despite their continual frustration, individual citizens and organisations did not stop approaching the courts. As with legal cases brought prior to 2000, these law suits had a number of pragmatic objectives that included securing freedom for political and civil society activists or, as in the case filed by Kuchera and his colleagues, seeking the courts to enforce specific orders. In other cases, however, the objective was not centred on the hope of a favourable ruling from the courts. Rather, it was about securing an authoritative record of events which could be used in order to get justice at some future date when a less compromised judiciary was in place. In this regard, the 2006 report by the MDC Secretary for Legal Affairs, David Coltart, noted,

The cases provide a valuable record for the future as they detail numerous human rights abuses including crimes against humanity. The time will come when this evidence will be used to secure Justice on the behalf of the thousands of Zimbabweans who have suffered under the brutal ZANU PF regime. The time will also come when the same evidence will be used to bring to justice those responsible for these human rights abuses and crimes against humanity.[50]

In other instances, filing cases in local courts was a necessary step in order to access international legal forums like the Southern African Development Community Tribunal or the African Commission for Human and People's Rights. These courts generally required that all local avenues for legal recourse be exhausted before they heard a case.

In addition to these pragmatic objectives, lawsuits brought by citizens were also assertions of a rights-based citizenship. Using the courts to assert one's rights as a citizen was especially important given the narrow and exclusionary definition of citizenship that the ZANU (PF)

---

[50] Ibid.

government had adopted in the post-2000 period. As Alexander's work on political prisoners has shown, ideas such as the 'rule of law' and 'rights-bearing citizenship' were important for recent political activists, as well as those of the liberation struggle in the 1960s and 1970s.[51] For Kuchera and his fellow litigants, their application was rooted in their belief that they were citizens whose rights were being violated on the grounds of their physical disability. It is worth noting that the original plan had been for the National Association of Societies for the Care of the Handicapped, the umbrella body which represented people living with disabilities, to be the main applicant in the case. However, the Association's board grew cold feet at the last moment, in part due to its reluctance to antagonise the government. Consequently, Kuchera, whose affidavit had been included in the papers that had been prepared for the original case, agreed to step up and be the main applicant.[52]

Despite the fact that their March 2008 application was dismissed with costs, Kuchera and his lawyers were not discouraged. After the elections, Kuchera and five visually impaired co-litigants filed a new case before the Supreme Court.[53] In this new law suit, they cited the President, the Minister of Justice, the Zimbabwe Electoral Commission and the Attorney General as respondents. The six maintained that their right to freedom of expression was being violated by Sections 59 and 60 of the Electoral Act, as well as SI 43/2008 which prevented them from being assisted in voting by a person of their own choosing. They also maintained that they had been discriminated against by the Electoral Commission on the grounds of their physical disability. Whereas other citizens were able to vote independently and in secret because they were provided with voting materials that they could read, they were prevented from enjoying the same rights because the Electoral Commission did not provide voting materials in braille or enlarged fonts. Almost two years later, in January 2010 the Supreme Court unanimously ruled in favour of the applicants, and struck off Section 60 (1) (a) and (b) of the Electoral Act on the grounds

---

[51] See Alexander, 'The Political Imaginaries', and Alexander, 'Nationalism and Self-government'.

[52] Interview with M. Kuchera, Harare, 3 September 2014.

[53] *M. Kuchera et al. v. President of Zimbabwe, Minister of Justice, Chairperson of Zimbabwe Electoral Commission and the Attorney General*, Case No. SC 106/08.

that it was in contravention of the Constitution.[54] The fact that the ruling went in Kuchera and his co-litigants' favour did not signify a fundamental shift in the stance of the judiciary. Rather it reflected a shift of the country's political climate. By 2010 the political tensions in the country had significantly dissipated and a government of national unity was in place; as such, the political stakes in the case were much lower than they had been in March 2008.

Much like the lawsuits of individual citizens, the court cases filed by organisations such as the MDC also gave expression to the values that they espoused. The 2006 report by Coltart clearly captured the ways that the party's litigation was rooted in its own alternative vision of the country's social and political order. In concluding the report, he explained: 'It has been absolutely vital that these cases be brought for the following reasons. 1) The cases reaffirm the MDC's commitment to respecting the rule of law even when the judicial system has been subverted by the regime. 2) The cases themselves had served a valuable purpose in destroying whatever legitimacy the regime may have had.'[55]

The circumstances of citizens who took on the government in court during the post-2000 period contrasted with those of the 1980s in a number of respects. In the first instance, they had the advantage that there was significant international attention directed at Zimbabwe, and there was a broader political movement from which to draw strength. In addition, there were a number of non-governmental organisations that assisted individuals who wanted to file law suits against the government with funding to cover their legal costs. The Zimbabwe Human Right NGO Forum, for example, had begun offering legal services to victims of government brutality in the wake of the 1998 food riots. After 2000 it continued to take up legal cases in local and international courts on behalf of victims of torture and political violence. By 2004, The Zimbabwe Lawyers for Human Rights (ZLHR) had also established a fund which was used to pay the legal costs of citizens who wanted to file human rights cases. The legal costs of the suit brought forward by Kuchera and others, for example, were paid for through this fund. The ZLHR also set up its human rights defenders programme which sought to provide expeditious legal representation

---

[54] Supreme Court order 28 January 2010, Constitutional Application No. SC106 of 2008.
[55] MDC Legal Affairs Department Report 2000 to 2005.

for any human rights activists who were subjected to political persecution, and many of the legal professionals who participated in this programme provided their services free of charge.[56] Although the language of post-2000 opposition and civil society activists was inflected by contemporary legal ideas, the instrumental and discursive mobilisation of the law in order to challenge the actions of the state was hardly new in Zimbabwean history. It was part of the political repertoire of earlier generations of citizens and activists.

Conclusion

To sum up, scholarly efforts to understand contemporary legal struggles in Zimbabwe must be founded on a deeper historicisation of such struggles. In their use of the law, state officials were drawing on older established institutional practices that had been developed under settler rule then adapted and built upon by the post-colonial government. The 'authoritarian rule of law' established by the ZANU (PF) government in the post-2000 period was in many ways an adaptation of the practices they had made use of in the 1980s. What is more, the practices they used in the 1980s were part of an older set of institutional practices they inherited from the settler state. Equally, in their efforts to deploy the law instrumentally and discursively in engagements with the state, citizens were drawing on older repertoires of action that had been utilised by earlier generations of political activists and 'ordinary' citizens. The boldness and tenacity reflected in the legal action by Kuchera and his colleagues had much in common with individuals like Swazini Ndlovu, a ZAPU official who sought to challenge his continued detention in the 1980s, and with Mqibelo Dube of Gokwe who sought legal recourse in order to resist the abuse of power by local authorities in Gokwe during the 1970s.

---

[56] Interview with Tinoziva Bere, Mutare, 28 April 2014.

Conclusion

This book set out to investigate the role played by law in the constitution and contestation of state power in Zimbabwean history between 1950 and 2008. The key to understanding this use of the law for opposing purposes, I have argued, lies in its 'fragmented hegemony'. Although law was used to impose and authorise specific economic, social and political arrangements, its power was always unstable and incomplete. In addition, it was available for appropriation and redeployment by the ruled for their own purposes. This fragmented hegemony of the law was, in part, rooted in the fragmented nature of the colonial and the post-colonial state. By examining a range of legal struggles between Africans and the state, and amongst Africans themselves, this study has cast a light on the multiple ways that law was employed and deployed by rulers and the ruled. In the process, it has also intervened in a number of key debates amongst historians of Africa about the connections between law, state power and agency. In concluding, I will summarise the four main reflections emerging from this study. To begin with, I make the case for an approach to African legal history that is attentive to both the coercive and the constitutive capacities of law, as well as their shifting interplay over time. Second, I argue for a revision of scholarly understandings of how 'customary law' was brought into the service of the state in colonial Africa. Third, I highlight the need to go beyond an understanding of African legal agency that focuses on the calculated use of law as a resource in specific social, economic and political struggles. Lastly, I point out how a historical study of legal struggles, of the kind that I have undertaken, can contribute to contemporary debates about human rights in Africa.

In examining the role of the law in constituting state power, I have employed an approach that merges the two dominant ways of thinking about the law in African history. The first treats law primarily as a coercive force which was deeply implicated in the physical and structural violence of colonial rule, while the second attends to

241

the symbolic, discursive and productive functions of law. The value of merging these two approaches goes beyond the fact that it allows for a much more nuanced account of the ways that law operated in Zimbabwean history. Given that law was integral to the constitution of the state itself, analysing how successive governments sought to balance law's coercive and legitimating capacity also provides a window onto the continuous process of state making and re-making.

From the early years of colonial occupation in Zimbabwe, law was an important means by which the state was constructed, and by which its influence was projected across space. The efforts in the 1890s to set up legal institutions, and to ensure that all inhabitants of the colony recognised these structures, were a key part of constituting the colonial state. When state sovereignty was challenged from the 1950s onwards, it was often through the courts that it was re-asserted. The trials of nationalists, for example, were meant to authorise the government's narrative of African nationalism which cast nationalists as criminals and terrorists. In addition, at the height of the guerrilla war, Special Courts were convened in areas where guerrillas were operating as a way of reasserting state sovereignty. Similarly, when the ZANU (PF) government assumed power in the 1980s, it used the 'primary courts' to re-establish the state's monopoly over the exercise of judicial authority after its erosion during the liberation war.

Law was also used to create, authorise and reproduce the social categories and hierarchies on which colonial rule was founded. Through the law, racial categories such as 'native', 'coloured', 'Indian', and 'European' were created and invested with rights and duties thus establishing the colonial social hierarchy. In addition, the law provided for the establishment of institutions that would reproduce this hierarchy, and it also sanctioned the use of violence in enforcing it. This was clear in the 1950s as Parliamentarians drafted laws that curtailed Africans' right to political participation, and provided state officials with greater powers to enforce the newly imposed restrictions. Significantly, the process of legislating drew heavily on colonial racial tropes. Africans who engaged in nationalist politics were initially characterised as errant children in need of a firm disciplining hand. However, over time they came to be described as 'wild animals' that deserved to be killed. This was accompanied by a corresponding shift in the punishments provided for in the law, and the mandatory death sentence soon came to be applied to a wide range of 'crimes' of commission and omission.

Underlying these developments was a shift in the balance of the use of law away from legitimation towards repression.

Whereas successive settler administrations had, up until the mid-1960s, used legalism as a way of legitimating state power, the ZANU (PF) government's primary means of legitimation was not the law, in and of itself. The new government's claims to legitimacy lay in its promises to eliminate the socio-economic legacies of colonial rule and to bring about modernisation and development. The role of law in this political project was that of an instrument to be used to fulfil these promises. Among the important changes of the period was the removal of the racial and gender-related barriers to full citizenship that had existed under settler rule. There was, however, a darker side to the use of the law during this period, one that had its roots in the political turbulence of the last decades of settler rule. The armoury of repressive legislation inherited from the settler state, ZANU (PF)'s authoritarian tendencies, and the simmering tensions of the 1980s came together to produce a toxic mix. Those who were deemed political enemies by the ruling party were discursively constructed as being outside the nation, and were thus rendered legitimate targets of state-directed violence. These individuals were denied the protection that the new Constitution was supposed to afford all citizens. The victims of this violence were, for the most part, ZAPU officials and supporters. However, after 2000 the members of the Movement for Democratic Change became the new victims of the ZANU (PF) government's authoritarian rule of law.

In thinking about the role of law in constituting state power, this study has also considered the place of 'customary law'. It has taken issue with the approach which emphasises ideas of top-down invention, and the legal centralist assumptions that are often embedded in it. In Southern Rhodesia, there was no effort to invent or to codify 'customary law'. The plans of successive administrations to bring chiefs' courts into the service of the state varied widely, and their success was never guaranteed. This was in large part because chiefs and their followers often had their own agendas, which tended to be opposed to those of the state. As such, I have adopted the concept of legal pluralism as a lens through which to examine the developments in the sphere of 'customary law' and its relations to that of state law. The experience of Zimbabwe might more usefully be thought of as a process of evolving legal pluralism characterised by the mutual appropriation of symbols, forms, and concepts between the 'customary' and state law. This was driven by the desire of state officials and traditional leaders to borrow legitimacy from the alternative legal system. At the same time, the different legal systems were also evolving as a result of internal contestation and the impact of broader social, economic and political changes in the country. Although there was a process of increasing interpenetration between the legal systems, there were also moments of reversal.

For the first five decades of colonial rule, indigenous legal systems in Southern Rhodesia enjoyed substantial autonomy. Formal efforts to draw local legal systems into the service of the colonial state were initiated through the Native Law and Courts Act of 1937. However, these initial moves were tentative, partly due to the opposition from Justice Ministry officials. Chiefs' jurisdiction was therefore limited to civil disputes, and there was no effort to codify 'customary law'. However, from the 1950s, there was growing consensus between chiefs and NAD officials that the former be accorded more judicial powers. This consensus reflected a desire by both parties to appropriate the symbols and forms of the legal system represented by the other. On the one hand, chiefs were well aware of their waning authority and prestige, and were therefore eager to appropriate the features of state law. They thus demanded written texts defining their powers, law books that were written in local languages, as well as courthouses and jails. On the other hand, state officials looked to traditional authorities in their effort to deal with the crisis of legitimacy that had been caused by the Native Land Husbandry Act of 1951. The product of this marriage of convenience was the 1969 African Law and Tribal Courts Act. However, as the case of Chief Ndanga's court shows, the state's designs were frustrated by the resistance from chiefs and their followers, as well as the pressure exerted by guerrilla fighters.

After independence the role of chiefs' courts had less to do with the state's need to borrow legitimacy. Rather, the new government sought to incorporate them into its broader modernising vision. As a consequence, the Customary and Primary Courts Act passed in 1981 initiated the most significant efforts to merge state and 'customary' law since 1890. Under the banner of modernising 'customary law', headmen and chiefs were marginalised, and their courts were replaced by a new system of 'Primary Courts'. In the process, many of the forms, symbols and concepts of state law were incorporated into these new courts. However, these ambitious efforts to overhaul the administration of 'customary law' were not accompanied by an effort to elaborate or codify 'customary law'. In addition, they were actively contested by chiefs and headmen. In the end, ZANU (PF)'s waning popularity and its desire to secure the support of traditional leaders, led to the dismantling of the Primary Courts system in 1990.

One of the central tasks of this study has been to explore the multiple dimensions of African legal agency, and press the scholarly insights about it further. It has done so by examining the development of African legal consciousness, and its expression through diverse forms of legal agency. It has also explored the connection between African legal consciousness and agency, and the state's uses of the law, showing how these impelled each other. Importantly, the study argues that Africans' use of the law reflected more than just its utility in specific social, economic or political struggles. It also gave expression to emergent political imaginaries, shifting ideas of personhood and alternative visions of the social and political order.

African legal consciousness was acquired through avenues such as education and prior experience in court as a litigant, a witness or a member of the gallery. In addition, personal networks also contributed to increasing knowledge about the legal system and ways of making use of it to pursue one's interests. Intermediaries such as court clerks, interpreters and lawyers also played an important role. One of the key forms that African legal agency took, was the use of law as a resource in struggles with state officials. Instead of complying with onerous or repressive orders issued by state officials, a substantial number of Africans chose to take matters up with the courts. Doing so invariably meant incurring significant financial costs, and there was often a price to be paid in the form of retribution from state officials. Such legal action was not limited to members of the social and political elite. As we have seen, 'ordinary' villagers in Mrewa, Gokwe, and Ndanga combined their resources and raised the money required to consult lawyers about government policies they disagreed with. Africans also deployed the language of the law in their engagements with the government. During the period of settler rule, critiques of the Rhodesian legal system were articulated by nationalists, guerrillas and African lawyers. These critiques drew on alternative ideas about law and justice, and unmasked the repressive nature of the Rhodesian state's legalism. Similarly, after independence, civil society and opposition party activists invoked ideas such as the rule of law, human rights, good governance and judicial independence in their critiques of the government.

There was also a performative dimension to African legal agency. From the early 1960s, nationalists and guerrilla fighters usurped courtrooms and used them as spaces for personal performances. Politicians like Joshua Nkomo engaged in behaviour that disrupted courtroom procedures and undermined the colonial authorities' efforts to use these trials as performances of state power. The nationalist cultural symbols that politicians and their supporters brought into the court also challenged the state's own symbols and rituals. The success of these different forms of legal agency is attested to by the increasing shift towards much more repressive laws, and by the undermining of procedural safeguards in the legal system by the Rhodesian Front government from the 1960s. The use of capital punishment and detention without trial became more widespread, and key principles of the rule of law such as access to legal representation and the presumption of innocence were substantially eroded. This decidedly repressive turn in the law led to a corresponding shift in nationalist and guerrilla soldiers' attitudes towards the courts. From the 1960s guerrilla fighters like Thomas Mutete Makoni and his colleagues regularly refused to be bound by the conventions of the Rhodesian courts and rejected their procedures as a parody of justice. Instead, they used the dock as a platform from which to assert their political convictions and put the settler state on trial. The impact of these performances was amplified by the local and international media that reported the trials to the world at large.

These instances of African legal agency should not be read solely in terms of the calculated use of the law in the pursuit of specific outcomes. The villagers of Mrewa who pooled their money in 1972 to seek legal advice, and persisted on this path, even after being detained by the police and knowing that they would incur the wrath of the DC, were clearly not taking the easiest path available. They were acting on the basis of an understanding that the law should limit state intrusions in their lives, and that it should constrain the power of state officials. These actions also reflected a particular conception of themselves in relation to the state, and their desired status in the polity. Such actions are especially significant when viewed in light of the efforts by the Rhodesian Front government in the 1960s and 1970s to define Africans as ethnicised, custom-bound subjects. These individuals were behaving like rights-bearing citizens, even if the state did not recognise them as such. This political imaginary remained important after independence and was clearly articulated by the ZAPU political detainee Swazini Ndlovu who remonstrated, 'My rights as a citizen have been curtailed and I am not told why.'

These emerging political imaginaries and ideas about personhood had their roots in long-term social and economic processes that were triggered or accelerated by colonisation. These included the spread of Christianity, rural-urban migration, education, entry into wage labour and membership in African social and political associations. These processes had an important influence on how Africans conceived of themselves in relation to each other and to the state. The political currents of the post-World War II period, which included ideas around national self-determination, universal human rights, socialism and Pan-Africanism, also influenced African political aspirations and imaginaries. These aspirations and imaginaries in turn found expression through their legal encounters with the state. Over time, these imaginaries and the forms of legal agency they inspired, became part of the political repertoire of citizens in their engagement with the state. As such, after independence, the state continued to be confronted by citizens who refused to have their rights violated and insisted that state power be exercised within the confines of the law.

This history of struggles for rights has much to offer to the search for ways to invigorate contemporary human rights discourse in Zimbabwe, and in Africa more broadly. The instances of villagers pooling resources to challenge the acts of state officials remind us that the struggle for rights need not be delegated to, and dominated by, donor-funded human rights NGOs. In the same vein, the broader range of ideas about law and justice invoked by citizens over the decades alert us to the possibilities for the struggle for rights and the attendant discourse to be defined from below. By recognising the links between contemporary human rights struggles and the older ones discussed in this book, it is also possible to further challenge the official narrative about the anti-colonial struggle that has been used to silence dissenting voices. This narrative has tended to elevate the land question and the role of Zanu (PF) political leaders and war veterans. By contrast, as this book has demonstrated, the contributions of 'ordinary' citizens were just as important, and questions of rights, justice and citizens' entitlements were intimately linked to the anti-colonial struggle. Ultimately, this longer history of legal struggles alerts scholars and activists alike to the rich repertoire of strategies and discourses that were employed and deployed in struggles against state repression in colonial and post-colonial Zimbabwe.

Bibliography

Interviews

Anderson, Chris, Harare, 14 April 2011.
Austin, Reg, Harare, 29 April 2011.
Bere, Tinoziva, Mutare, 28 April 2014.
Chakona, J., Jerera, 4 February 2011.
Chidyausiku, Godfrey, Harare, 14 March 2011.
Chief Ndanga, Ndanga, 6 February 2011.
Chihambakwe, Simplisius, Harare, 15 March 2009.
Chihambakwe, Simplisius, Harare, 16 March 2011.
Chimuka, N., Zaka, 31 March 2009.
Chin'ozho, S., Chiredzi, 31 March 2009.
Dhlula, Agnes, Bulawayo, 29 November 2010.
Dzoro, Lovemore, Zaka, 30 March 2009.
Dzoro, P., Chiredzi, 30 March 2009.
Elliot, Bryant, Harare, 4 April 2011.
Gubbay, Antony, Harare, 14 April 2009.
Kanter, Harry, Harare, 15 April 2011.
Kuchera, Masimba, 3 September 2014.
Kunodziya, C. M., Zaka, 31 March 2009.
Mabusela, Constance, Bulawayo, 29 November 2010.
Magora, M., Ndanga, 2 February 2011.
Mahlangu, Polyanna, Bulawayo, November 2011.
Mapuranga, C. M., Jerera, 6 February 2011.
Masterson, Alex, Harare, 28 April 2011.
Mberi, Kudakwashe, Zaka, 31 March 2009.
Mbuya Machakata, Jerera, 5 February 2011.
Mbuya Muyocha, Jerera, 4 February 2011.
Mbuya Tazvivinga, Jerera, 5 February 2011.
Mkushi, Honour, Harare, 23 March 2011.
Mr Chikwanda, Jerera, 4 February 2011.
Mr Hama, Jerera, 5 February 2011.
Mr Matara, Zaka, 31 March 2009.
Mrs Charinda, Ndanga, 6 February 2011.

Mubako, Simbi, Harare, 26 April 2011.
Mufuka, Moffat, Jerera, 4 February 2011.
Mutambanengwe, Simpson, Harare, 13 April 2011.
Mutape, F., Ndanga, 2 February 2011.
Mutero, Betty, Harare, 22 March 2011.
Muteti, B. M., Zaka, 31 March 2009.
Ndanga, Reuben, Ndanga, 6 February 2011.
Ndanga, Rueben, Ndanga, 18 April 2011.
Ndume, Celestine, Ndanga, 2 February 2011.
Ngwaru, J. B., Ndanga, 2 February 2011.
Pichanick, Alwyn, Harare, 8 April 2009.
Ranger, Terence, Oxford, 27 September 2011.
Reagan, Ken, Harare, 13 April 2011.
Regedzayi, William, Jerera, 4 February 2011.
Rukwava, V., Zaka, 1 April 2009.
Sekuru Mbizi, Chiredzi, 31 March 2009.
Shamunyarira, Nathan, Harare, 24 March 2011.
Sibanda, Siwanda Kennedy Mbuso, Bulawayo, 28 November 2010.
Sibanda, Siwanda Kennedy Mbuso, Bulawayo, 30 November 2010.
Simpson, Harry, Harare, 16 April 2009.
Smith, George, Harare, 16 April 2009.
Stewart, Julie, Harare, 12 April 2011.
Tshuma, Josphat, Bulawayo, 11 September 2013.

Manuscripts and Archival Sources

National Archives of Zimbabwe

NAZ-Bulawayo, Local Government District Nkai, Chief Dakamela's Court, Loc 29/6/3R, Box 28926.
NAZ-Masvingo, File: Local Government District Administration Chiefs and Headmen.
NAZ-Masvingo, Zaka Community Court Civil Records, Loc 7-1-8F, Box 3563.
NAZ-Masvingo, Bikita Magistrates Court Civil Records 1–90, Loc 9-5-3R, Box 5251.
NAZ-Masvingo, Zaka Community Court Maintenance Cases 1985, Loc 10-6-6R, Box 3567.
NAZ-Masvingo, Bikita Magistrates Court Maintenance cases 1990.
NAZ-Masvingo: CHK & HM 14 1975–1982.
NAZ-MS587/4, Untitled File.
NAZ-MS589/7/3 Kurehwandada Muzheri vs The State.

NAZ-MS590/15 Political Trials.

NAZ-MS591, Ian Smith's Hostages.

NAZ-MS591/2/4, Legal Sheridan.

NAZ-MS591/2/7 Ian Smith's Hostages, Geneva Press Conference October 1976.

NAZ-MS591/4 Political Prisoners Box.

NAZ RG4, Committee of Enquiry into the Legal Profession, Provisional Report, April 1978.

NAZ-S2796/2/1, Assemblies of Chiefs General.

NAZ-S2796/2/4, Assemblies of Chiefs Matabeleland 1951–1958.

NAZ-S2824/11, Minutes of the Working Party 'C'.

NAZ-S2827/1/19 Report of the Working Party 'C' Chiefs Courts.

NAZ-S2930, Vol. 1 African Law and Tribal Courts.

NAZ-S3331/17/12 Criminal Matters: 1962–1966.

NAZ-S3332/2/2 Law and Maintenance Order Amendment Bill 1963–1964.

NAZ-S3385 Salisbury High Court Criminal Cases 11496–11502.

NAZ-S3642/2, Sipolilo Magistrate's court: Cases appealed by Africans 81/58–111/58.

NAZ-S3700/15 Legal Status of African Women.

NAZ S3700/16, *Kwangware & 47 Others v. State*

NAZ-S3700/40 Tribal Land Authorities.

NAZ-S3700/43, TTL Authorities: Disputes 1973–1976.

NAZ-S3700/103/1, African Law and tribal Courts Act: Policy:

NAZ-S3700/103/2, Tribal Courts: Court Clerks, Training: Allowances.

NAZ-S3700/103/4/2, District Commissioner's Court Rules.NAZ-ORAL/239 Leo Baron.

Sibanda Private Archives

SPA File, Bulawayo Law and Order Cases.

SPA File, Law Society 1983.

SPA File, Sledge Muradzikwa and 8 others vs Emmerson Mnangagwa.

SPA File, State vs Swazini Ndlovu.

SPA File, State vs Timothy Dube and Elias Sakana.

British National Archives

BNA DO35/7726, H W Chitepo, first Southern Rhodesian African Barrister.

BNA FCO36/741, Tangwena Dispute.

BNA FCO 36/1273, Commutation of Death Sentences in Southern Rhodesia.

Rhodes House Library

Terence Ranger Papers, Trial of Michael Mawema

Printed Primary Sources

Newspapers

African Daily News
Rhodesia Herald
The Economist
The Herald
The Sunday Mail
Zimbabwe News
Zimbabwe Review

Government Documents

Southern Rhodesia Parliamentary Debates
Rhodesia Parliamentary Debates
Zimbabwe Parliamentary Debates
Zimbabwe Senate Debates
African Law and Tribal Courts Act, Statute Law of Rhodesia 1969, Salisbury, 1970.
Report of the Courts Inquiry Commission, Government of Rhodesia, Salisbury, 1971.
Constitution of Zimbabwe 1979 (Lancaster House)
The Training of Community Court Presiding Officers and Clerks, Ministry of Justice, Harare,1982.
'The Law and the Judiciary in Zimbabwe', Department of Information Press Statement, 20 August 1984.
'Chiefs Trial Courts not legal yet', Department of Information Press Statement, 6 July 1990.
'State of Emergency to go – Mahachi', Department of Information Press Statement, 23 July 1990.
'President Announces General Amnesty', Department of Information Press Statements, 1 August 1990.
Public Order and Security Act 2002 [Chapter 11: 17]

Printed Reports and Collections of Primary Documents

Nyangoni C. and G. Nyandoro (eds), Zimbabwe Independence Movements: Select Documents, (London, 1979).

Lawyers' Committee for Human Rights, *Zimbabwe: Wages of War, A Report on Human Rights* (New York, 1986).

Breaking the Silence, Building True Peace: A Report on the Disturbances in Matabeleland and the Midlands 1980–1988, Catholic Commission for Justice and Peace and Legal Resources Foundation (Harare 1999).

Gubbay A., 'The Light of Successive Chief Justices of Zimbabwe in Seeking to Protect Human Rights and the Rule of Law', Miriam Rothschild and John Foster Human Rights Trust Annual Lecture 2001.

Zimbabwe Human Rights NGO forum, 'Enforcing the Rule of Law in Zimbabwe', Special Report 3, September 2001.

Media Institute of Southern Africa (MISA) and Article 19, 'The Access to Information and Protection of Privacy Act: Two Years On', September 2004.

Solidarity Peace Trust, 'Subverting Justice: The role of the Judiciary in denying the will of the Zimbabwean Electorate since 2000', March 2005.

Solidarity Peace Trust, 'Policing the State: An Evaluation of 1981 political Arrests in Zimbabwe – 2000–2005', December 2006.

Solidarity Peace Trust, 'Destructive Engagement: Violence, Mediation and Politics in Zimbabwe', July 2007.

Solidarity Peace Trust, 'Punishing Dissent, Silencing Citizens: The Zimbabwe Elections 2008', May 2008.

Printed Secondary Works

Abel R., *Politics by Other Means: Law in the Struggle against Apartheid, 1980–1994* (New York, 1995).

Adewoye O., *The Legal Profession in Nigeria 1865–1962* (Nigeria, 1977).

Agamben G., *State of Exception* (Chicago, 2005).

Alexander J., *The Unsettled Land: State-making and the Politics of Land in Zimbabwe, 1893–2003* (Oxford, 2006)

'Political Prisoner's Memoirs in Zimbabwe: Narratives of Self and Nation', *Cultural and Social History*, 5 (2008), 395–409.

'The Political Imaginaries and Social Lives of Political Prisoners in Post 2000 Zimbabwe', *JSAS*, 36 (2010), 483–503.

'Nationalism and Self-government in Rhodesian Detention: Gonakudzingwa, 1964–1974, *JSAS*, 37 (2011), 551–69.

'View from the Liberation Movement Camps in Zambia', paper presented at the Britain Zimbabwe Research Day, June 2012.

Alexander J., J. McGregor and T. Ranger, *Violence and Memory: One Hundred Years in the 'Dark Forests' of Matabeleland* (Oxford, 2000).

Anderson D., 'Policing the Settler State: Colonial Hegemony in Kenya, 1900–1952', in D. Engels and S. Marks (eds), *Contesting Colonial Hegemony: State and Society in Africa and India* (London, 1994), 248–66.

Histories of the Hanged: Britain's Dirty War in Kenya and the End of Empire (London, 2005).

'Punishment, Race, and "The Raw Native": Settler Society and Kenya's Flogging Scandals, 1895–1930', *JSAS*, 37 (2011), 479–97.

Arrighi G., 'Labour Supplies in Historical Perspective: A Study of the Proletarianization of the African Peasantry in Rhodesia', *Journal of Development*, 6 (1970), 197–234.

Banana C., (ed), *Turmoil and Tenacity: Zimbabwe, 1890–1990*, (Harare, 1989).

Barnes T., 'The Fight for the Control of African Women's Mobility in Colonial Zimbabwe, 1900–1939', *Signs*, 17 (1992), 586–608.

Batezat E., M. Mwalo and K. Truscott, 'Women and Independence: the Heritage and the Struggle' in C. Stoneman (ed), *Zimbabwe's Prospects: Issues of Race, Class, State and Capital in Southern Africa* (London, 1988), 153–73.

Berry S.,'Hegemony on A Shoestring: Indirect Rule and Access to Agricultural Land', *Africa*, 62 (1992), 327–55.

Bhebe N. and T. Ranger (eds), *Society in Zimbabwe's Liberation War* (Harare, 1996).

Bhebe N. and T. Ranger (eds), *Soldiers in Zimbabwe's Liberation War* (Harare, 1995).

Biti T., 'The Judiciary, the Executive and the rule of law in Zimbabwe', in S. Kayizzi-Mugerwa, A. O. Olukoshi, L. Wohlgemuth (eds), *Towards a New Partnership with Africa: Challenges and Opportunities* (Uppsala, 1998), 66–81.

Bourdieu P., 'The Force of Law: Towards a Sociology of the Juridical Field', *Hastings Law Journal*, 38 (1987), 805–53.

Branch D.,'Imprisonment and Colonialism in Kenya, c.1930–1952: Escaping the Carceral Archipelago', *The International Journal of Historical Studies*, 38 (2005), 239–66.

Broun K., *Black Lawyers, White Courts: The Soul of South African Law* (Athens, 2000).

Bundy C., *The Rise and Fall of the South African Peasantry* (London, 1979).

Chanock M., *Law, Custom and Social Order: The Colonial Experience in Malawi and Zambia* (Cambridge, 1985).

'Writing South African Legal History: A Prospectus', *JAH*, 30 (1989), 265–88.

'The Lawyer's Self: Sketches on Establishing a Professional Identity in South Africa, 1900–1925', *Law in Context Special Issue*, 16 (1999), 59–79.

The Making of South African Legal Culture 1902–1936: Fear Favour and Prejudice (Cambridge, 2001).

Chidyausiku G., 'The Quality of Administration of Justice in Zimbabwe', *Legal Forum*, 2 (1988), 3–5.

Child H. F., *The History and Extent of Recognition of Tribal Law in Rhodesia*, (Salisbury, 1973).

Chikuhwa J. W., *A Crisis of Governance: Zimbabwe* (New York, 2004).

Chung F., *Reliving the Second Chimurenga: Memories from the Liberation Struggle of Zimbabwe* (Stockholm, 2006).

Clayton A. and D. C. Savage, *Government and Labour in Kenya 1895–1963* (London, 1974).

Cohen D. W., '"A Case for the Basoga": Lloyd Fallers and the Construction of an African Legal System', in K. Mann and R. Roberts (eds), *Law in Colonial Africa* (London, 1991), 239–53.

Cole D. H., '"An Unqualified Human Good": E. P. Thompson and the Rule of Law', *Journal of Law and Society* 28 (2001), 177–203.

Comaroff J. L., 'Colonialism, Culture and the Law: A Foreword', *Law and Social Enquiry*, 26 (2001), 305–14.

'Governmentality, Materiality, Legality, Modernity: On the Colonial State in Africa', in J. Deutsch, H. Schmidt and P. Probst (eds), *African Modernities: Entangled Meanings in Current Debate* (Oxford, 2002), 107–34.

Comaroff J. and J. Comaroff, 'Law and Disorder in the Postcolony: An Introduction', in J. Comaroff and J. Comaroff (eds), *Law and Disorder in the Postcolony* (Chicago, 2006), 1–56.

Cooper F., *Colonialism in Question: Theory, Knowledge, History* (Berkeley, 2005).

Cooper F. and A. L. Stoler, 'Introduction: Tensions of Empire: Colonial Control and Visions of Rule', *American Ethnologist*, 16 (1989), 609–21.

Crisp J., *The Story of an African Working Class: Ghanaian Miners' Struggles, 1870–1980* (London, 1984).

Currie M. E., *The History of Gill, Godlonton and Gerrans, 1912–1980* (Harare, 1982),

Deutsch J.-G., 'State of Normalcy', Paper presented at the Violence in Colonial and Post-colonial Africa Workshop, 1 June 2012.

'Celebrating Power in Everyday Life: The Administration of Law and the Public Sphere in Colonial Tanzania, 1890–1914', *Journal of Cultural Studies*, 15 (2002), 93–103.

Drinkwater M., *The State and Agrarian Change in Zimbabwe's Communal Areas* (New York, 1991).

Dumbutshena E., 'Justice the People's Rights', *Legal Forum*, 2 (1990), 5–8.

Ehrlich E., 'The Sociology of Law', *Harvard Law Review*, 36 (1922), 130–45.

Elkins C., *Britain's Gulag: The Brutal End of Empire in Kenya* (London, 2005).

Ellman S., 'Law and Legitimacy in South Africa', *Law and Social Inquiry*, 20 (1995), 407–78.

Engels D. and S. Marks, 'Introduction: Hegemony in a Colonial Context', in D. Engels and S. Marks (eds), *Contesting Colonial Hegemony: State and Society in Africa and India* (London, 1994), 5–15.

Englund H., *Prisoners of Freedom: Human Rights and the African Poor* (Berkley, 2005)

Evans I., *Bureaucracy and Race: Native Administration in South Africa* (Los Angeles, 1997).

Falk R., 'The Power of Rights and the Rights of Power: What Future for Human Rights?', *Ethics and Global Politics*, 1–2 (2008).

Feltoe G., 'A Survey of Major Legislation in the period 1980–1984, ZLR, 1 & 2 (1983–84), 278–85.

Fields K., *Revival and Rebellion in Colonial Central Africa* (Princeton, 1985).

Foucault M., *Discipline and Punish: The Birth of the Prison* (London, 1975).

Gluckman M., *The Judicial Process among the Barotse of Northern Rhodesia* (Manchester, 1955).

Godwin P. and I. Hancock, *'Rhodesians Never Die': The Impact of War and Political Change on White Rhodesia c. 1970–1980* (Oxford, 1993).

Gould J., 'Strong Bar, Weak State? Lawyers, Liberalism and State Formation in Zambia', *Development and Change*, 37 (2006), 921–41.

Grady P., 'Autobiography and the "Power of Writing": Political Prison Writing in the Apartheid Era', *JSAS*, 19 (1993), 489–523.

Gubbay A. R., 'Speech delivered at the Opening of the 1991 Legal Year', *Legal Forum*, 3 (1991), 5–9.

Guha R., *Dominance Without Hegemony: History and Power in Colonial India* (Massachusetts, 1997).

Gupta A. and A Sharma, 'Rethinking Theories about the State in an Age of Globalisation', in A. Gupta and A. Sharma (eds), *The Anthropology of the State: A Reader* (Oxford, 2006), 1–41.

Hansen T. B. and F. Stepputat, 'Introduction: States of Imagination', in T. B. Hansen and F. Stepputat (eds), *States of Imagination: Ethnographic Explorations of the Postcolonial State* (London, 2001), 1–38.

Hatchard J., *Individual Liberties and State Security in the African Context: The case of Zimbabwe* (Harare, 1993).

Hay D., 'Property, Authority and the Criminal Trial', in D. Hay *et al* (eds), *Albion's Fatal Tree: Crime and Society in Eighteenth Century England* (Middlesex, 1975), 17–63.

Herbst J., *State Politics in Zimbabwe* (Harare, 1990).

Hirsch S., 'Khadi Courts as Complex Sites of Resistance: The State, Islam and Gender in Post-colonial Kenya', in M. Lazarus-Black and S. F. Hirsch (eds), *Contested States: Law, Hegemony, and Resistance* (New York, 1994), 207–30.

Holleman J. F., 'Law and Anthropology: A Necessary Partnership for the Study of Legal Change in Plural Systems', *Journal of African Law*, 23 (1979), 117–70.

Hynd S., 'Killing the Condemned: The Practice and Process of Capital Punishment in British Africa, 1900–1950s', *JAH*, 49 (2000), 403–18.

Jeater D., *Marriage, Power and Perversion: The Construction of a Moral Discourse in Southern Rhodesia, 1894–1930* (Oxford, 1993).

'"Their Idea of Justice is so Peculiar": Southern Rhodesia, 1890–1910', in P. Coss (ed.), *The Moral World of the Law* (Cambridge, 2000), 178–95.

Law, Language and Science: The invention of the "Native Mind" in Southern Rhodesia, 1890–1930 (Portsmouth, 2007).

Kalinga O. J. M., 'The 1959 Nyasaland State of Emergency in Old Karonga District', *JSAS*, 36 (2010), 743–63.

Kanyongolo F. E., 'The Rhetoric of Human Rights in Malawi: Individualization and Judicialization', in H. Englund and F. Nyamjoh (eds), *Rights and the Politics of Recognition in Africa* (London, 2004).

Karekwaivanane G. H., 'It shall be the duty of every African to obey and comply promptly': Negotiating State Authority in the Legal Arena, 1965–1980', *JSAS*, 37 (2011), 333–49.

'"Through the Narrow Door": Narratives of the First Generation of African Lawyers in Zimbabwe', *Africa: Journal of the International African Institute*, 86 (2016).

'Les juristes entre "Africanisation" et transition politique: transformations du champ juridique dans le Zimbabwe postcolonial, 1980–1995', *Politique Africaine*, 138 (2015).

Kazembe J. L., 'The Women Issue', in I. Mandaza (ed), *Zimbabwe: The Political Economy of Transition 1980–1986* (Harare, 1986), 377–404.

Killingray D., 'The "Rod of Empire": The Debate over Corporal Punishment in the British African Forces, 1888–1946', *JAH*, 35 (1994), 411–37.

Kostal R. W., *A Jurisprudence of Power: Victorian Empire and the Rule of Law* (Oxford, 2005).

Kriger N. J., *Zimbabwe's Guerrilla War: Peasant Voices* (Cambridge, 1992).

'The Politics of Creating National Heroes: The Search for Political Legitimacy and National Identity', in N. Bhebe and T. Ranger (eds), *Soldiers in Zimbabwe's Liberation War* (Oxford, 1995), 139–62.

Ladley A., 'Changing Courts in Zimbabwe: The Customary Law and Primary Courts Act', *Journal of African Law*, 26 (1982), 95–114.

Lardner-Burke D., *Rhodesia: The Story of Crisis* (London, 1966).

Lawrence B. N., E. L. Osborn, R. L. Roberts (eds), *Intermediaries, Interpreters, and Clerks: African Employees in the Making of Colonial Africa* (Madison, 2006).

LeBas A., *From Protest to Parties: Party-building and Democratization in Africa*, (Oxford, 2011).

Litowitz D., 'Gramsci, Hegemony and the Law', *Brigham Young University Law Review*, 515 (2000), 515–51.

Lonsdale J., 'Kenyatta's Trials: Breaking and Making and African Nationalist', in P. Coss (ed), *The Moral World of Law* (Cambridge, 2000), 196–239.

Machingaidze V. E. M., 'Agrarian Change from Above: The Southern Rhodesia Native Land Husbandry Act and the African Response', *The International Journal of African Historical Studies*, 24 (1991), 557–88.

Mamdani M., *Citizen and Subject: Contemporary Africa and the Legacy of Late Colonialism* (Princeton, 1996).

Manase W. T., 'Grassroots Education in Zimbabwe: Successes and Problems Encountered in Implementation by the Legal Resources Foundation of Zimbabwe', *Journal of African Law*, 36 (1992), 11–18.

Mandela N., *Long Walk to Freedom* (London, 1995).

Mann K. and R. Roberts, 'Introduction', in Mann and Roberts (eds), *Law in Colonial Africa* (London, 1991), 3–58.

Martin D. and P. Johnson, *The Chitepo Assassination* (Harare 1985).

Matyszak D., 'Democratic Space and State Security: Zimbabwe's Public Order and Security Act', unpublished paper.

Mazarire G. C., 'Discipline and Punishment in ZANLA: 1964–1979', *Journal of Southern African Studies*, 37 (2011), 571–91.

McCracken J., 'In the Shadow of Mau Mau: Detainees and Detention Camps during Nyasaland's State of Emergency', *JSAS*, 37 (2011), 535–50.

McCulloch J., *Black Peril, White Virtue: Sexual Crime in Southern Rhodesia, 1902–1935* (Bloomington, 2000).

Merry S. E., 'Legal Pluralism', *Law and Society Review*, 22 (1988), 869–96.

'Anthropology, Law and Transnational Processes', *Annual Review of Anthropology*, 21 (1991), 357–79.

'Law and Colonialism', *Law and Society Review*, 25 (1991), 889–922.

'Courts as Performances: Domestic Violence Hearings in a Hawai'i Family Court', in M. Lazarus-Black and S. F. Hirsch (eds), *Contested States: Law, Hegemony, and Resistance* (New York, 1994), 35–58.

'Resistance and the Cultural Power of Law', *Law and Society Review*, 29 (1995), 11–25.

'Transnational Human Rights and Local Activism: Mapping the Middle', *American Anthropologist*, 108 (2006), 38–51.

Mlambo A. S., 'From the Second World War to UDI, 1940–1965', in B. Raftopoulos and A. Mlambo (eds), *Becoming Zimbabwe: A History from the Pre-colonial Period to 2008* (Harare, 2009), 75–114.

Mlambo E., *Rhodesia: Struggle for a Birthright* (London, 1972).

Moore S. Falk, 'Law and Social Change: The Semi-Autonomous Social Field as an Appropriate Subject of Study', *Law and Society Review*, 4 (1973), 719–46.

Social Facts and Fabrication: Customary Law on Kilimanjaro (Cambridge, 1986).

Mungazi D., *Colonial Education for Africans: George Stark's Policy in Zimbabwe* (New York, 1991).

Munochiveyi M., *Prisoners of Rhodesia: Inmates and Detainees in the Struggle for Zimbabwean Liberation, 1960–1980* (New York 2014).

Munro W., *The Moral Economy of the State: Conservation, Community Development and State Making in Zimbabwe* (Ohio, 1998).

Ncube W., 'The Decision in Katekwe v Muchabaiwa: A Critique', *ZLR*, 1 & 2 (1983–84), 217–28.

'Customary Law Courts Restructured', *ZLR*, 7 (1989–1990), 9–17.

Ndhlovu-Gatsheni S. and W. Willems, 'Making Sense of Cultural Nationalism and the Politics of Commemoration under the Third Chimurenga in Zimbabwe', *JSAS*, 35 (2009), 191–208.

Neocosmos M., 'Can a Human Rights Culture Enable Emancipation? Clearing Some Theoretical Ground for the Renewal of a Critical Sociology', *South African Review of Sociology*, 37 (2006), 356–79.

Nhongo-Simbanegavi J., *For Better or for Worse: Women and ZANLA in Zimbabwe's Liberation Struggle* (Harare, 2000).

Nkomo J., *Nkomo: The Story of My Life* (London, 1984).

Nyagumbo M., *With the People: An Autobiography from the Zimbabwean Struggle* (London, 1980).

Oguamanam, C. and W. Wesley Pue, 'Lawyers', Colonialism, State Formation and National Life in Nigeria, 1900–1960: "the fighting brigade of the people"', *Social Identities: Journal for the Study of Race, Nation and Culture*, 13 (2006), 769–85.

Oomen B., *Chiefs in South Africa: Law, Power and Culture in the Post-Apartheid Era* (Oxford, 2005).

Palley C., *The Constitutional History and Law of Southern Rhodesia, 1888–1965* (Oxford, 1966)

'The Judicial Process: UDI and the Southern Rhodesian Judiciary', *The Modern Law Review*, 1 (1967), 263–87.

'Law and the Unequal Society: Discriminatory Legislation in Rhodesia under the Rhodesian Front from 1963 to 1969, Part 1', *Race and Class*, 12 (1970), 15–47.

Palmer R. and N. Parsons (eds), *The Roots of Rural Poverty in Central and Southern Africa* (Berkeley, 1977).

Passmore G. C., *The National Policy of Community Development in Rhodesia: With Special Reference to Local Government in the African Rural Areas* (Salisbury, 1972).

Peck A. J. A., *Rhodesia Accuses* (Salisbury, 1966).

Pete S. and A. Devenish, 'Flogging, Fear and Food: Punishment and Race in Colonial Natal, *JSAS*, 31 (2005), 3–21.

Peterson D. R., 'Morality Plays: Marriage, Church, and Colonial Agency in Central Tanganyika, ca.1876–1928', *American Historical Review*, 111 (2006), 983–1010.

Phimister I., *An Economic and Social History of Zimbabwe, 1890–1948: Capital Accumulation and Class Struggle* (London, 1988).

Phimister I. and C. van Onselen, 'The Labour Movement in Zimbabwe: 1900–1945', in B. Raftopoulos and I Phimister (eds), *Keep on Knocking: A History of the Labour Movement in Zimbabwe* (Harare, 1997).

Pierce S., 'Punishment and the Political Body: Flogging and Colonialism in Northern Nigeria', *Interventions*, 3 (2001), 206–21.

Raftopoulos B., 'Nationalism and Labour in Salisbury, 1953–1965', *JSAS*, 21 (1995), 79–93.

'The Labour Movement and the Emergence of Opposition Politics in Zimbabwe', in B. Raftopoulos and L. Sachikonye (eds) *Striking Back: The Labour Movement ant the State in Zimbabwe 1980–2000* (Harare, 2001), 1–24.

Raftopoulos B. and L. Sachikonye (eds), *Striking Back: The Labour Movement and the Post-Colonial State in Zimbabwe, 1980–2000* (Harare, 2001).

Raftopoulos B. and T. Yoshikuni (eds), *Sites of Struggle: Essays in Zimbabwe's Urban History* (Harare, 2001).

Rajah J., *Authoritarian Rule of Law: Legislation, Discourse and legitimacy in Singapore* (Cambridge University Press, 2012).

Ranger T., 'The Invention of Tradition revisited: The Case of Colonial Africa', in T. Ranger and O. Vaughan (eds), *Legitimacy and the State in Twentieth Century Africa: Essays in Honour of A. H. M. Kirk-Greene* (London, 1993), 62–111.

Are we not also Men? The Samkange Family and African Politics in Zimbabwe 1920–1964 (London, 1995).

Voices from the Rocks: Nature, Culture and History in the Matopos Hills of Zimbabwe (Oxford, 1999).

Rao A. and S. Pierce, 'Discipline and the Other Body: Correction Corporeality and Colonial Rule', *Interventions*, 3 (2001), 159–68.

Rathbone R., 'Law, Lawyers and Politics in Ghana', in D. Engels and S. Marks (eds), *Contesting Colonial Hegemony: State and Society in Africa and India* (London, 1994), 227–47.

Rich Dorman S.,'NGOs and the Constitutional Debate in Zimbabwe: From Inclusion to Exclusion', *JSAS* 29, (2003).

Roberts R.,'Text and Testimony in the Tribunal de Premiere Instance, Dakar, during the early Twentieth Century', *JAH*, 31 (1990), 447–63.

Ross S. D.,'Rule of Law and Lawyers in Kenya', *Journal of Modern African Studies*, 30 (1992), 421–44.

Saada E., 'The Empire of Law: Dignity, Prestige, and Domination in the "Colonial Situation"', *French Politics, Culture and Society*, 20 (2002), 98–120.

Sachs A., *Justice in South Africa* (London, 1973).

Sadomba W. Z., *War Veterans in Zimbabwe's Revolution: Challenging Neo-colonialism and Settler International Capital* (Suffolk, 2011)

Scarnecchia T., *The Urban Roots of Democracy and Political Violence in Zimbabwe: Harare and Highfield, 1940–1964* (Rochester, 2008).

Schmidt E., 'Negotiated Space and Contested Terrain: Men, Women, and the Law in Colonial Zimbabwe, 1890–1939', *JSAS*, 16 (1990), 622–48.

Shadle B. L., '"Changing Traditions to Meet Current Altering Conditions": Customary Law, African Courts and the Rejection of Codification in Kenya, 1930', *JAH*, 40 (1999), 411–31.

Shamuyarira N., *Crisis in Rhodesia* (New York, 1966).

Sharafi, M., 'A New History of Colonial Lawyering: Likhovsky and Legal Identities in the British Empire', *Law and Social Inquiry*, 32 (2007), 1059–94.

Sherman T. C., 'Tensions of Colonial Punishment: Perspectives on Recent Developments in the Study of Coercive Networks in Asia, Africa and the Caribbean', *History Compass*, 7 (2009), 659–77.

Shutt A. K., '"The Natives are Getting Out of Hand": Legislating Manners, Insolence and Contemptuous Behaviour in Southern Rhodesia, c.1910–1963', *JSAS*, 33 (2007), 653–72.

Sithole M., *Zimbabwe: Struggles Within the Struggle, 1957–1980* (Harare, 1999).

Smith R., '"Money Breaks Blood Ties": Chiefs' Courts and the Transition from Lineage Debt to Commercial Debt in Sipolilo District', *JSAS*, 24 (1998), 509–26.

Snyder F. G., 'Colonialism and Legal Form: The Creation of "Customary Law" in Senegal', *Journal of Legal Pluralism*, 49 (1981), 49–90.

Spear T., 'Neo-Traditionalism and the Limits of Invention in British Colonial Africa', *JAH*, 44 (2003), 3–27.

Steele M. C., *'The Foundations of a "Native" Policy: Southern Rhodesia, 1923–1933'* (PhD Thesis, Simon Fraser University, 1972).

Stewart J., 'Legal Age of Majority Act Strikes Again: Chihowa v Mangwende SC 84.87', *ZLR*, 4 (1986), 168–72.

Stoler A. L., 'Colonial Archives and the Arts of Governance', *Archival Science*, 2 (2002), 87–109.

Stoneman C. (ed), *Zimbabwe's Inheritance* (New York, 1982).

Tendi M., *Making History in Mugabe's Zimbabwe: Politics, Intellectuals, and the Media* (Oxford, 2010).

Thompson E. P., *Whigs and Hunters: The Origins of the Black Act* (New York, 1975).

Tredgold T., *The Rhodesia That Was My Life* (London, 1968).

Trubek D. M., 'Max Weber on Law and the Rise of Capitalism', *Wisconsin Law Review*, 720 (1972), 720–53.

Tsanga A., 'Reconceptualizing the Role of Legal Information Dissemination in the Context of Legal Pluralism in African Settings', in A. Hellum et al. (eds), *Human Rights, Plural Legalities and Gendered Realities: Paths Are Made by Walking* (Harare, 2007), 437–58.

'The Professional Trajectory of a Human Rights Lawyer in Zimbabwe between 2000 and 2008', *JSAS*, 35 (2009), 977–91.

Turrell R., 'Kimberly: Labour and Compounds, 1871–1888', in S. Marks and R. Rathbone (eds), *Industrialisation and Social Change in South Africa: African Class Formation, Culture and Consciousness, 1870–1930* (Essex, 1982), 45–76.

van Onselen C., *Chibaro: African Mine labour in Southern Rhodesia 1900–1933* (London, 1976).

Weinrich A. K. H., *Chiefs and Councils in Rhodesia: Transition from Patriarchal to Bureaucratic Power* (Columbia, 1971).

Werbner R., 'Smoke from the Barrel of a Gun: Postwars of the Dead, Memory and Reinscription in Zimbabwe', in R. Werbner (ed), *Memory and the Postcolony: African Anthropology and the Critique of Power* (London, 1998).

Tears of the Dead: The Social Biography of an African Family (Edinburgh, 1991).

West M., *The Rise of an African Middle Class: Colonial Zimbabwe* (Indianapolis, 2002).

White L., *The Assassination of Herbert Chitepo: Texts and Politics in Zimbabwe* (Bloomington, 2003).

Unpopular Sovereignty: Rhodesian Independence and African Decolonization (Chicago, 2015).

Wiener M., *An Empire on Trial: Race, Murder and Justice under British Rule, 1870–1935* (Cambridge, 2009).

Windrich E., 'Rhodesian Censorship: The Role of the Media in the Making of a One-party State', *African Affairs*, 78 (1979), 523–34.

Yoshikuni T., *African Urban Experiences in Colonial Zimbabwe: A Social History of Harare before 1925* (Harare, 2007).

Zimudzi T., 'African Women, Violent Crime and the Criminal Law in Colonial Zimbabwe, 1900–1952', *JSAS*, 30 (2004), 499–517.

Zvobgo E., *The Role of Law as an Instrument of Oppression* (Melbourne, 1973).

   'Notes on Cases: Smith N. O. and Lardner Burke N. O. *v.* Wonesayi', *Rhodesian Law Journal*, 12 (1972).

Unpublished Theses

Edsman B., 'Lawyers in Gold Coasts Politics c. 1900–1945' (PhD Dissertation, University of Uppsala, 1979).

Feltoe G., 'Law, Ideology and Coercion in Southern Rhodesia' (MPh Thesis, University of Kent, 1978).

Verheul S., 'Performing the Law: Plays of Power in Harare's Magistrates Court Zimbabwe' (MPh Thesis, University of Oxford, 2011).

Index

Books in This Series